Every Time I Feel the Spirit

QUALITATIVE STUDIES IN RELIGION

GENERAL EDITORS: Penny Edgell Becker *and* Mary Jo Neitz

The Qualitative Studies in Religion series was founded to make a place for careful, sustained, engaged reflection on the link between the kinds of qualitative methods being used and the resulting shape, tone, and substance of our empirical work on religion. We seek to showcase a wide range of qualitative methodologies including ethnography; analysis of religious texts, discourses, rituals, and daily practices; in-depth interviews and life histories; and narrative analyses. We present empirical studies from diverse disciplines that address a particular problem or argument in the study of religion. We welcome a variety of approaches, including those drawing on multiple qualitative methods or combining qualitative and quantitative methods. We believe that excellent empirical studies can best further a critical discussion of the link between methods, epistemology, and social scientific theory, and thereby help to reconceptualize core problems and advance our understanding of religion and society.

Evangelical Christian Women: War Stories in the Gender Battles
Julie Ingersoll

*Every Time I Feel the Spirit: Religious Experience and Ritual
in an African American Church*
Timothy J. Nelson

Every Time I Feel the Spirit

Religious Experience and Ritual in an African American Church

Timothy J. Nelson

NEW YORK UNIVERSITY PRESS

New York and London

NEW YORK UNIVERSITY PRESS
New York and London
www.nyupress.org

© 2005 by New York University

Library of Congress Cataloging-in-Publication Data
Nelson, Timothy Jon.
Every time I feel the Spirit : religious experience and ritual
in an African American church / Timothy J. Nelson.
p. cm. — (Qualitative studies in religion)
Includes bibliographical references and index.
ISBN 0–8147–5819–3 (hardcover : alk. paper) —
ISBN 0–8147–5820–7 (pbk. : alk. paper)
1. African American women—Religious life.
2. AfricanAmerican women—Religion.
I. Title. II. Series.
BR563.N4N454   2004
248.4'082'0973—dc22   2004015008

New York University Press books are printed on acid-free paper,
and their binding materials are chosen for strength and durability.

Manufactured in the United States of America

c 10 9 8 7 6 5 4 3 2 1
p 10 9 8 7 6 5 4 3 2 1

To our Charleston family

Contents

Acknowledgments

I would like to thank the following scholars who gave me initial direction and advice on this project: Martin Marty, Martin Riesebrodt, Gerald Suttles, William J. Wilson, and Robert Wuthnow. Jim Spickard and one anonymous reviewer offered generous encouragement and timely guidance, and I couldn't have asked for a better editorial team than Penny Edgell, Mary Jo Neitz and Jennifer Hammer; because of their efforts this is a far better book. I am very grateful to Reverend Wright and the people of Eastside Chapel who opened their hearts and lives to me while I was researching this project. It was truly a life-changing experience.

Introduction

It was mid-August when my wife and I first went to the Saturday night prayer service at Eastside Chapel AME Church in Charleston, South Carolina.[1] The summer evening was oppressively humid—the kind of weather that once led local novelist Pat Conroy to describe a stroll through the streets as akin to "walking though gauze"—and the Palmetto bugs (large, cockroach-like creatures with the disconcerting ability to fly) lazily scuttled across the sidewalks. We were transplanted Northerners—"Yankees" now—new to the South Carolina Lowcountry and not acclimated to the heat, the moisture, or these repugnant-looking insects who seemed to migrate to the pavement on hot summer evenings with alarming regularity. We were to be in Charleston for exactly one year, my wife to interview low-income single mothers for her project on welfare and work, and me to begin my research on African American churches.

The prayer service was scheduled to begin at 10:30 p.m., which is exactly when we arrived. Upon entering the sanctuary we were surprised to discover that we were the first ones there. Well, almost the first. Reverend Wright, Eastside Chapel's thin, dark-skinned, and serious-looking pastor, was on the dais in a lime-green Fila sweat suit, adjusting the microphones and playing a gospel tape over the sound system. He greeted us warmly (both of us had met him in his study earlier that week) and we chatted for a few minutes before sitting down in one of the front pews to wait for everyone else to arrive. After a few minutes a young twenty-something man came into the church and settled into the pew right behind us. My wife and I turned to greet him. He introduced himself as Ronald and gave us a brief but bright smile followed by a handshake. Ronald then immediately went down to the floor on both knees, squeezing his eyes shut and praying silently for a few minutes. Observing this ritual (which some others, though not everyone, performed as they entered the sanctuary later), I worried that our own entrance had been too casual (we didn't stop to kneel or to pray) and that our sociability had interrupted Ronald's normal routine.

At 10:40, a cluster of nine or ten people, most of them women wearing long denim skirts or summer dresses, arrived all at once and greeted us and each other. After they settled into scattered groups in the front pews, Reverend Wright looked over the assembled group with a stern face and announced that he was going to have to put the meeting time back to 10:00 because certain people didn't seem to be able to arrive on time. After a brief pause while this reprimand settled over the group, he informed us that we weren't going to go down to Folly Beach to pray (the night's scheduled activity) until the following week because "that takes too much preparation." He announced, much to my surprise, that we were going over to Colonial Lake instead to pray and asked us all to assemble there as soon as we could. Colonial Lake was right by our apartment building and lies just above Broad Street, the line that separates Charleston's oldest and "best" white families from the rest of the not-quite-so genteel (but still very white and affluent) population on the southern end of the peninsula.

As a recent expatriate of Chicago, which had just then been labeled by sociologists as America's most racially segregated city, I was puzzled that this group of African Americans did not seem to feel intimidated at the idea of assembling in an upscale white neighborhood. We *were* in the South now, weren't we? I knew all about the Civil Rights Movement and the brutal tactics of repression practiced by Southern whites. I had seen *Eyes on the Prize* with the footage of dogs, fire hoses, and the contents of sugar canisters poured over the heads of peaceable African Americans sitting at lunch counters. I was nervous, even if they didn't seem to be. It was my first indication that race relations don't seem to work the same way in the South, at least in the urban areas, as they do in Chicago, where I had been in graduate school, or in California, where I had spent most of my childhood. Not that they really seemed to be *better* in the South—just somehow *different*.

As we stood up and headed back toward the doors of the sanctuary, my wife asked our new acquaintance Ronald if he wanted a ride. He gladly accepted the offer, as he had walked to the church from the northern end of the neighborhood, just on the other side of the Silas Perlman Bridge that bisects the Eastside and connects the peninsula to Mt. Pleasant. Retracing our path back to Colonial Lake with Ronald in the back seat, we found out that he wasn't actually a member of Eastside Chapel. He had listened to "Pastor's Prayer Time," Reverend Wright's weekly gospel radio program on a local AM station, earlier that week, and when this evening's prayer service was announced, he "felt called" to come down and join in. Ronald is in the construction business—he works with plaster and stucco—which, along with painting and bricklaying, is a traditionally African American trade in the Charleston area that goes back to slavery times. He told us that he and his wife, who had not accompanied him this evening, normally attended a nondenominational church across town. In fact, although Ronald came to Eastside Chapel on a fairly regular basis over the next twelve months, I never did see his wife with him.

In just ten minutes we were pulling up to Colonial Lake. Although poetic, the name of this small body of water is really a double misnomer, for it is not really a lake and was built much more recently than the colonial era. Originally a pond for the sawmills that operated on that part of the peninsula, it is now an artificial pool fed underground by the tidal Ashley River and surrounded by a concrete apron ringed with palmetto trees and oleander bushes. Its quarter-mile perimeter forms a track that is a favorite spot during the day for joggers, dog-walkers, and a still-common sight: black nannies pushing strollers with their white charges. Despite the fact that it was now 11:00 p.m., the August heat had drawn out several older white couples from nearby homes who were strolling around the water. Perhaps because my self-consciousness was heightened by being with this group of African Americans in a very white part of town, I sensed that these white couples were curious and more than a little suspicious of us—particularly when they spied two whites, my wife and me, among the group. There were now about twenty-five of us assembled, mostly women and only about five or so men besides Reverend Wright, Ronald, and me. One of these men was quite noticeably drunk, and, I found out later, had been brought right off a street corner by one of the other men. Like Ronald, about three or four people had come from other churches after hearing about the event on Reverend Wright's radio program.

We assembled in a loose knot around "Rev," as he was known by those closest to him in the church, who asked us if anyone had anything to share that would benefit the group. After a few moments of silence, several people began to share stories of how their faith had led them through difficult times of poor health and financial uncertainty. A few others said that they had received a dream or vision for the ministry of the church. As people talked I realized that they meant those terms "dream" and "vision" in a literal, spiritual sense and not, as I was typically used to hearing them, as fancy language for an organizational mission statement. As I look back on it now, this was my first clue that the experience of the supernatural was going to play a much larger role in my understanding of this church than I yet realized.

After allowing people to speak for about twenty minutes, Reverend Wright gave the assembled group a few words of instruction as to what to pray for, and then sent us on our way around the perimeter of the lake. He directed us to walk "either by yourself or in twos and threes." So off we went, mostly in one big clump that thinned out when we were about halfway around the lake. Given that it was now about 11:30 at night and we were in a public area on a residential street, I had assumed that people would pray silently, or at least in subdued tones, as they marched. But as we walked most people began to pray out loud, and some of the women began to achieve a rather considerable volume. One woman in particular started praying in tongues in a loud and agitated voice and at the same time she began to have what looked like mild convulsions. She was helped along by two companions on either side, and nobody seemed to pay much attention to it, except perhaps the white people still strolling by and working hard to retain an uninterested air of nonchalance.

After two laps around the lake, which took about fifteen minutes, we assembled back in a group and Reverend Wright asked us if the Spirit had spoken to anybody. Hesitantly, a few people shared some vaguely worded spiritual affirmations that Reverend Wright received soberly and without comment. When they finished, he paused for a few moments and then declared that while we were walking and praying, the Lord had spoken to him. "God," he announced,

> told me that souls of his children—and particularly black people—are "dusty." God said that he missed the praises and dancing of his people. And so we are going to have an all-night praise celebration on this coming Friday. For if the people of the world can party all night and praise their god Satan, we Christians should be able to show that we can have just as much tenacity in praising the true, living God!

This announcement was greeted with what looked like genuine enthusiasm from the gathering, who seemed to be quite excited at the prospect of an all-night praise meeting.

Reverend Wright then said that we should "bless each other" for a while and instructed each of us to find somebody, pray over them for a few minutes, then move on to someone else. So we began, and by the time it was over I had prayed with about a dozen different people, each one in the same way: they came at me with both arms outstretched, gripped my hands tightly, squeezed their eyes shut, and prayed out loud—sometimes in English, sometimes in an unrecognizable "prayer language." Most appeared to be quite fervent, and several people hugged me and praised God for my wife and my coming to their group. Then they dropped my hands and went to find another prayer partner.

During all of this praying and partner switching, which reminded me in an odd way of square dancing, I suddenly noticed one male voice that floated above the choppy waves of sound created by all of that simultaneous praying. Turning around to find its source, I saw that Reverend Wright had latched on to the drunk man off the street and was loudly rebuking the "spirit of alcoholism" in him. I looked nervously for the older white couples, but they seemed to have melted back into the humid Lowcountry night. Finally, some time after midnight, we formed one big circle and held hands for the closing prayer. Reverend Wright gave a short benediction and then announced that we would meet at 9:00 p.m. the following week for the prayer time at Folly Beach. Kathy and I collected Ronald and gave him a ride back to his apartment, then compared notes about the evening's experience on the drive back to our side of town.

This Saturday night prayer meeting (or midnight prayer meeting as it was sometimes called) was my first exposure to the congregation that I am calling Eastside Chapel, and it gave me a taste of just about everything else that I would observe over my next twelve months in Charleston. The dreams and visions, the prophetic word from God about "dusty souls," the speaking in tongues and mild convulsive movements while "in the spirit"—I would hear stories of countless similar episodes during my interviews and witness firsthand many of the same actions during prayer meetings, Sunday worship services, and revival meetings. In fact, the very next day during the morning worship service I observed several women engaging in extended episodes of "shouting" or paroxysmal dancing under the influence of the Holy Spirit that only ended when they "fell out" or fainted and lay prostrate on the floor in a semiconscious state.

If you're not used to it (and I certainly wasn't), watching people dance ecstatically in the aisles for over ten minutes and then appear to pass out cold in church can be somewhat disconcerting. And it's not like I was completely unprepared for anything like this. I had been to Protestant charismatic churches before as part of my religious upbringing, and my father had even taught for a while at a charismatic seminary in Orange County, California. But those were white, mostly middle-to-lower-middle-class establishments, and there was never any spontaneous dancing or hollering. I had only seen people being "slain in the spirit" once before, as a teenager, when a friend took me to his Foursquare Gospel church. And even that was more orderly, as people lined up in the front of the pulpit fell backwards one by one when the pastor walked by them with his arm outstretched, like mechanical ducks in a shooting gallery. By comparison, the seemingly spontaneous eruptions of shouting, dancing, and general carrying on at Eastside Chapel seemed far more chaotic, uncontrolled, and unpredictable. I was fascinated.

I think that this initial fascination came from the fact that this religious world seemed so familiar and so foreign to me at the same time. True, in the churches of my youth there were no seventy-year-old women in fancy dresses and hats pogo-ing to an organ riff that sounded more Fats Domino than George Beverly Shea. But the people here at Eastside talked a lot of the same language as the folks I knew growing up: about being "born again," the importance of being "filled with the Holy Spirit," the process of "sanctification," how to avoid the "temptations of the world," and other phrases that mark the more theologically conservative wing of American Protestantism. This combination of familiar theology packaged in an exotic (to me at least) and energetic cultural form proved irresistible. So instead of feeling threatened by it or dismissing it as simply nonsensical or as a form of mass hysteria (as many scholars, both black and white, have done), I wanted to know more. So much so, in fact, that I changed the entire focus of my research.

The Research Process

Although I had come to Charleston that summer to study the African American church, the original purpose of the research was very different from what it became. As a graduate student at the University of Chicago just finishing my coursework, I had recently encountered William Julius Wilson and his book *The Truly Disadvantaged* (1987), as well as other writings on what was then being called the urban "underclass." As a pastor's kid with a personal as well as professional interest in the sociology of religion, I was curious to understand the role of churches in the high-poverty African American neighborhoods that Wilson and others were talking about. My plan was to target one such community and its churches for investigation and to gauge the nature and extent of mutual influence between neighborhood and congregation. After a brief foray to Charleston in February, I used tract-level census data to select a community on the peninsula that appeared to fit the standard "underclass" criterion of having 40 percent or more of the individuals living below the poverty line. When we packed our U-Haul trailer and moved to the city in July, I got out the Yellow Pages and began to call pastors.

My first visit was to a black United Methodist congregation on Meeting Street. This seemed like a good (i.e., nonthreatening) place to start, as it was a larger, established church affiliated with a mostly white denomination and was situated on a major artery bordering the neighborhood, almost directly across from the brand new visitor's center that the city was putting up. After attending this and a few other middle-class and relatively stuffy congregations on the periphery of the neighborhood—both United Methodist and African Methodist Episcopal (AME)—I called Reverend Wright and found myself at the Saturday Night Prayer Service at Colonial Lake. It was at this point that my research started to shift from a church-and-community project to one centered on religious experience and ritual.

I should reiterate that it was actually my wife and I who attended that prayer service. After all, she was the reason that we were in Charleston in the first place. She is also a sociologist, and her work on low-income single mothers in Chicago had attracted some foundation money to extend that research to three other sites chosen carefully according to varying economic and social welfare conditions. So we had come to Charleston, sight unseen, because it was a city with a strong economy and low AFDC benefits. We never dreamed that we would become so taken with the town— its history and architecture, and the little church in a neighborhood that most whites were afraid to drive through.

I spent the next twelve months at Eastside Chapel, and during that time my initial sense of strange familiarity only deepened. When I listened to people recount their often complex and symbolic spiritual dreams to me, accepted folk medical advice for healing cuts (by draping them with spider webs), heard stories about "seeing colors" while in church (in which everything seemed to turn pink), and of course, observing the "shouting" and "falling out" on Sunday mornings, I often felt how white, middle-class and Northern (or, more accurately, non-Southern) I really was. Yet, as all ethnographers know, spending time with people allows you to see them as just that—people—and to discover the myriad ways in which we are all essentially similar. Through the course of researching this book, my wife and I became very close to several families in the church. As well as being an academic exercise then, this book also serves as a kind of scrapbook that documents a very significant year in our personal lives.

Which raises the question, Why this book? Although certainly not as common as books on diets or management techniques, there are a number of good works on African American religion that have been published in recent years. Why add another one to the growing pile? Every author should have something unique to contribute, and with *Every Time I Feel the Spirit*, I am trying to achieve several things. First, I want to provide a window into the tremendously important yet still largely overlooked world of African American religion as the faith is lived by ordinary believers. Whatever else religion is (and it is many things—a set of beliefs, a moral code, a community of the like-minded, a tax-exempt voluntary organization) it is, at its most fundamental and profound level, a way of understanding and experiencing the world. It is also a way of orienting one's actions based on these understandings and experiences, and this is where the subject of religious ritual comes in. Eastsiders, as I quickly discovered, have an intimate and powerful connection to the spiritual realm, a connection that is seen in both their individual encounters with God and in their collective expressions of worship. In fact, I had been at Eastside Chapel only a week or two when I met the strange and mysterious Dr. Alexander Palmer (a taxi driver and herbologist with, he said, a degree in "metaphysiology"), who said that he had "a word from the Lord" for me and my research in the church. "The book you are going to write," he prophesied, "is going to touch a lot of people and reveal to the white community the depth of the relationship between black Christians and God." It sounded good to me (particularly the part about "a lot of people"), and, upon reflection, this is a pretty fair characterization of the final product.

I should say up front that this is a book about black religion *as religion*. The italics in that last sentence might puzzle readers from outside of the academic world, who may be forgiven for naively assuming that this is a rather obvious point. Let me explain. For decades, scholars have been preoccupied, one might even say obsessed, with one issue regarding African American religion: the relation between black Christianity and political consciousness and/or social activism. The ghostly voice of Karl Marx, heard now only in distant echoes in most rooms of the sociological mansion, is still quite loud and clear in the closet devoted to the study of the

African American church. It seems that one of the burdens oppressed peoples must forever carry is the paternal concern of academics, who constantly worry that a robust spiritual consciousness interferes with the far more important business of developing a political one.

Of course there is nothing inherently wrong with investigating the effects of religion on political and social activism, as long as one recognizes that it is a very limited perspective that does not engage most of what is central to religious belief and practice. More importantly, it misses (and all too often dismisses) what religious people themselves think is important about their faith. The best example of the constraints imposed by this kind of approach is Peter Goldsmith's (1989) otherwise wonderful anthropological study of two Sea Island African American congregations off the coast of Georgia. In the first part of the book he presents a beautifully nuanced and in-depth comparison of the histories and the ritual practices of these churches—one Baptist and one Holiness. But his analysis is hamstrung by a single-minded reliance upon the Marxist notion of hegemony, which forces the theoretical conclusions along very predictable channels of "false consciousness."

As long as I am stating what this book is not about, let me say that there are a few other debates that I don't intend to engage in here. The first is the issue of African versus European influence in the traditional worship style of black religion. Is shouting purely an African survival, or did the enthusiasms of the racially mixed Methodist camp meetings contribute to this form of expression? This is a difficult (and probably impossible) question to answer definitively, given the lack of appropriate historical sources that could shed light on the matter. More interesting to me is how black Christians themselves have approached this issue and how they have construed "shouting," the use of drums and other elements of worship as racially distinctive. On a related front, the debate over whether enslaved Africans really did adopt their masters' religion or simply appropriated the outward forms of it for their own purposes is outside the scope of this study. Not only is this question also probably impossible to settle empirically, but it is a question better situated in the ideological field of racial politics than in an any purely academic debate.

Some readers may mistakenly assume that this book fits into the growing genre of sociological research called "congregational studies," an understandable assumption, given that one congregation was the setting for most of the fieldwork. However, this is not an exercise in religious organizational sociology, and I do not pay very much attention to the general structure of the church, its status hierarchies or social cleavages, its history and development as an independent entity, or even its gender dynamics. Nor is the overall culture of the congregation much on display here, at least as an anthropologist might approach such a task. For example, I do not thoroughly or systematically explore the belief system of the congregation or its use of symbols except as they relate to experience or ritual.

Instead, I have limited my focus to individual members' religious experiences in their daily lives, and the collective experience of worship, with a particular emphasis on the Sunday morning service. My justification for this approach is that these two aspects of religious life have remained understudied and undertheorized within the social sciences. Less defensibly, at least from an academic standpoint perhaps, is that they were also the aspects of Eastside Chapel that I found endlessly fascinating.

Of course, the religious experiences of these individuals are profoundly shaped by their membership in the social organization called Eastside Chapel, and particularly through the informal comments and formal teachings of Reverend Wright. But they were also shaped, as the story of Mother Gadsden in chapter 5 makes quite clear, by contacts outside of the congregation, and even, in significant ways, by exposure to the larger cultural world of religious broadcasting and print media. It is the members of Eastside Chapel and their experiences that are the essential units of analysis in the first part of the book, and individuals are never completely, or even primarily, encapsulated by one organization, even one as seemingly all-consuming as a sectarian church.

In the second part of the book I expand the focus from the personal to the collective experience of worship, with an emphasis on analyzing the Sunday morning service. Because this is the ritual centerpiece of religious life and what most people visualize when someone mentions the word "church," one can easily be misled into the idea that to study the Sunday morning worship service is to study the congregation directly (Goffman 1961: 12). There are several inadequacies in this belief. First and most obviously, the active membership of the organization is never perfectly coterminous with the participants in any particular worship service, even on the first Sunday of the month, when most Eastsiders try to be there. Second, there are differences between being a member of a church and a participant in a ritual. For example, there is no one-to-one correspondence between those in positions of authority in the congregation and those who dominate ritual occasions. The senior pastor of course has a relatively unique position in that he or she wields a great deal of both organizational and ritual control. However, other persons in positions of authority and power in the church (trustees, for example, or large financial contributors) may never stand up in front of the church and be content to wield their considerable influence "behind the scenes," while choir directors, musicians and other ritual specialists on display every Sunday may have little actual say in the life or direction of the church as an organization. Likewise, conflicts between segments of the church membership are of considerable import to the church, but these fault lines are seldom openly exposed, or even quietly alluded to, in public ritual.

On a more positive note, let me say a few things about what I *am* trying to accomplish here. First, I let the analyses in this book emerge from my observations and interviews in Eastside Chapel. As I stated before, I had arrived in Charleston with a much different research agenda in mind. It is no great tribute to my keen sensitivities as a field-worker that I abandoned the church-community project and began to focus on the spiritual experiences of Eastside members and the dynamics of the worship services. As the reader will see, these topics were pretty much thrust upon me continually as I became involved in the life of the church and I would have to have been extraordinarily dull or stubborn to have avoided them.

Although this book attempts a faithful description of the religious world of Eastside Chapel, this does not mean that it is simply a collection of stories and observations. It is, after all, a work of sociology, and I do have some theoretical ambitions—namely to extend and refine sociological understandings of religious ritual and religious experience. Chapter 1 gives a description of Eastside Chapel and its setting—both in the geography of the South Carolina Lowcountry and in the culture and history of black religion in the United States. Those squeamish about theory will be relieved to discover that most of it is confined to chapter 2 in which I try to engage the concepts of experience and ritual in as brief and jargon-free a manner as possible. Chapter 3 discusses Eastsiders' experiences of God and his activity in their everyday lives, while chapter 4 turns to Eastsiders' conception of Satan and the spiritual battle they see around them. After this, the focus of the book shifts from experience to ritual in chapters 5 and 6, particularly showing how religious experience is incorporated into the Sunday morning service and other collective gatherings. Chapter 7 turns to the social location of the congregation and its influence in shaping both ritual and experience. Finally, the conclusion offers a summary of the book's approach to religious experience and ritual and points out some implications for the study of religion in general.

God's House in the Holy City

The past, someone once observed, is another country. Perhaps this is why Charleston seemed so foreign and exotic to me the first time I drove down South Carolina's Route 61, past the Ashley River plantations with their quaint formal gardens and ghostly rice fields and onto the streets of the narrow peninsula. For in this city, history is a constant and talkative companion who continually interrupts the routines of daily life with reminders of its 300-odd years of existence. Every trip through the compact grid of downtown streets and alleys, whether to the grocery store or post office, is like a journey through Southern history, and one must pass the house of this Confederate general or that signer of the Declaration of Independence just to mail a letter or buy some milk and eggs. The description of a visit to Charleston as "walking through the pages of a history book" (Stevens 1939) are as applicable now as they were when they were written during the Great Depression, and I soon found that the greatest challenge of driving here was avoiding the horse-drawn carriages that constantly plied the lower half of the peninsula, filled with sun-burned tourists marveling at the nation's largest collection of pre-Revolutionary structures.

As one who had spent most of my thirty-something years in southern California, where any building older than the Second World War seemed like an ancient relic, I found this history-on-display quite remarkable, sometimes astonishing and frequently disturbing. For mixed in the urban landscape with these venerated and meticulously preserved buildings, there are reminders of another past that is not so glorious. The physical remains of this legacy are sprinkled throughout the city's historic district in such sites as the Old Jail, a crumbling concrete fortress in the middle of an African American housing project and built on the very site of the work house once used to punish slaves. There is the Old Slave Mart on Chalmers Street, site of the largest slave auction house in the South and a museum for a brief time, but now shuttered after Hurricane Hugo tore the roof off in 1989. There is Market Hall on Meeting and Market Streets, standing at the epicenter of Charleston tourism and recently renovated, with a museum devoted to the Daughters of the Confederacy. And of course, there are the remains of Fort Sumter, a constant brooding presence in the harbor and a silent testament to the war waged to defend that "peculiar institution" of slavery.

Here in the Lowcountry, the boundary between past and present was more permeable than any place I had ever been, and it seemed particularly true of this twisted and tangled relationship between blacks and whites. Unlike the North, which didn't accommodate significant numbers of African Americans until after 1910, the races have over three hundred years of continuous history together in the South, and the physical legacies of this complex past are all but unavoidable. Even the drive from our apartment building on Colonial Lake to Eastside Chapel was like a guided tour of the brutal, tragic, and often ironic history of southern race relations: past the statue of John C. Calhoun the ardent "fire-eating" separatist whose passionate rhetoric helped spur South Carolina to become the first state to withdraw from the Union; past the Old Citadel, an institution with its origins in the establishment of a city militia following the aborted slave uprising in 1822 led by Denmark Vesey (and serving, in the 1980s and 1990s, as the county welfare office before its current incarnation as an Embassy Suites hotel); past Emanuel AME Church, one of the first and most important independent black churches in the South, and the base of Vesey's recruitment for that slave insurrection that never happened.

Although Eastside Chapel itself is hardly historic—it was founded and built in the 1940s—the surrounding community has a unique place in African American history as one of the oldest urban black settlements in the country. The Eastside neighborhood actually comprises several historic suburbs—Mazyckborough, Wraggsborough, and Hampstead—which were annexed to the city in 1849. Although furthest away from the old section of city, the Village of Hampstead was the first of the three to be developed, laid out in the 1760s by Henry Laurens, a slave trader and millionaire several times over and perhaps one of the wealthiest men in the American colonies at that time (Fraser 1989). Laurens modeled his ninety-nine acres after an English suburb, complete with a central grassy square that still remains. Mazyckborough was developed next, in 1786, and subdivided into exceptionally wide streets to help control the fires that plagued the narrow cramped quarters of old Charleston. Finally, Wraggsborough was laid out in the 1790s with an open mall off Meeting Street for public use (Grimes et al. 1987).

Because contemporary American cities tend to be so segregated by race and class, it is sometimes difficult to imagine how diverse the population of the Eastside was for most of its history. In the early 1800s wealthy white planters Joseph Manigault and William Aiken built mansions (both of which still stand) in the Mazyck-Wraggsborough districts, and Hampstead was the summer home of several successful planters and merchants. Interspersed among these wealthier families were many middle and working-class whites who moved into the neighborhood in the 1830s and 1840s, some displaced by the fire of 1838 in nearby Ansonborough. When white immigrants from Ireland, Bavaria, and France poured into the already crowded area in the 1850s, they lived with sometimes as many as 16 under one roof (Grimes et al. 1987). The homes that were built during this period, from 1830–1860, were patterned after the "single house" which predominated in the lower part of the city, so called because they are one room wide and two rooms deep on each floor, with porches (called "piazzas" by Charlestonians) on the sides to catch the summer breezes.

The "Neck" as this portion of the peninsula was then known, also attracted many African Americans. After the Ansonborough fire Charleston passed an ordinance requiring that all new structures were to be built with brick, with the result that the Neck (which was still outside the city limits) became, according to one observer, "rapidly filled with small cheap wooden houses." Many slaves whose masters had permitted them to live on their own (a growing practice at this time in the urban South) sought housing in this lower-rent district (Wade 1964). Here they lived alongside free blacks, a group that made up almost a quarter of the Neck's African American population in 1850 (Jenkins 1998). In addition to the attraction of cheap rents, the area was also further from police surveillance and thus appealed to "runaways, slaves 'passing as free,' and other people eager to expand their margin of liberty" (Grimes et al. 1987: 3). The growing numbers of slave and free blacks in the Neck was a constant worry to authorities, and the area was annexed to the city in 1849 partly to establish more control over this population (Powers 1994). In 1850, whites made up about 46 percent of the Neck's population, slaves comprised another 45 percent, and free persons of color the additional 9 percent.

After the Civil War the city's black population increased rapidly as freed slaves left the rural plantations and streamed into the urban centers of the South, and Charleston's total African American population grew by 57 percent between 1860 and 1870. The black population of the Neck grew by 79 percent during the decade while losing only about 3 percent of its whites (Jenkins 1998). Throughout the first half of the twentieth century, Charleston remained one of America's most residentially integrated cities, with African Americans spread throughout every district (Taeuber and Taeuber 1969). In 1900, the three wards that comprise the current Eastside were 31 percent, 36 percent, and 37 percent black, nearly perfectly coinciding with African Americans' representation of 36 percent in Charleston overall. Residential integration was the norm here, to the extent that Cabbage Row, the black tenement renamed "Catfish Row" in Dubose Heyward's 1925 novel, *Porgy and Bess,* was located below Broad Street in Charleston's wealthiest enclave.

While Charleston became progressively more segregated in the early decades of the twentieth century, it still had the lowest segregation index of any American city until 1960 (Taeuber and Taeuber 1969). Several factors contributed to this slow but steady racial separation of the city. First, there was a steady attrition of blacks employed as domestic servants by wealthy white families. These servants, who generally lived in or near their places of employment, relocated to the upper wards of the city. The lower wards also began to restore their large historic houses, with the effect of raising property values and forcing out low-income blacks. Finally, the construction of the Wraggsborough public housing complex in the Eastside during the 1940s and 1950s drew a uniformly poor and black population to the area (Zierden 1990; Powers 1994).

At some point in the 1960s, probably coinciding with enforcement of desegregation in the Charleston School District, residential turnover reached a tipping point and there were dramatic changes in the racial complexion of the neighborhood. In 1960 the Eastside held almost 10,000 people, about 60 percent of them African American, and the median income of the nonwhite population was only slightly below that for the non-white population in the larger metropolitan area. By 1970 all but a handful of whites had left and there was a slight decrease in the black population as well. The result was that the Eastside lost over 40 percent of its overall population and became 98 percent black within a few short years. With a poverty rate of 65 percent, the remaining black residents were significantly poorer than those in the larger Charleston area, which had a rate of about 50 percent. These trends continued for the next two decades, so that by the time I began my research the neighborhood was down to about 3,400 residents—a 65 percent loss in population since 1960. While the fortunes of

Charleston's African Americans improved greatly after the Civil Rights era, the Eastside increasingly became the repository of the elderly and impoverished. The poverty rate for the neighborhood's African Americans was 55 percent, down from its height in 1960, but still far above the cutoff of 40 percent that social scientists had established for identifying neighborhoods of "extreme poverty" (Jargowsky and Bane 1990), and a full 25 points higher than the rate for the region's African Americans as a whole.

In short, when I first came to Eastside Chapel the neighborhood around the church had become Charleston's most notorious and dangerous slum. Directly across the street from the church property there was an abandoned house, sagging and weary with neglect, almost every chip of paint weathered from the gray boards. Every block had at least two or three of these boarded-up and abandoned properties, rotting like bad teeth between the occupied dwellings, some of which didn't look in much better shape. These crumbling houses, many between 90 and 150 years old, are the legacy of neighborhood's white and black flight over the past forty years. In the late 1990s, the Eastside Neighborhood Council mapped 115 abandoned buildings in one part of the community (Maybank 2001). In addition to population loss and neglected housing stock, the Eastside has become increasingly plagued by the social problems that seem inevitably to accompany inner-city poverty—unemployment, fatherless families, crime, drug abuse, and social isolation. Nearly 12 percent of the Eastside's adult men were unemployed when I began my study, compared to 7 percent of African American men in the greater Charleston area (and only 2 percent of white men). When they were able to find employment, close to 40 percent of Eastside adults worked in service occupations—almost twice the rate for other blacks in the region. This may reflect the lack of education among the population, as over 60 percent of the neighborhood adults over twenty-five years of age had not graduated from high school, a rate that was a third higher than the rate for African Americans throughout Charleston. Finally, almost a third of the families in the neighborhood were headed by single mothers, and close to a third of all the families had some income from public assistance (U.S. Bureau of the Census 1990).

In this impoverished environment dealing drugs is a tempting occupation for many of the Eastside's male residents. Opportunities to do so are particularly plentiful in Charleston, as it is the seventh busiest seaport in the United States and serves as an entry point for the South American, Asian, and Mexican narcotics destined for distribution in the Southeast. A half a block to the south of the church there is a tiny corner store where boisterous young men tend to gather and carouse on weekend evenings, sometimes loudly enough to distract from Eastside Chapel's Sunday evening services or the midnight prayer service on Saturday nights. In addition to the usual (and generally unheeded) signs that prohibit loitering in front of the store, a hand-lettered message on the front door warns: "There will be no drug dealing in and around this establishment. A hint to the wise should be sufficient. Leave your drugs at home or somewhere else." Several of Eastside Chapel's men—including several church leaders—were either former dealers or still struggled, sometimes unsuccessfully, with the temptation to go back to the trade.

Where there are drugs, there is crime. Shortly before I began studying the church, Lt. Ronald Hamilton, head of the Charleston Police Team One unit whose boundaries include the Eastside, told the Charleston *Post-Courier,* "Crime on the Eastside is out of control" (Dorothy Givens, "Policeman Gives Grim Report on East Side Crime," Nov. 15, 1990). In the same article a local merchant reported that his store had been broken into over fifty times in a two-year span. Just five days later the paper ran an article with the headline "Eastside Heavy on Homicides," with figures showing that the majority of the sixty homicides in Charleston from 1983 (the year that the popular but eccentric police chief Rueben Greenberg took office) to 1990 had occurred in the Eastside (Charles Francis, Nov. 20, 1990). Much of the crime was drug-related, and the worst drug infested corner in the county was right on the park that had once served as Hampstead's village green 200 years earlier. The many abandoned houses in the area also attracted addicts who used them as "shooting galleries"—a problem so bad that the city started seizing properties identified by police and residents as the worst of the "drug havens" and boarding them up (*Post-Courier* April 9, 1992). In 1992 the Federal government chose the Eastside, now recognized as the drug and crime capital of the Lowcountry, as a demonstration site for its "weed and seed" program and began to initiate community policing and other neighborhood programs, with mixed results.

Although the Eastside continues to have more than its share of poverty and the many social problems that accompany it, the neighborhood is not wanting for religious resources. One of Charleston's oldest nicknames is "the Holy City," a moniker earned, so the guidebooks speculate, because of the many churches within its borders. If this interpretation is true (the label may be an ironic one, given the city's historic reputation for drunkenness, debauchery, and general wickedness), then the Eastside can perhaps be considered its most sacred community. Within the small area defined by the neighborhood boundaries (about one mile long and a half mile wide), I counted no fewer than fifteen active black congregations when I first explored the community, in the fall of 1991. Although racially homogenous, these churches were quite diverse in denominational affiliation: one Catholic, two Baptist, two United Methodist, three African Methodist Episcopal, one Christian Methodist Episcopal, one Reformed Episcopal, one Church of God in Christ, and four independent Holiness or Pentecostal congregations. They ranged in size from the massive presence of Emanuel AME (the flagship church of the denomination in the South), to the small and struggling independent churches where sometimes fewer than a dozen of the faithful worshipped together on a Sunday morning. Still, the vitality and dedication of these congregations stood in stark contrast to the poverty, crime, and hopelessness that surrounded them.

Although such a concentration of black churches in poor urban communities is certainly not unique (McRoberts 2003), the African American congregations of the Eastside have spiritual roots that go deeper than those in virtually any other North American community. Charleston was the scene of three decisive events in the development of black Christianity: the historic encounter between John Wesley and a converted African that led to the first Christian outreach to the slaves; the discovery of the Denmark Vesey slave rebellion, which closed independent black churches throughout the South for decades; and the landmark meeting that launched the coordinated mission to the slaves in the contentious years before the Civil War. Though these events have mostly receded into obscurity—only the Vesey incident has remained an important touchstone for some of the region's black population—their legacy has powerfully shaped the religious landscape of African Americans today, in Charleston and throughout the nation.

It was on the first Sunday in August in 1736 when John Wesley, who had been in the colonies for less than six months, delivered a sermon at St. Philip's Church in Charleston. Wesley had been invited to preach by Anglican minister Alexander Garden, the Commissary of the Bishop of London and a long-time advocate of religious education for slaves. Following the service, Wesley—probably on his own initiative—approached one of the few Africans in attendance, an older woman who had been converted to Christianity by her mistress. Conversing with her for some time, Wesley became increasingly distressed at her inability to answer what he considered the most basic questions of Christian teaching. Reflecting later upon the conversation, he anguished, "When shall the Sun of Righteousness arise on these outcasts of men, with healing in His Wings?" This event had a deep impact on Wesley and tremendous significance for the future Christianization of African Americans, as this encounter in Charleston marks the beginning of the evangelical Protestant mission to the slaves (Frey and Wood 1998: 89).

When Wesley preached that sermon in 1736, Africans had been in the Lowcountry of South Carolina for over sixty years, arriving in Charlestown, as it was then known, with the first boatload of displaced Barbadians in 1670. In a very real sense, the history of African Americans in Charleston is the history of Africans as a people in North America, as scholars estimate that well over 40 percent of all the slaves reaching the British mainland colonies between 1700 and 1775 first touched the New World here. Historian Peter Wood provides the metaphor:

> Here was a thin neck in the hourglass of the Afro-American past, a place where individual grains from all along the West African coast had been funneled together, only to be fanned out across the American land-scape with the passage of time. Sullivan's Island, the sandy spit on the northeast edge of Charlestown harbor where incoming slaves were briefly quarantined, might well be viewed as the Ellis Island of black Americans. (1974: xiv)

As a major port of entry for African slaves, the nonwhite population of South Carolina grew rapidly, particularly with the successful introduction of rice in the late seventeenth century and the rising demand for workers from West Africa who knew how to cultivate the profitable crop. Around 1708, within one generation of the colony's founding, the black population outstripped the white through continued importation. By 1720, persons of African descent comprised 65 percent of South Carolina's population, and the density of the black population in the colony was the highest of any in North America. Upon landing in Charlestown a year after Wesley's visit, one Swiss immigrant remarked, "Carolina looks more like a Negro coun-try than like a country settled by white people" (Wood 1974: 132).

There had been some attempt to convert the growing numbers of en-slaved Africans to Christianity before the Wesleys—and George Whitefield after them—brought Methodism to the slaves. The Anglican Church had established the Society for the Propagation of the Gospel to Foreign Parts (SPG) in 1701 for the express purpose of evangelizing Native Americans and African slaves, but this effort failed for several reasons. First, the Anglican brand of Christianity was book-oriented, which not only clashed with the more experiential African religious style, but also meant that SPG missionaries placed an emphasis on teaching the slaves to read—a practice staunchly opposed by most slaveholders, particularly following the Stono Rebellion of 1740 (Creel 1988). As a result, many slave owners actively opposed slave conversion and refused to let missionaries onto their property or allow the slaves to meet for Sunday services. Because the SPG workers drew their salaries from these same planters, they were hardly in a position to force the issue. Second, American colonists were not an especially religious lot themselves and showed little outward concern for their own souls, let alone those of their bondspeople. This indifference to Christianity did not escape the notice, nor the condemnation, of the SPG missionaries who diverted their religious zeal toward saving the colony's white population. Missionary Francis Le Jau wrote to his London supervisor in 1713 that he had been forced to spend much of his energies not on converting the "pagan" Africans but on combating the "visible progress of atheism, irreligion and immorality" among the English colonists (Bowes 1942: 17).

African Americans not only outnumbered whites in South Carolina for most of their almost 200 years of slavery, but they were also densely settled and relatively isolated on rice and cotton plantations. One observer of the Lowcountry region remarked that these segregated living arrangements, combined with the continued importation of Africans into the nineteenth century, had allowed slaves to "more easily preserve their heathenish ideas and customs" (Powers 1994: 19). This is certainly true of the Gullah dialect, a Creole language that developed in Charleston and the Sea Islands to the south, and which is still spoken in some of the more remote areas of the region. Native African religious practices, primarily Islam and tribal-based animist cults, were also preserved under these conditions.

Thus, when the converted slave woman encountered John Wesley at St. Philip's Church, she was in the distinct religious minority of African Americans. It was not until the explosive growth of evangelical Christianity during the Great Awakening and the institutionalization of the Methodist church in America during the 1780s that the conversion of African slaves began in earnest. The success of the Baptists and Methodists in recruiting African slaves is attributable partly to the fact that their theology and ritual forms had a much greater affinity to African religious sensibilities than did the more formal and literary Anglican tradition. The success is also attributable to the outspoken anti-slavery attitudes of many evangelical leaders, particularly Wesley. However, it was the organized revival meetings and the developing system of itinerant preachers and missionary organizations that began to yield large harvests of African converts, beginning in the 1780s and gaining momentum throughout the early part of the nineteenth century. Between 1800 and 1815 the number of black Methodists doubled from 20,000 to over 40,000—or roughly a third of the entire Methodist population in America (Frey and Wood 1998: 149). The success of Methodists among Charleston's African Americans was particularly pronounced: conference records from 1800 show that 20 percent of the entire black population of Charleston belonged to the denomination. By 1817 the city had the largest Methodist society in North America, and black Methodists represented close to half of the city's African American population (Frey and Wood 1998).

With the phenomenal expansion of Methodism among both blacks and whites, racial tensions within the church were inevitable. Richard Allen, a free African American in Philadelphia, was barred from praying one morning in 1789 at his customary spot in a Methodist church. He and other aggrieved black parishioners withdrew their membership to form an independent African church that later evolved into the African Methodist Episcopal denomination, founded in 1817. That same year in Charleston, the white pastor of Bethel Methodist Church tried to restrict his black parishioners from collecting and managing their own tithes and offerings. Two free African Americans in the church, Morris Brown and Henry Drayton, were dispatched by black congregants to Philadelphia to be ordained as ministers in the newly formed AME Church. They returned to establish a branch in Charleston, and by 1818, four-fifths (4,367) of the African American members had left the white Methodist churches to join Charleston's new Emanuel AME, a figure that included most of the black deacons and represented almost a third of Charleston's African American population (Poole 1994).

For a short time this southern branch of the AME, second in size only to the mother church in Philadelphia, met in a hearse house on the Methodist burial grounds. In 1817 the church petitioned the state legislature for permission to worship in a church building that they had erected in Hampstead, part of the current Eastside neighborhood. The petition was granted, over the objections of the delegation from Charleston, but this novelty—the only legal all-black association in the entire state—was immediately regarded with hostility and suspicion by whites who started a campaign of harassment against the young church. Hundreds of blacks were arrested during one church meeting for "engaging in a species of worship which the neighborhood found a nuisance" (from the Charleston *City Gazette,* quoted in Wikramanayake 1973: 126). Six months later an additional 143 were arrested for the same reason. Eight of the ministers were given the option of receiving ten lashes each or paying a fine of five dollars, and Morris Brown and the other church leaders were sentenced to one month in jail. In 1820 a group of white citizens accused Emanuel of promoting abolitionism and petitioned the state legislature to close the church. This charge was never substantiated, but the discovery of the Denmark Vesey plot of 1822 sealed the fate of the church. Vesey, a former slave who had purchased his freedom through lottery winnings, was inspired by the successful slave revolt in Haiti in the 1790s. He and almost seventy other blacks, slave and free, had developed a plan to overpower the guards around the city arsenal, distributing arms to slaves in Charleston and the surrounding countryside before torching the city and killing the entire white population (Powers 1994). The conspiracy was betrayed before it was acted upon, and when officials arrested the organizers of the plot, they found that many, including Vesey, were leaders in the Emanuel AME congregation. The church was ordered closed, and the building was destroyed (Wikramanayake 1973).

No independent black churches were allowed in Charleston until the close of the Civil War forty-three years later. But the seeds of the AME had been firmly planted in what would prove to be very fertile soil for the denomination. Though Emanuel's building was destroyed and the congregation officially outlawed, worshippers went underground and continued to meet in small groups in private homes in the Hampstead area (Wikramanayake 1973). For public worship, African Americans were forced back into churches controlled by whites, and on any given Sunday during the 1840s about half of Charleston's black population attended services. It appears that most urban slaves were allowed to attend the church of their choice, and congregations within the wealthier denominations—Episcopalian, Presbyterian, Lutheran, and Congregationalist—drew fewer African Americans to their more restrained and intellectually oriented services. Yet even in these churches slave and free blacks comprised roughly half of the congregation, and they wholly dominated the Baptist and Methodist memberships. In 1845 the three Baptist churches in the city had a combined membership of 2,495, of whom almost 80 percent were African American. The three Methodist churches had an even smaller white minority, as 4,115 out of 4,751, or roughly 87 percent, of Charleston's Methodists were black (Clarke 1979). Although blacks and whites were members of the same congregation and attended Sunday worship services together, black congregants had their own classes and class leaders who functioned as preachers and pastors to the African Americans under their spiritual care.

The Christianizing of African Americans during this period was not limited to the Methodists or Baptists. For example, between 1840 and 1845 the proportion of blacks in the Presbyterian Church in South Carolina doubled and in 1845 constituted 28 percent of the denomination's total membership (Fickling 1924). By that time the issue of evangelizing the slaves had generated so much general interest that in May of that year there was a historic three-day conference held in Charleston to organize missionary efforts among the Southern denominations. Charles Colcock Jones, Charles Cotesworth Pinckney, William Capers, and other leaders in this movement were in attendance at this meeting on Chalmers Street, just down the street from one of the largest slave markets in the South (Clarke 1979). For the most part, this mission was targeted toward slaves on plantations, but there were also two separate black churches founded in Charleston in 1850: Anson Street Presbyterian Church (which evolved into Zion Presbyterian) and Calvary Episcopal. Both of these missionary congregations were under the care of white pastors.

Despite the intensification of evangelization efforts after 1845, the effectiveness of the missionary movement is difficult to determine. The Southern Methodists and Baptists claimed to almost double their black membership from 1846 to 1861 (Raboteau 1978), but other figures tell a different story, particularly in South Carolina. In 1840, about 17 percent of the state's slaves were members of the four major Southern denominations. The Methodists claimed exactly half of these, while the Baptists held about a quarter, the Episcopalians about 4 percent, the Presbyterians 3 percent, with the rest divided into the smaller denominations. Over the next twenty years, despite the great expansion of mission activity and denominational funding, the proportion of church members in the slave population grew by only 3 percent.

At the close of the Civil War several developments set the pattern for the segregated religious institutions that have carried over to today. Denominations that had split in the 1840s over slavery into Northern and Southern branches now began to divide below the Mason-Dixon line into parallel black and white institutions. The exodus of African Americans from the Southern denominations was swift and the losses to the white church were enormous. In South Carolina the Southern Methodists counted 50,000 black communicants in 1860. Six years later only 16,000 of them remained, and these were soon to be lost to the Colored Methodist Episcopal church (CME) when that denomination was established in the 1870s.

In 1865 missionaries from Northern denominations followed the Union Army into the defeated Confederate states. The missionaries' initial purpose was the same as the Federal government's—to rebuild the war-ravaged South into the image of the victorious North—but it was a moral and religious reconstruction that they sought. The Northern Methodists, for example, were particularly concerned to redeem their white coreligionists and make them see the error of their ways (Williamson 1965). The Southern Methodists, however, were less than welcoming to these crusading Yankees, whom they regarded as little more than religious carpetbaggers, and refused to cooperate. The rebuffed Northern missionaries quickly turned their evangelistic zeal to the black population and in this they were quite successful, primarily because they publicly advocated absolute racial equality within the church—a very appealing doctrine to the newly freed slaves and a position that would have been impossible had the missionaries succeeded in their original effort to recruit Southern whites. By the time of their first conference in 1866, the Northern Methodists claimed 2,750 African Americans in South Carolina, over half of whom lived in Charleston (Williamson 1965: 184).

Though the Northern Methodist Church in South Carolina held firmly to racial equality throughout the Reconstruction period, it was the denomination's leadership in the North that began to move toward recognition of racial distinctions. This development further eroded the competitive edge of the Northern Methodists over their strongest rivals among the region's African Americans—the reestablished Southern branch of the African Methodist Episcopal Church. After the closure of Emanuel AME in 1822, the denomination had no official presence in the Southeast until 1865, and it was under the leadership of Daniel Alexander Payne that the AME became the dominant religious institution among Charleston's African Americans. Born in Charleston in 1811 to free parents, Payne established a school for free black children when he was only nineteen years old. When South Carolina outlawed the teaching of both free and slave black children in 1834, Payne left Charleston and headed North. Thirty years after his departure from the city Payne returned as a bishop and missionary in the African Methodist Episcopal Church. He organized the South Carolina Conference in May of 1865 and its growth was immediate. One year from its founding, the AME boasted a membership of over 22,000, most of whom were South Carolinians. By the end of Reconstruction in 1877, the AME was the second largest black denomination in the state, with 44,000 members and 1,000 ministers (Williamson 1965).

Ironically, the growth of the AME was facilitated by support from the white Southern Methodists. Although the denomination was reluctant to let go of their black members, when they saw that such a separation was inevitable they preferred to send them to the African Methodists rather than to their would-be reformers in the Northern Methodist Church. In Charleston the Southern Methodists allowed the African Methodists to use Trinity Church while Emanuel AME was under construction. That church, so symbolic of the struggle for African American freedom, was rebuilt immediately after the Civil War and was one of the first buildings to go up in post–Civil War Charleston. It was established in a new location on Calhoun Street and constructed according to a design by architect Thomas Vesey—Denmark's son.

The AME has maintained a strong presence in South Carolina since that time. In 1906, forty years after the denomination returned to the South, the U.S. census of religious bodies counted a national membership of almost 500,000. South Carolina's two conferences reported 423 churches with over 55,000 members, or just over 10 percent of the membership. The AME is particularly strong in the coastal area of the state, which is one of the few regions in the country that have more black Methodists than Baptists.

Eastside Chapel

When Emanuel AME Church was closed by the authorities in 1822, the building was destroyed and the debris carted away. The lot on which it had stood was sold, and over the next century private homes were built and a Jewish cemetery was established nearby on the same block. In 1942, 120 years after the destruction of Charleston's first independent black church, another AME church was built almost directly on top of where the landmark structure had been. That church is the one I call Eastside Chapel and it was founded by the Reverend John Simmons. Although he died in 1995 at the age of 102, Reverend Simmons was still living when I was researching this book. Confined to a wheelchair and barely able to move or speak, he was wheeled over from his house next door to the church to attend the occasional special service, but otherwise did not take an active role in the congregation. In 1938 Reverend Simmons was pastoring an AME church in another part of the city when the presiding bishop of the local AME conference assigned him to a small congregation whose church building had just been destroyed by a hurricane. After renting several different halls for the church to use, the denomination negotiated for the current Eastside property and the main part of the church building was completed in 1942. (The fellowship hall wing was added later.) Reverend Simmons stayed for sixteen years as pastor of Eastside Chapel before going on to found four other AME churches on the Sea Islands off the Carolina coast—two on Edisto Island and two on Wadmalaw Island. Reverend Simmons's daughters Nazarene and Elizabeth, and his grandchildren Vertelle and Michael were all leaders in the congregation during my year in Charleston. The current pastor, the Reverend Roger L. Wright, was the ninth to succeed Reverend Simmons as Eastside's senior pastor.

By all accounts, Eastside Chapel's building hadn't changed much since Reverend Simmons founded the church fifty years earlier. It is a modest L-shaped structure built of wood and brick and sits on a treeless corner lot enclosed by a wrought-iron fence, with ample room for parking on the mostly dirt yard. The sanctuary itself holds about two hundred worshippers and is decorated according to the standard form of so many small Southern churches: white walls, red carpet, and few adornments. A computer-generated paper banner on the south wall features a rendition of praying hands next to the caption "What a Mighty God We Serve," while a similar banner in the front of the church reminds the congregation, "We've Come This Far By Faith." Behind the pulpit, slightly elevated and hidden behind a low wall, is the organ and a small choir loft. To the front of the church, stage left, is a small drum kit and a pair of congas.

A fellowship hall—used for children's Sunday School, overflow seating during worship and revival services, and Tuesday night Bible study—forms the leg of the L on the right hand side of the sanctuary, just about even with the pulpit. There are several small offices here—one for the pastor's study and one for storing files and office supplies. A wall across from these rooms displays a sheet of paper that lists current members of the Usher Board, and next to it is a schedule showing which of the many church organizations is responsible for leading the Sunday morning service for the next six months. Gray linoleum tile covers the floor, and metal folding chairs and collapsible tables serve as furniture. Although no pictures of Jesus are visible (the mural of a white Christ behind the choir loft was painted over several years before I came), there is a small triptych of Martin Luther King, Jr., Nelson Mandela, and Malcolm X clustered along one wall. A compact kitchen, where fried chicken dinners sometimes appear on Sunday afternoons, completes the room. A door from the fellowship hall allows congregants to step down and into the front yard, a small area nestled in the shadow of the building's two wings. There are no banks of flowers here or any other attempt at landscaping, just some hardscrabble grass and a well-worn dirt path back to the sidewalk.

Of the fifteen churches in the neighborhood, Eastside Chapel's building is just about in the middle of the range in size and amenities. On the one end of the continuum there are several small and dilapidated wood frame or cinder block structures that are not much larger than the average suburban living room and without such conveniences as a bathroom or central heating. (I spent a Sunday morning in December in one of these small churches and left with a revised estimation of how cold Southern winters could become.) At the other end of the continuum are the other AME and United Methodist churches, the CME congregation, and one of the Baptist churches, which are all housed in more substantial buildings. Although its congregation was founded in 1870, Meeting Street United Methodist has the only structure newer than Eastside Chapel's. The newer church was built in 1962. Emanuel AME is the oldest, erected in 1865, and most of the other churches were built in the early decades of the twentieth century.

Although middling in the size of its building, Eastside Chapel rivaled most of its larger neighbors in attendance at the typical Sunday morning service, and support for the midweek prayer meeting and Bible study was quite impressive. In fact, to say that Eastside Chapel is an active congregation would be quite an understatement. When I began this project, I was not prepared for the sheer volume of weekly church-related events, and I say this as a pastor's son who grew up in about a half-dozen predominantly white churches of varying sizes and denominational affiliations. And, unlike those in the white church culture with which I was familiar, none of these many services at Eastside Chapel lasted for less than two hours. Sunday School began the week's regularly scheduled events, followed by the Sunday morning worship service (which began at 11:00 and often lasted until 2:30 or 3:00 in the afternoon) and then the occasional 6:00 Sunday evening service that lasted until at least 9:00. After a few days' rest, Thursday night brought a double-header—prayer service and Bible study—and then on Saturday nights there was the midnight prayer meeting (which actually started at 10:00 and lasted until well after midnight). But that's just the first layer of the cake. In addition to these regular services, Reverend Wright and his four assistant ministers were frequently asked to preach at other congregations (often as far as ninety miles outside of Charleston) for their revivals and Sunday evening services, and a handful of members always traveled with them to these engagements.

The Senior Choir (about twenty-five members) and the John Simmons Evangelistic Choir (about fifteen members) held weekly rehearsals and were often invited to other churches to participate in their worship services or other special events. In addition to the adult choirs, the Youth Choir (twenty members in their teens and early twenties) and the Rainbow Choir (fifteen primary-school-aged children) held rehearsals twice a month and sang on alternating Sundays. The eight administrative organizations (Steward Board, Trustee Board, Stewardess Board, Missionary Society, Commission on Evangelism, Pastor's Aide Board, Usher Board, and Women's Auxiliary) had between eight and eighteen members each and held regular meetings. Then there were the two "prayer bands": the Israelite Prayer Band and Prayer Band No. 5, which were informal but recognized groups who were often called upon to lead the singing and worship at revivals and other special meetings, both at Eastside and in neighboring churches. In addition to their regular meetings, many of these organizations also sponsored one-night, three-night, or even week-long revivals, as well as yearly anniversaries and many special fund-raising services. These services depended upon the participation of other invited congregations and often centered on a numerical theme (e.g., 100 Men in Black, 100 Women in White, Twelve Tribes of Israel, Seven Speakers Program, etc.) that determined the number of other congregations invited to send one or more representatives and the structure of the service itself. In return, other congregations often invited Eastside Chapel to participate in their fund-raising services.

Like most congregations, Eastside Chapel had an easier time drawing members to church on Sunday mornings than at other times during the week. However, the turnout for prayer services and special meetings was considerably greater than that of the other two neighborhood AME congregations and the one United Methodist church I observed, even though these higher-status churches had much larger memberships to draw upon. The Sunday morning service at Eastside was usually filled to capacity, particularly on the first Sunday of the month when Reverend Wright was sure to preach, communion service was held, and class dues were collected. Sometimes folding chairs even had to be set up in the center aisle to accommodate overflow crowds. The Thursday night Bible study and prayer service drew an average of twenty to twenty-five members who filed in over the course of the evening, and even the Saturday night prayer service consistently brought out between ten and fifteen of the faithful. The many special services and revival meetings tacked onto this already-full calendar were also quite well attended.

Participation in Eastside Chapel was costly, not only in the amount of time members spent at these various activities, but in financial terms as well. Each worship service and revival meeting included at least one offering, every choir member was required to own several robes, and all church boards and auxiliaries charged monthly dues over and above the "class dues" of $10 a month assessed of each adult parishioner. For the congregation's fiftieth anniversary, every member was supposed to contribute $250 (although it was understood that many would not be able to reach that goal). When I first came to the church I was a graduate student with no income, and my wife and I subsisted on what we thought of as a meager stipend from her research grant. Consequently, I found the financial expectations associated with church attendance to be quite intimidating and I came to have great respect for those church families who contributed a substantial portion of their income to the church. Most of them earned less than we did.

Members in good standing were supposed to tithe, or give one-tenth of their earnings to the church, to be involved in at least some of the church's organizations, and to attend the annual revivals, fund-raisers, and weekly Bible study in addition to the Sunday morning service. Upon joining the church, new members are handed an information packet that contains a short history of the AME denomination, a schedule of services, and two handouts explaining that every good Christian should offer a portion of his or her time, talents, and treasure to the church. Reverend Wright often communicated these expectations regarding participation and financial giving in sermons, Bible studies and in other forums, and there were several structures in place for monitoring and maintaining these commitments. Reverend Wright frequently chastised the congregation for not turning out in greater numbers for some weekly services—particularly Bible study—and in one instance even singled out Lenard Singleton during Sunday morning worship as someone who should have been present at an event that had taken place the previous day. The six leaders of the adult classes were responsible for contacting their members when they did not appear in church and for collecting their monthly class dues.

Before I came to Eastside Chapel, I took it for granted that the amount I placed in the offering basket each Sunday was between me and God and the Internal Revenue Service. Thus I was quite surprised to find that the act of giving, cloaked in secrecy in most churches I was familiar with, was very much on display at Eastside Chapel. The tradition practiced there is for worshippers to file to the front of the church one row at a time in order to place their offering in the collection plate—a historically African American practice with no historic parallel among white congregations (Puckett 1931). After a few embarrassing experiences of being caught during an offering either with no cash or only $20 bills I was unwilling to part with, I always attended services with a few dollars in my wallet. And for the those who thought they could conceal their meager offerings in the envelope provided with the Sunday morning bulletin, there was another practice at Eastside Chapel that I had never seen before: publishing the prior week's offering—not just a total, but a list of every name and the exact amount given—and putting it in that same bulletin that was handed to every person who walked through the door. When I first visited the church in July, I was given a bulletin insert with a financial report for the month of June, with the names of 127 adults (husbands and wives listed individually and with separate amounts) and how much each had put in the offering over those four weeks. I calculated the monthly total for these adult members (not including children and visitors, who are also listed) at $5,748.03, which works out to a mean of $45.26 for each person over the entire month. That average, though, is highly misleading, because the amounts range from $1 to $400, and there are plenty of $5 offerings listed next to those for $50 and even $150.

Aside from these traditions that increase the visibility (and therefore public pressure) on giving to the church, revivals and other special meetings are structured to elicit maximum collections. The Seven Speakers Program is a traditional one in the African American religious community. Twining and Baird's (1980) description of the program as "a contest whose outcome is decided by the amount of the collection" is perhaps a bit simplistic and cynical, at least judging by the one that I attended, but the offering does figure prominently in the service. The format is a simple one: seven preachers from various congregations are invited by a host church to come give a short sermon, usually on a Friday or Saturday evening. The invited preachers generally bring along a coterie of members (about half a dozen each at the one I saw) from their congregations. After each visiting preacher has delivered a sermon, the preacher and his or her supporters file to the front of the church to make a financial contribution. At the end of the service, the treasurer from the home church (which is the beneficiary of the money) announces the total offering from each visiting church as well as a grand total—a competitive structure that certainly increases the amount raised by the host church.

The emphasis on contributions of both time and money, and the monitoring of these contributions, may seem exploitative to some (and certainly are cited by others in the neighborhood as a reason for their alienation from organized religion), especially given the relatively low earnings of the congregation. Eastside Chapel drew most of its 300 or so members from the surrounding neighborhood, but this is not to say that the social composition of Eastside Chapel exactly reflected that of its environment. Unlike many in the Eastside, almost all of the adults in the church held low-wage jobs and only a few of the single mothers collected public assistance.[1] Most of the men were employed as unskilled and semiskilled laborers in the construction trades or in service occupations like catering or janitorial service. Many of the older women had been private household workers, and several had been cooks for local schools. As Reverend Wright put it to me,

> This is a low-income crowd. . . . We don't have high-dollar workers. I think we've got some people that work for the phone company, and one of the ladies works at job services and does counseling. Those are the more lucrative jobs you'd find in this congregation. Everybody else is basically running a cash register for somebody, working in somebody's kitchen, or cleaning motel rooms.

But it is precisely because of these relatively low earnings that such an emphasis on giving is seen as necessary. This is especially true because of the large numbers of churches in the black community that need supporting. Decades ago one of the standard questions addressed by research on African American religion was, in the words of a chapter title in Mays and Nicholson's landmark book *The Negro's Church* (1933), "Is the Negro Overchurched?" Observers had often commented on the large numbers of black churches relative to the population, even becoming, according to Mays and Nicholson, "a subject of ridicule and laughter for many people"

(p. 198). The authors calculated, using the 1926 federal census of church bodies in seven southern cities, that Charleston was behind only Houston in how thinly spread its adult members were across congregations (207 adult members per church). In order to stay in business, some of these smaller and poorer congregations had to work almost constantly to elicit contributions of time and money, hence the evolution of the many traditions regarding offerings, special services, and other fund-raising techniques.[2]

What Do Eastsiders Believe?

Although I have spent some time elaborating on the issue of contributions, Eastside Chapel is not just an organization that elicits time and money from its members. It is first and foremost a religious institution that promotes and disseminates a particular set of beliefs and doctrines. In order to be received as a member within the African Methodist Episcopal denomination, one must answer "yes" to the following questions:

> Do you believe in the God the Father Almighty, Maker of heaven and earth; and in Jesus Christ, His only begotten Son, our Lord; and that He was conceived by the Holy Spirit, born of the Virgin Mary; that He suffered under Pontius Pilate, was crucified, dead, and buried; that He arose again on the third day; that He ascended into heaven and sits at the right hand of God the Father Almighty; and from there He shall come again at the end of the world to judge the quick and the dead?
>
> And do you believe in the Holy Spirit, the Church Universal, the communion of saints, the remission of sin, the resurrection of the body, and everlasting life after death? (AME Church Hymnal, 1986)

The most important of the spiritual realities is the existence of God. While God is held to be one being, the doctrine of the Trinity holds that he (for God is definitely a male deity at Eastside) is actually three persons: Father, Son, and Holy Spirit. This Trinitarian doctrine is expanded upon in the first four points of the Articles of Religion of the AME church and is considered important enough to be included in an informational pamphlet published by Eastside Chapel called *About Our Church*.

1. OF FAITH IN THE HOLY TRINITY

There is but one living and true God, everlasting, without body or parts, of infinite power, wisdom and goodness: the maker and preserver of all things, both visible and invisible. And in unity of this God-head, there are three persons of one substance, power and eternity: the Father, the Son, and the Holy Ghost.

This is a traditional affirmation of Christian monotheism—one supreme God, creator of heaven and earth, made up of three persons within "one substance." The "Articles of Religion" go on to be more specific about the nature of the second person of the Trinity.

2. OF THE WORD OR SON OF GOD, WHO WAS MADE VERY MAN

The Son, who is the Word of the Father, the very and eternal God, of one substance with the Father, took man's nature in the womb of the blessed Virgin; so that two whole and perfect natures, that is to say, the God-head and manhood, were joined together in one person, never to be divided, whereof is one Christ, very God and very man, who truly suffered, was crucified, dead and buried, to reconcile his Father to us, and to be a sacrifice, not only for original guilt, but also for actual sins of man.

The culmination of Christ's earthly work is singled out for special recognition:

3. OF THE RESURRECTION OF CHRIST

Christ did truly rise from the dead, and took again his body with all things appertaining to the perfection of man's nature, wherewith he ascended into heaven, and there sitteth until he return to judge all men at last day.

Of the third person of the Trinity, the "Articles" have much less to say:

4. OF THE HOLY GHOST

The Holy Ghost, proceeding from the Father and the Son, is of one substance, majesty and glory with the Father and Son, very and eternal God.

This basic set of Christian beliefs, particularly the emphasis on the divinity of Christ and his literal resurrection from the dead, is characteristic of that wing of the faith known as evangelicalism (Hunter 1983). Although scholars and others have used the term "evangelical" primarily in connection with white Protestant churches, many, if not most, African American Christians share this same profile of conservative beliefs (Roof and McKinney 1987).

Though considered absolutely essential, the formal set of doctrines outlined above constitute only the skeletal structure of the specific beliefs and total worldview espoused by members of Eastside Chapel and other local congregations. In addition to the Trinitarian conception of God as three "persons," Eastsiders believe in a somewhat larger cast of spiritual characters than those mentioned in the AME book of discipline. They believe in the existence of angels, who are primarily thought of as God's messengers to human beings, as in, for example, Gabriel's annunciation to Mary that she was to give birth to Jesus, and the appearance of angels to the shepherds in Bethlehem. Angels are also believed to engage in spiritual warfare, and the book of Revelation places angels around God's throne, worshipping him night and day. In terms of status and power, angels rank between God and human beings, although the Bible gives some indication that at the Last Judgment Christians will be elevated above the angels. The most famous—or infamous—of these angelic beings is Lucifer, who even before the earth was created, defied God and was thrown out of heaven with his cadre of followers. Lucifer, also known as Satan, (or, more often, "the enemy") commands this band of renegade angels called demons who continually work against God's purposes in heaven and earth.

According to this theology, human beings are caught in the middle of this struggle between God and Satan, or good and evil. Adam and Eve were the first humans, created pure and without sin, to be in relationship with God. However, Eve and Adam were tricked by Satan into defying God's commandment not to eat from the Tree of the Knowledge of Good and Evil, and thus sin was brought into the world. Because of their disobedience, Adam and Eve's relationship with God was severed, and all subsequent human generations are tainted with this corruption. This belief is known as the doctrine of original sin. All of this is recorded in the book of Genesis. The rest of the Bible is devoted to documenting God's efforts to win back his rebellious creatures, first by choosing the nation of Israel for himself from the descendants of Abraham, then by sending his son to die on the cross, for the sin of all humankind.

Sources of Theological Knowledge

How do members of Eastside Chapel come to their views about the nature of spiritual reality and its relation to the visible world? Undoubtedly, the ultimate source of knowledge for both pastors and laypersons is the Bible itself. The translation that Eastsiders used most often (but did not hold to as dogmatically as congregations in white fundamentalist churches did) was the authorized King James Version. As far as I could determine, every family owned at least one copy of a King James Bible, and Eastsiders frequently brought their Bibles to Sunday morning service, as none were provided in the pews. No hymnals were provided either.

Much of the liturgy, including the AME Call to Worship, the reading of the Decalogue, the Gloria Patri, the doxology, the Lord's Prayer, and of course the weekly selections of Scripture reading, as well as the words of many of the hymns, are lifted directly from Biblical texts. Pastor Wright, like most conservative Protestant pastors, organized his sermons around key sections of Scripture, and the stories of the Old Testament prophets, Jesus, and his disciples provided much of the material for his sermon illustrations. The AME Sunday School material that Eastside used was also organized around Biblical passages. Most members I talked to professed to read the Bible at least once a day on their own, although some admitted that this was an ideal that they often fell short of. Deborah Watson, one of the more zealous members of Eastside, told me that she had her Bible with her and accessible at all times, "so when I'm walking by [it] and trying to get my daily chores done and my business taken care of, [I can read something out of it]. So that's a continuous thing that I always keep as a habit."

For those who wanted to participate in a more in-depth study of the Scriptures beyond daily devotional readings, Reverend Wright conducted a weekly Bible study on Thursday evenings in the fellowship hall of the church. After attending similar Bible studies at other AME and African American United Methodist congregations in the Eastside neighborhood, I had expected a turnout of about six or seven people, and was surprised when the meeting averaged over twenty people for the nights I was able to attend. Perhaps due to the size of the meeting or to Reverend Wright's leadership style, the Bible studies were not run as informal discussion groups. Rather, they had a definite classroom atmosphere to them, a feeling enhanced by the fact that Reverend Wright ran the study from behind a schoolteacher's desk positioned at the head of the fellowship hall, perpendicular to several rows of folding tables and chairs for the rest of the attendees. Almost everyone brought notebooks and pens as well as Bibles to these studies and took notes throughout the meeting.

The content of the study consisted partly of background and historical information relating to a particular book of the Bible, which the Reverend took from commentaries, dictionaries, and other published reference sources. For example, the first meeting I attended was devoted to studying the book of Deuteronomy. Reverend Wright began by informing the group of Israel's situation at the time it was written and told them that the book's title was a compound Latin word meaning "second law." He then explained the place of Deuteronomy within the five books of the Bible known as the Torah. For the most part, however, the Reverend had a volunteer read a chapter out loud, then ask those assembled about a particular phrase or passage and what they thought it meant in relation to other portions of Scripture or how they might apply it to their lives. Much of the time, Reverend Wright would expound on various themes at length until the Bible study sometimes seemed to consist of a series of short sermons. Weekly Bible study was an important part of congregational life and Reverend Wright tried to emphasize the fact that sound Biblical knowledge was an important but neglected aspect of African American church life. One Sunday morning he addressed the congregation as a whole with this admonition:

> I thank God for those people who are coming out and learning about the Bible. Those people who are coming out and learning about the Bible are being richly blessed. They are growing beyond those persons who are not coming to learn what's in the Word of God. They are surpassing you. They are growing above you. They are understanding what you don't understand. And it's simply because they have a desire to know what's in the Word of God. And [because] they're going to be Christians, they want to be Christians standing on something. Not a Christian because they're a member of the Church, but they want to know the rules, the principles, the laws of the Church of which they are members. And so I praise God for them.

One of the things about Reverend Wright that many members valued was that they saw his teaching as grounded in the Bible. Evidently this was not the case with some other pastors whom members had encountered, either at Eastside before Reverend Wright's tenure, or at other churches. When I asked Mother Gadsden what her favorite part of the Sunday morning service was, she replied in terms of what she felt was the most important aspect of the service—the fact that Reverend Wright preached from the Bible.

> I think the most important is—give 'em the Word! See a lot of the ministers not even preaching what's in my Bible. I don't know where they get their sermons from. But I mean, when you got a minister that you open your Bible and you read the same thing that's in his—a lot of people don't know what thus saith the Lord. Scriptures will be quoted wrong [by some ministers, and they] may say the Scriptures say this and the Scriptures [really] say something else. So [they] don't have it like the Bible say.

This insistence on having it "like the Bible say," or a literal interpretation of Scripture was a view shared by members and leaders alike. It was almost taken for granted at Eastside Chapel that the Bible was the literal Word of God transmitted through human writers (in fact, like Mother Gadsden, members frequently referred to the Bible with the shorthand phrase "the Word"). This view of Scripture was almost taken for granted, but not quite, as Reverend Wright and other members did seem aware that there were other stances of Biblical interpretation. For example, in his introduction to the book of Deuteronomy during Bible study, Reverend Wright emphasized the fact that the miracles recorded in the book were literally true and were not "fairy tales." However, the adoption of a literal reading of the Bible did not seem to be taken in the militant spirit normally identified with white fundamentalist churches, and I can only surmise that a demystifying approach to Scripture has made little inroads into this population.

Another important belief about the Bible was that, although it was an ancient book, because it was God's Word and because the basic condition of people's hearts has not changed over the millennia, it still could speak to contemporary issues and concerns. As Reverend Wright stated one Sunday before announcing the Biblical text for his sermon:

> Everything in the Bible still exists. [For every] current event there's [an equivalent event that's discussed in the Bible]. And this morning the Bible is a mirror. One thing about a mirror, a mirror never lies. A mirror tells you exactly what's being shown. . . . That's why all of us have mirrors in our home, because we want to see ourselves. And that's why we bring our "mirrors" to church, because we want to see ourselves.

While the Bible is considered the primary source of truth concerning God, there are several important secondary sources of theological knowledge, which both supplement the Bible and shape members' interpretations of it. Reverend Wright did attend seminary, as all AME pastors are required to do. The assistant pastors of Eastside were in the process of attending Allen Seminary, which met on the campus of the Trident Technical College in North Charleston. Although seminary knowledge was sometimes evident in the sermons of Reverend Wright (such as an occasional exposition of a New Testament passage in Greek, or extended discourse on a particular theological puzzle), for the most part this aspect of Reverend Wright's training remained submerged. This was in keeping with his philosophy about theological training, for he thought that too much education tended to distance pastors from the concerns of their parishioners, and he once remarked to me in an interview that "education should be like underwear—it should support without being seen."

Church leaders and members are also connected to a larger evangelical Christian culture through the media. Eastsiders often read books by Christian authors and watched religious programming on television, and many of these authors and television personalities were white Pentecostals—Benny Hinn was a particular favorite, as was Charles Stanley. The Bakkers were also watched by many until the scandals of the late 1980s, and a few of the older parishioners were members of the 700 Club and had even purchased time-share units at the organization's resort in nearby Charlotte, North Carolina.

However, more important than any of the secondary sources of theological knowledge I have listed so far—official AME doctrines, seminary learning disseminated by the pastors, Sunday School booklets and other denominational material, and Pentecostal authors and television personalities—was the informal and orally transmitted African American religious culture shared between Eastside Chapel and the many other African American congregations in the area. While it is true that the tendency among some scholars to treat the black church as a monolithic institution can grossly oversimplify what is a complex and very diverse range of religious expressions in the African American community, there is a shared tradition of informal African American theology that crosses denominational and geographical divisions. I base this observation on several sources: visits to other black congregations in various traditions within the Charleston area, the published accounts of historians, anthropologists and sociologists concerning African American religious beliefs and practices

across decades and geographic regions, and finally, an admittedly nonsys-
tematic exposure to nationally distributed black gospel music tapes,
widely televised preachers and evangelists, and (mostly local) radio
preachers.

This shared religious culture is remarkable because of both its resilience
and its ubiquity, at least among the more traditional lower- and working-
class churches of African Americans. When reading Drake and Cayton's
classic *Black Metropolis* (1945) or Hylan Lewis' *Blackways of Kent* (1955),
and their samples of prayers and testimonies from Chicago and North
Carolina, I was struck to find that they were almost word-for-word repro-
ductions of the words and phrases I was hearing on Sunday mornings in
Charleston during the 1990s. During my stay in the Lowcountry, I attended services at Black Baptist, United Methodist, AME, and Holiness
congregations from Mt. Pleasant to Goose Creek to John's Island, and I
heard largely the same songs and the same types of prayers, testimonies,
and sermons at each of these churches, all drawn from the same supply of
well-known concepts and rhetorical styles, even down to the repeated and
predictable use of certain stock phrases. This is not to say that these religious rituals were simply a tired rehash of the same old thing, for the genius of these performances, both collective and individual, is to take this
common stock of words and ideas and make them alive and immediate.

The reason for this amazing resilience and ubiquity of African American religious culture is because it is routinely enacted across denominational and geographic boundaries in many different forms. In the year I
conducted my fieldwork, Reverend Wright spoke at other churches' revivals and special meetings almost every week. These trips took the Reverend and accompanying members (usually about a dozen) all over coastal
South Carolina and even, on one occasion, to an AME church in Lanham,
Maryland. This geographic breadth was not unusual. The first Sunday I attended Eastside, the visiting preacher was an AME pastor from Cambridge, Massachusetts, and the special speaker at Eastside's fall revival was
the pastor of a Fire Baptized Holiness church in Newark, New Jersey.
When the Reverend (or the assistant pastors, for they also gained experience by speaking for other congregations) was not traveling somewhere,
Eastside had many special events of its own that it would invite other congregations to attend. These occasions, like the Twelve Tribes of Israel, the
100 Women in White, the 100 Men in Black, the Tom Thumb Weddings,
the Seven Speakers Programs and the numerous anniversary programs of

various churches, choirs, usher boards, missionary boards, and so on, were institutionalized throughout the black church community. As I mentioned before, these were often thinly disguised attempts to raise money for the host church, and invitations were sent to all types of congregations within a hundred-mile radius. However, despite their financial impetus, these occasions also served to reproduce traditional African American religious culture across all types of churches and over large geographic areas.

Aside from these influences, the religious culture of Eastside Chapel was also shaped by its current pastor, the Reverend Roger Wright. Because of his dominant personality and strong leadership style (welcomed by some but certainly not universally admired among the members, particularly those connected to the founding pastor's descendents), Eastside Chapel would have seemed a quite different place had I been there in the years before or after he came. When I began my research Reverend Wright had been the pastor for almost three years. With his relative youth and seemingly boundless energy, Reverend Wright had already accomplished quite a bit at the church by the time I met him. He had initiated several outreach programs at Eastside Chapel, raised money to pay off the church's mortgage and buy a church van, renovated the sanctuary, and bought an abandoned house across the street he intended to turn into a halfway house for drug-addicted men. The congregation had grown by about a third since Reverend Wright had come to Eastside Chapel, and toward the end of my research time there, there was talk of building a new sanctuary.

Reverend Wright grew up in the "Accabee" section of Charleston, a black working-class community that borders North Charleston. His father was a steelworker and his mother a seamstress, and they lived with their seven children in a two-bedroom house. Reverend Wright grew up attending a "sanctified" church affiliated with the House of God denomination. Although a good student, he dropped out of high school in his junior year because it was the first year of integration in Charleston's schools. He recalled, "I just could not adapt to the predominantly white teachers" when he had been used to the nurturing of black teachers. He was married at seventeen and worked at the medical university until enlisting in the Air Force a year later. In the service, Reverend Wright got his GED and began taking college-level courses. After he was discharged from the service, he went to Charleston Southern University (then called Charleston Baptist College) to complete his liberal arts degree in Religious Studies. He began studying for the ministry in 1985 as an itinerant deacon of an AME church in Vance, South Carolina, and pastored three congregations before taking the position at Eastside Chapel.

It was on a sultry Monday afternoon in midsummer that I walked into Eastside Chapel for the first time and met Reverend Wright. I had arranged on the phone for an appointment with him to introduce myself and tell him about my plans for studying the relationship between the neighborhood and the local churches. This was to be my third interview with a pastor of an Eastside neighborhood congregation, and just the week before I had interviewed two of the other pastors—Reverend Ellison at Emanuel AME and Reverend Sumter of Meeting Street United Methodist. Coming through Eastside Chapel's sanctuary, I entered the fellowship hall and saw Reverend Wright through his open office door, sitting behind a desk that almost completely filled the small room and poring over a large Bible dictionary. He stood and greeted me with a formal courteousness—polite, certainly, but not exactly warm—and invited me to sit down. My first impression was that he was quite different from Reverend Sumter, my first interviewee, who had already come to represent my image of what a Southern black pastor looked and sounded like.

Reverend Sumter was in his sixties, his soft voice still tinged with an upcountry Pee Dee accent and his speech garnished with colorful down-home phrases. He spoke more slowly than I was used to, like the drawling speech of Southern stereotypes, and was given to telling comical stories—often breaking into a low, rumbling laugh as he shared a humorous tale from his many years as a country pastor.

Reverend Wright offered a stark contrast. First, he was quite a bit younger (thirty-eight) and had a restless energy and drive that propelled his conversation, as well as his numerous ideas for projects that the church should initiate, and (as I later found out) his crowded schedule of speaking engagements. Although raised in a neighboring county to Reverend Sumter, Reverend Wright had no trace of an accent and no time for rambling tales about country folk, though he too had served at several rural churches. In a business-like way, Reverend Wright began to answer my basic questions about Eastside Chapel—how long had the church been there, what was the schedule of services, what was the usual attendance, and so on. However, it wasn't long before he turned the interview toward his two great interests, the twin topics that I would hear about many times in the coming year and that certainly shaped the life of the church under his leadership. The first of these surfaced when I asked about the weekly schedule of the church. He mentioned that they had a "midnight prayer service" on Saturday nights, adding "we usually have about twenty-five people who turn out for that, ranging in age from thirty-five to eighty. At the prayer service, we talk about the dreams and visions that God has given people during the week." My curiosity was aroused by that phrase "dreams and visions," and so I asked him what the AME's position was concerning such spiritual gifts. He replied,

> The AME is very accepting of diversity. We have very conservative churches like Emanuel, and a lot of very charismatic churches. We believe here [at Eastside Chapel] in the gifts of the spirit—in tongues and the laying on of hands for healing. See, the AME used to practice these gifts in the early 1800s, but then Bishop Payne in the 1840s didn't approve of this kind of jubilation and put an end to it. Now many AME churches are only into educating the mind instead of also edifying the heart. I'm trying to get the people here to recognize that this is their heritage in the AME before the 1840s.

He went on to say that he was criticized by some in the church for encouraging people to speak in tongues and shout, practices that they associated with Holiness and Pentecostal churches and considered alien to historic Methodism. Later in the year I inadvertently gave him some ammunition in this personal crusade when I lent him my copy of Lincoln and Mamiya's book *The Black Church in the African American Experience* (1990). Turning on the radio a few weeks later to catch his program, "Pastor's Prayer Time," on the local AM gospel station, I heard him read a section of the book on the "emergence of Pentecostalism." With a careful emphasis, Reverend Wright read aloud over the airwaves: "Just as Methodism was originally a part of the Puritan movement within the Anglican church, so did *Holiness* originate as a reform movement within *Methodism*" (p. 78).

He was very critical, however, of contemporary white Pentecostals because of the history of racial exclusion in what had started as an integrated religious revival. Referring back to the Azusa Street origins of the Pentecostal movement in turn of the century Los Angeles, Reverend Wright explained:

> The Pentecostal movement started among black people, and whites were coming to Los Angeles from all over—even from England—to be a

part of what was going on at this black mission on Azusa Street. Well, pretty soon other whites started calling these white folks "nigger lovers" and oppressing them, so that finally they withdrew to their own church. They didn't want to, but they were getting hassled so much by the other white people—see, there was so much racism in the beginning of this century. Now the first two ministers in this new white group were consecrated by the black bishop—and this was how the Assemblies of God churches came into being—right out of the Church of God in Christ. Now the thing I have against [Jimmy] Swaggart, and [Jim] Bakker, and those guys is that they're racist. They may not think of themselves as such, but racism goes at a deeper level—you can have unconscious racial attitudes. Now what I hold against Swaggart and them is that they never acknowledge where their church came from, that they came out of the black Pentecostal tradition.

Standing up, Reverend Wright grabbed a history of Azusa Street from his bookshelf and went into the tiny room next door, motioning for me to follow. He turned on the small Xerox machine and began to photocopy several pages for me from the book, which he had purchased at a Church of God in Christ bookstore in Tennessee. The copies were from a section entitled, "The Azusa Mission: The Greatest Pentecostal Outpouring Ever Known" and included early accounts of the revival meetings and the interracial nature of their participants.

Having introduced the theme of race, the other subject (besides the Methodist roots of the Holiness movement) that he was passionate about, Reverend Wright warmed to the topic when we returned to his office. While some African Americans in Charleston seemed uncomfortable in discussing race in mixed company (one young African American man had hesitantly used the word "Caucasian" in conversation and then made sure I wasn't offended), Reverend Wright was always very candid and outspoken on the subject, both in private talks and in sermons and Bible studies. In that first meeting with him, Reverend Wright recommended that I read Chancellor Williams's *The Destruction of Black Civilization* and J. A. Rogers's *From Superman to Man*, books he had purchased at a local black consciousness bookstore in Charleston.

In this way, Reverend Wright was very much a "race man," unlike most of the other pastors I met in Eastside churches, and every one of my conversations with him sooner or later turned to the topic of American race relations or to some aspect of black history. In Bible studies he sometimes talked about the Old Testament Jews as an African people, but this was never definitively stated as an article of belief. As much as he was Afrocentric in his biblical interpretation and his support of what he thought of as traditionally African forms of worship (shouting and other forms of enthusiasm), he was also capable of being very critical and derisive of what he considered negative racial traits. In Bible studies and other small group settings he would often refer to the black race as "negroes" with mild scorn in his voice, and make statements like, "nobody is as hardheaded and mistrustful as us—I know how hard it is to lead negroes."

This critical orientation could also find expression on a personal level, and Reverend Wright was often quite hard on people in his congregation, particularly those who were his most loyal allies. On several occasions he called people out by name from the pulpit and chastised them for not being at a particular event or for some perceived mistake in belief or action. He admitted to me in private that he often "beat up" on the congregation in public, which was his way of trying to hold them to very high standards of conduct, but, he added, "I always support and love them too."

Whether Eastsiders appreciated Reverend Wright's leadership style, which some clearly did, or found it to be overly authoritarian, a view that others just as clearly subscribed to, there is no doubt that he put his mark on the church during the years he was there. His own background in the Pentecostal tradition, his continued emphasis on personal holiness, and his elevation of such practices as shouting and other forms of spiritual experience certainly shaped the church at the time I was doing this research. In sum, Eastside Chapel, like all congregations, is an institution molded by its history, influenced by its social and cultural environment, and pushed in different directions by the force of charismatic individuals like Reverend Wright.

* 2 *

Religious Experience and Ritual

Mother Evelyn Gadsden was almost seventy years old when she joined Eastside Chapel. Although a lifelong member of a larger and more affluent AME church several blocks from Eastside Chapel, she had often visited the congregation under several of the previous ministers, because, she explained, "they always had good services over here." After her daughter Theodosha joined Eastside in the late 1980s, Mother Gadsden finally transferred her membership to the smaller church, over the vigorous protests of her friends in the other congregation. When my wife and I began attending Eastside Chapel, Mother Gadsden was already a class leader—a congregational position of authority unique to Methodism— and when we joined the church later in the year, Reverend Wright added us to her class list. This meant that she was responsible for collecting our monthly dues, seeing that we came to church regularly, and generally keeping an eye on us.

When Mother Gadsden phoned to welcome us as new class members, I took the opportunity to set up an interview with her in her Westside apartment just above the Crosstown Expressway, which bisects the peninsula. I learned that she had retired from the school district after working for decades cooking lunches at Buist Academy, a magnet school on the peninsula and the only predominantly white public school in peninsular Charleston. A widow for almost twenty years, she was now quite active in the church and, in addition to serving as class leader and as a member of several boards, was one of several volunteers that answered mail and telephone calls (usually prayer requests) generated by Reverend Wright's gospel radio program.

I didn't find these things out until much later in the interview, though, because several minutes after we began talking, just after declaring that she had been "saved and Holy Ghost filled" in 1975, she was struck by a sudden inspiration: "I am going to give you a copy of my testimony!" Jumping up excitedly and leaving the room for just a moment, she hurried back with two photocopied sheets of text that had been hand-lettered on lined notebook paper. Across the top were the words "February 2, 1976. 10 p.m." Under this it read, in part:

> A change from darkness to light with more understanding. Blessed be the name of the Lord. I've lived in darkness for many a year. But thank God I see the light before it got too late, as it is later than we think. The light is Jesus. So many of us is in darkness, but you will have to be concern about your self and your soul before you can see the light which is Jesus.

This continued for another dozen or so sentences, some of which were paraphrased Bible verses like, "Those that are born of the flesh are flesh. Those that are born of the spirit and truth, you are in Jesus." The last page concluded, "This is my message. This is my testimony." As an exhortation to nonbelievers, Mother Gadsden's written testimony is very direct and passionate. But the most remarkable thing about this document is her story about where the message came from. As she handed me this copy, she exclaimed, "God is so good!" She paused for just a moment, relishing the memory, and then said:

> When the Lord gave me that testimony that night, he woke me up. He said, "Well, get up!" And everything I wrote I heard in my left ear. Every word on this [paper] I heard in my left ear and I wrote it down. That was on Tuesday. And on Thursday I had a dream about having copies made and distributing it. That testimony is now all over [Charleston]. Every time the Lord would tell me to have copies made and distribute it, somebody would give me two dollars, and then I would have two dollars' worth of copies to hand out.

By the time I interviewed Mother Gadsden in the late spring of my year in Charleston, I was no longer surprised to hear about this kind of direct communication from God. All of my experiences in the church, including participation in worship services, informal interactions and taped interviews with church members had shown me that this kind of occurrence was far from an uncommon one among Eastsiders. In fact, when I first began questioning church members with my prosaic inquiries about the organizational life of the church and their participation in it, they would use any opportunity to tell me about a recent dream they felt was prophetic, how God had shown them something at the last midnight prayer meeting or revival service, or how Satan had been playing nasty tricks on them. As I listened to these narrations, the agents of the spiritual world seemed as vital and active at Eastside Chapel as the fictional characters on any daytime soap opera, with just as much drama and intrigue.

What particularly caught my attention was that, in addition to direct forms of communication with God, like dreams, visions, and words of prophecy, Eastsiders also talked quite a bit about how God operated in their everyday lives by working through ordinary people and situations for His own ends. Deborah Watson was in her mid-thirties and a relative newcomer to Eastside Chapel when I interviewed her. Although from a different background than most in the congregation (she had recently moved from Indiana and was raised in a Holiness church), she was a faithful and active participant—a key member of the Bible study and Saturday night prayer service. After some general discussion about her background and how she became involved in the church, my conversation with her turned to the practice of tithing. Deborah firmly believed that God rewarded Christians who regularly gave 10 percent of their earnings to the church. To support this assertion she recounted one of her own experiences.

> Because I had $200 [on Sunday], I gave God $20. I went to work Monday—and I work at this warehouse, the only black worker, the only black person there. And I had a man-type job because I would lift up boxes, put them through a UPS machine, load them up for the UPS when they come. Put the product in the boxes, take them down, put them on the weight, scale th[...] to do all that by myself. So the two other white guys that were [...] what I was doing, they figured it was going to be easy, they gonn[...], kick back [thinking], "We got somebody here that can do it." [...] anyway. I didn't do no complaining, I did it anyway. They left [...] e in the warehouse by myself. . . . My boss says "You ought to [...] ay." I said "Dave, I'm gonna quit as soon as I get this row done, [...] hen I come in the morning I know what I'm faced with. So l[...] ead and complete it now 'cause I know I have it all out the way. [...] aid "I tell you what then, I'm gonna take you home, after you [...] rk." . . . I got in the car and on the way he said, "I really appreci[...] aning my warehouse up for me, I really do." He said, "Deb, you're a good worker. A real good worker." I said "Thank you." He said "That's why I'm gonna give you this money here and I want you

to get something for you and your kids for dinner." I said "No, I can't take that David. I really can't." He say, "Yes, you can. Because the Bible say 'You giveth and you taketh and thou shall receive.' So, I want you to receive it as a blessing." And when he said that, I thought about my tithe. So you see there, people don't realize it until after it happens, but God bless you double portions for what you give.

Now Deborah might have interpreted this event in several different ways: she could have attributed it to her supervisor's generosity or considered it a reward for her own hard work in the face of her coworkers' laziness (and perhaps racism and sexism as well). Yet she didn't attach these purely human meanings to this event. Although her supervisor was the only other party physically present during this exchange, and the money did come out of his wallet, to Deborah this was a transaction between her and God. She acknowledged to me that her spiritual interpretation of the event was triggered by her supervisor's quote from the Bible, yet once she applied that interpretation to this event, his status was transformed from being the source of the money to simply that of the mediary through whom God had acted to reward her faithfulness.

Throughout my year at Eastside Chapel I heard many of these kinds of stories, often told through testimonies during worship services, but also in casual conversations and during formal interviews. The most interesting aspect of these narratives to me was how often God, Satan, and other spiritual beings appeared in them. More importantly, God and Satan appeared in these accounts not simply as objects of belief, but as objects of their everyday experience. That is, they existed as *agents* whose actions were perceived to be just as knowable, just as real, and just as consequential in the day-to-day lives of Eastside members as those of human beings were.

Often Eastside Chapel members experienced this agency in terms of a direct encounter between themselves and the supernatural, as did Mother Gadsden and her left-ear testimony. Salvation and being "filled with the Holy Ghost" are, of course, both extremely important normative experiences that involve a direct encounter with God. "Shouting," or highly stylized ecstatic dancing accompanied by an altered state of consciousness, is also defined by Eastsiders as a powerful and intimate experience of the Holy Ghost. Likewise, almost all the church members could recount spiritual dreams or visions in which they felt God had spoken to them, either through ordinary language or through symbolic imagery. Furthermore, they seemed to consider such direct experiences and communications as essential to the normal life and development of Christian spirituality.

However, as Deborah Watson's story illustrates, many Eastsiders reported that some of their most significant experiences of supernatural agency take place not in church or in prayer but in their everyday lives at home, work, or school. These experiences are not interpreted as direct encounters with God or with other spiritual beings. Rather, Eastside members perceive the hand of God or the interference of Satan in the midst of such "ordinary" events as getting or losing a job, becoming sick, or receiving some unexpected money to pay an overdue bill. Because they attribute these events to the working of supernatural forces, the events become significant religious experiences. This extends to occurrences in the natural world as well. When Hurricane Hugo ripped through the Lowcountry in 1989, Eastsiders interpreted the violent storm not simply as a physical phenomenon, the natural result of a particular combination of atmospheric conditions and forces, but as a punishing and warning act of God toward the wicked city of Charleston.

All of this points to a very important but insufficiently recognized and analyzed aspect of religion: systems of spiritual belief—whether loosely organized cults or highly rationalized world religions—not only add a sometimes extensive cast of spiritual characters to the drama of social life (God or gods, spirits, ancestors, saints, demons), but also often imbue these beings with the capacity and the inclination to intervene in the ongoing affairs of the social and physical world. Thus, religion makes it possible for believers to interact with spiritual beings and to interpret events—whether unusual or bizarre or, as is often the case, simple and mundane—as the result of their direct intervention. While some people might attribute being laid off, becoming ill, or breaking the good china to "bad luck" or to the operation of impersonal social or natural forces, to the religious-minded there is always the possibility of a spiritual interpretation.

Religious Experience

While I was in the field recording the spiritual experiences of my interviewees, I decided to investigate what sociologists and other academics had to say about the topic. I was, after all, supposed to be conducting academic research even if it had moved in a somewhat unexpected direction, and I had to get up to speed on the literature. What I found right away as I began to go to the library was that there was very little there, at least within my discipline of the sociology of religion. From my reading, it appeared that most sociologists had avoided the topic with something of the same embarrassed determination with which Victorians had shunned discussions of sex—and for somewhat the same reason. Much as the proper gentlemen and ladies of the nineteenth century had regarded sexuality, sociologists seemed to consider religious experience an intensely private and individual affair, something that clearly fell within the jurisdiction of the psychologist (or perhaps the psychiatrist, given the general academic opinion about the rationality of belief in the supernatural). And with a few exceptions (most notably Rodney Stark and Andrew Greeley), sociologists had indeed left the subject of religious experience to the psychologists. So I began reading the psychological literature, beginning with the genteel, literary-philosophic approach of William James and moving to the "just the facts, ma'am" school of variables and significance testing in the *Journal for the Scientific Study of Religion*. There was an in-depth literature here, to be sure, but one that I increasingly felt captured only a small part of the lived experiences of the Eastside congregation, and by extension, other large sections of Christendom.

The problem was not in the empirical work itself, which was rigorous and seemed (to this quantitatively challenged ethnographer at least) methodologically sophisticated. Rather, I felt that the inadequacy was rooted more deeply, in the very concept of religious experience that these studies relied upon and the assumptions that lay underneath this concept. Perhaps the easiest way to convey this is by reviewing the actual questions used in quantitative studies of religious experience in both sociology and psychology. The oldest of these is Stark's 1963 survey of congregation members in Northern California in which he asked whether they had "ever as an adult had the feeling that [they] were somehow in the presence of God" (Stark 1965). Bourque (1969) and Back and Bourque (1970) asked their respondents: "Would you say that you have ever had a 'religious or mystical experience'—that is a moment of sudden religious awakening or insight?" a question later used in the Gallup poll (Gallup 1978; Gallup and Newport 1990). Several years later, Andrew Greeley (1974) posed this query: "How often have you had one of the following experiences? Felt as though you were very close to a powerful, spiritual force that seemed to lift you out of yourself?" This same question was used in many later studies, including Hay and Morisy (1978), Thomas and Cooper

(1978), McClenon (1984) and in the General Social Surveys of 1983, 1984, 1988, and 1989 (Davis and Smith 1991).

Now, these are not necessarily bad questions—people do talk about these kinds of experiences, and these studies reported that a significant portion of the American public claim to have had them. But it did leave me wondering if that was really all there was to religious experience. The questions seemed both too vague and too restrictive at the same time, and the generality of such terms as a "moment of sudden religious awakening" or feeling "close" to an unnamed and undefined "powerful, spiritual force" left me confused. How would Mother Gadsden have answered these questions? ("Yes," would be my guess, though I never asked her.) But would such an affirmative response have captured anything significant about her actual experiences? Do all religious conversions qualify as a "moment of sudden religious awakening" even if nothing unusual seems to happen? Would people who shout or speak in tongues automatically translate those particular experiences into the more vague and abstract language of the surveys? Or what about the many testimonies I had heard about being healed from illness and disease, or how Jesus had "come through" to resolve a difficult financial situation? These kinds of experiences seemed to be just as significant and as miraculous to Eastsiders as the more cognitively oriented moments of "sudden insight," whatever that phrase might mean.

Thinking about my conversations with Eastside members helped me to identify another thing that bothered me about these survey items: they seemed to consider only those experiences that were qualitatively distinct and clearly set apart from "ordinary" experiences as potential candidates for the adjective "religious." By emphasizing the relatively infrequent and fleeting episodes in which people sense that they are somehow "in contact" with the spiritual or brief moments of insight into the nature of the universe, they emphasize a discontinuity between religious experiences and those of everyday life, and this is a distinction based on the quality of the experience itself. Some extra money given from a supervisor to a worker (whether accompanied by Biblical quotations or not) is nobody's idea of a "mystical experience" in that respect, yet one that perhaps taught Deborah Watson more about the nature of God and his care and provision for her than any more dramatic episode accompanied by flashing lights and tingling sensations.

As I thought about the mismatch between what the psychologists and sociologists seemed to mean by the term "religious experience" and the stories that Eastsiders were telling me (and, much more importantly, one another) I happened to pick up Wayne Proudfoot's book *Religious Experience* (1985) in the College of Charleston library. As I read it, my confusion began to subside and one idea in particular came sharply into view, a concept that seemed to offer the link between the literature on religious experience on one hand and my observations in the field on the other. That concept is "attribution," a common enough notion, and well known to any undergraduate in social psychology. But in this context it seemed to be a gate that opened onto some very interesting paths.

Attribution theory was first developed within general psychology by Heider (1958) and later applied to religious experience by Proudfoot and Shaver (1975). The basic idea is that one's beliefs about the causes of particular experiences play an integral role in shaping the meanings of those experiences and, thus, in shaping the experiences themselves. According to this perspective, a religious experience is any event that a subject attributes at least partially to the operation of supernatural forces, and over the past fifteen years, scholars have developed this approach in attempting to predict when an individual will apply a spiritual interpretation to everyday events (see Gorsuch and Smith 1983; Spilka and Schmidt 1983; Spilka, Shaver, and Kirkpatrick 1985; Lupfer, Brock, and DePaola 1992).

Because it is the nature of the attribution that defines an experience as religious and not its qualitative distinctiveness from everyday modes of being, two conclusions necessarily follow. First, unusual and powerful cognitive, emotional, and physical sensations may not necessarily be interpreted by the subject as the result of spiritual forces, in which case they would not be a religious experience. For example, one might have an experience of being "lifted out" of oneself or even see visions of angelic beings and other conventionally religious objects after taking hallucinogenic drugs. Yet one might still deny that this was a religious or mystical experience and might explain these sensations simply as the "natural" effects of the chemicals upon the nervous system. Thus, no matter how unusual the emotional or cognitive states, how intense the physical sensations, or how overtly spiritual the symbolism or imagery, if the individual does not consciously connect them to the operation of spiritual beings or forces, then the individual has not had a religious experience. The crucial relationship of attribution to religious experience parallels Howard Becker's famous observations about smoking marijuana: a user who fails to connect his or her experiences to the effect of the drug cannot achieve the state of being "high" (Becker 1963).

If it is the attribution and not the quality of the experience itself that makes one's experience religious, then the second conclusion that can be drawn is that *any* experience, no matter how ordinary or mundane it may seem, can be religious if the individual attributes some aspect of the event to the operation of spiritual beings or forces. If the defining aspect of the experience is its attribution to a supernatural cause, not the singularity of the effect, then one implication is that doctrine matters: those who believe in a more active spiritual world will be likely to attribute spiritual causation to those events that others might explain in wholly natural or social terms. This is borne out by Gorsuch and Smith (1983) who conducted experimental research using written scenarios that incorporated various positive and negative outcomes. They found that "Fundamentalists made more attributions of responsibility to God than did Non-fundamentalists, [and] this occurred regardless of how extreme or mild or how probable the outcomes were perceived to be" (p. 349).

Because we can attribute events only to causes that we believe in, systems of belief are the ultimate sources of experience. I can hardly attribute that noise in the attic to the presence of a ghost if I don't believe in such things. In the same way, systems of religious belief—called doctrines in their codified form—define the possible cast of characters that exist on the natural and supernatural stage. Usually, of course, religious doctrines do much more than simply posit the reality of particular spiritual beings. They also imbue each of them (as good novelists do to their fictional creations) with a history, a character, and a set of motivations for good or ill—particularly with regard to the social world of human beings and the natural environment in which we live.

Belief systems are usually quite explicit about what kinds of religious experiences are humanly possible, and, going even further, advise their practitioners which of these possible experiences are to be sought after or avoided. For example, Pentecostal Christians advocate the experience of speaking in tongues, which they feel is not just spiritually beneficial and psychologically therapeutic, but actually a hard and fast prerequisite for personal salvation. At the other end of the spectrum, possession by a spiritual being (other than the Holy Spirit) is the worst possible thing that could happen to a person (and groups differ as to whether it is even *possible* for a true Christian to be possessed by a demon), but is an experience celebrated by occult and neo-pagan groups who will try to "channel" spiritual beings as a matter of course.

Because particular experiences depend upon particular beliefs, Proudfoot argues that those with differing beliefs must have different experiences. While we can agree with Eliade that, in a very general sense, those
who are religious live in a different experiential world from those who are
not, we must recognize that the religious do not all live in the *same* alter-
nate reality. "Religions do not all inhabit the same world, but actually
posit, structure, and dwell within a universe that is their own," William
Paden (1994: 51) rightly observed, and he might have added that within
each of the major religious traditions there are what we may call "sub-
worlds," and these can actually differ from one another as much as (or
even more than) the major faiths differ from one another. For example,
the Protestants who read the newspaper and scratch their heads over the
personal ads thanking St. Jude "for favors granted" live in a parallel Christian universe from Catholics who depend on his intercession in their daily
lives (Orsi 1997), and mainline Protestants with their relatively disen-
chanted worldview may have more in common experientially with Reform
Jews than they do with the Pentecostal Christian demon chasers and their
"puke-and-rebuke" exorcisms (Cuneo 2001).

These examples highlight another important point about beliefs: they
must be made available to individuals if they are to operate as sense-mak-
ing devices in their everyday lives. Doctrine, which is by its very nature
abstract and removed from immediate experience, must come into play
within specific domains of ordinary existence in order to transform the
ordinary forms of experience into the religious variety. How do believers
connect the events of their everyday lives to such abstract theological
ideas as the struggle between God and Satan, or the redemptive intervention of God within human history? Or, to ask the question the other way
around, how does this cosmology become grounded within the everyday
experiences of individual believers? At Eastside Chapel, the heuristic device of metaphor seems to mediate between the realms of immediate experience and abstract ideas. That is, theological principles are grasped in
terms of metaphors that translate these intellectual propositions into
more familiar domains. These metaphors provide ready-made templates
that members can use to make sense of their experiences within a spiritual
framework. Of course, all forms of human experience are necessarily mediated through some sort of symbolic system, but it seems that experiences attributed to spiritual beings are particularly in need of such trans-
lators.

The anthropologist James Fernandez (1986a, 1986b) has shown how metaphoric identities work to shape behavioral imperatives. For example, members of a Christian group that considers itself "God's soldiers" will understand their individual and collective mission as fighting all forces they consider opposed to God. Metaphors of identity can thus imply a particular blueprint for organizational and individual action (or at least the cultural norms for talking about such actions). Fernandez's point is a good one. Here, however, I want to explore the flip side of this issue as well, because metaphors, and particularly relational metaphors, are double-edged. They have implications not only for one's own behavior but also for expectations about the behavior of others. For example, I may consider myself a child of God. This means that I have a certain status, and I implicitly accept the responsibilities of that status, in this case those of a dutiful child toward a heavenly parent (however the content of those responsibilities may be culturally construed). According to the same metaphoric logic, however, it also means that I have assigned God the status of parent, and I can expect God to act in a parental manner toward me and my spiritual bothers and sisters. These expectations in turn form the basis of my interpretations of God's actions in my life.

When the believer's connection with God is interpreted according to a relational metaphor, then he or she will be particularly quick to notice and highlight everyday events that seem to confirm the nature of that relationship. For example, if I see God as a father in the sense that he takes responsibility to meet the needs of his children, I will attribute the provision of a steady job and place to live to the fatherhood of God. This process of "metaphoric selection" means that belief and experience become mutually sustaining forces. In the words of Basil Bernstein (1964: 258), "Language marks out what is relevant affectively, cognitively and socially, and experience is transformed by what is made relevant," and he might have added that this cycle reinforces both the power of the language and its connection to commonsense reality among its users.

While metaphor is a device that powerfully shapes believers' expectations—and therefore their perceptions—concerning the actions of spiritual beings in the world, metaphors are not merely static constructs. They are incorporated into ongoing narratives of God's action in human history and in the lives of particular groups and individuals. Biblical narratives are particularly important in this respect, because they offer specific examples of historic characters whose lives were touched by divine or diabolic intervention. In fact, most of the Bible consists not of abstract doctrine but of *stories*—tales of God, Jesus, angels, Satan, and demons and their actions in the lives of specific individuals. The recounting of these stories in sermons, Bible studies, and Sunday School lessons encourages believers to identify with these Biblical characters, but not merely as models of correct behavior (or, more commonly it seems, incorrect and humanly fallible behavior). Biblical accounts of "heroes of the faith" like Moses, David, Peter, and Paul most clearly illustrate not how they acted as pillars of individual character and moral strength, but how they *reacted* to God's intervention or Satan's interference in their lives. These stories then sensitize believers to look for signs of spiritual agency in their own lives and to respond to these experiences as people of faith.

Biblical stories are not the only narrative sources that Eastsiders and other Christians may draw upon in understanding how God and Satan have worked in the past. In the past few decades, religious programming on television and radio, as well as the multi-million dollar Christian publishing industry has exposed even more of these stories, some of them quite sensational, to an international audience. Taken together, these narratives provide templates that believers may use to identify and label the actions of spiritual agents within the realm of their past, present, and future experience. The narrative foundation of religious experience works on multiple levels, not only integrating the disparate events of individual lives into a continuously unfolding narrative of a relationship with God or a continuing struggle with Satan, but also folding these personal stories into the larger cosmic drama of God's redemptive action in human history.

Perhaps the most powerful source of these narratives and metaphors is the worship service of the local congregation. It is here that the participant learns the spiritual history of the church and the larger denomination. It is in this context that the weekly testimonial accounts of other members—particularly pastors and other church leaders—expose believers to claims about how God or Satan has worked (and may continue to work) in the experiential world. Sermons, the centerpiece of the Protestant ritual experience, are often composed almost entirely of these metaphoric references to spiritual beings and narratives of their workings in human life and experience.

Religious Ritual

It was a balmy Sunday in May, just after 11:00 in the morning, when I walked into Eastside Chapel, took a bulletin from the usher's white-gloved hand, and surveyed the scene inside the sanctuary. It looked something like this:

Congregants mill around the room, greeting one another and making their way into the pews. It is going to be crowded today, as it is the first Sunday of the month. This means that Reverend Wright is sure to preach (while there may be a guest speaker on other Sundays), there will also be communion and collection of class dues. The appearance of the sanctuary and the worshippers indicates the special nature of this first Sunday service: the ushers are wearing their white uniforms, the church mothers who occupy the first several rows are dressed in white dresses and white hats, and the pulpit furniture is draped with white cloth. Organist James Ravenel, seated at his instrument directly behind and slightly above the level of the pulpit, plays a rendition of "Because He Lives," a white Southern Gospel number by Bill and Gloria Gaither. As Ravenel plays, he is joined by drummer Tony Green whose kit is set up on the floor to the left of the pulpit.

After about five minutes, just as people are settling into their seats, a loud buzzing noise erupts from the sound system. Ravenel and Green both wait patiently while Lenard Singleton, who runs the sound equipment and tapes the sermons, locates the source of the trouble. When he is done fixing it, Ravenel begins playing the refrain to the Isaac Watts hymn "Alas! And Did My Savior Bleed," more popularly known as "At the Cross." This cues the processional and the congregation rises to sing: "At the cross, at the cross, where I first saw the light, and the burden of my heart rolled away. It was there by faith I received my sight, and now I am happy all the day." Two boys of about nine or ten carrying brass candle-lighters lead the procession, marching quickly and without ceremony up the center aisle. When they reach the front they split left and right and ascend each side of the platform, quickly light the candles, and then beat a hasty retreat. The boys are followed by, in order, Senior Pastor Reverend Wright, then assistant pastors Miriam Lesesne and Bernard Jackson, senior church mother Ruby Simmons, and finally minister-in-training Anthony Scott. Reaching the front, Mother Simmons crosses to her seat on a short pew against the left-side wall, a place known as the "amen corner."

The ministers mount the platform. Lay minister Scott and Reverend Jackson take chairs placed slightly in front of the pulpit and facing one another on either side of the dais. Reverends Wright and Lesesne go to the more elaborately appointed chairs that face the congregation from directly behind the pulpit, just in front of the organ. Upon reaching these seats, the ministers don't sit down immediately, but kneel in front of their chairs first, elbows resting on the bottom cushion, for a quick word of prayer.

After Reverend Wright completes his own silent prayer (a slightly longer one than the other three) he steps to the pulpit and joins with the congregation, which has continued to sing "At the Cross" during this process. After the song ends, Reverend Wright remains silent, letting the echoes of the music fill the room. He clears his throat and then declares, "And the worship was called to order. And the people stood and sang a doxology, 'Praise God from whom all blessings flow.'" Following this pronouncement, the musicians play and the congregation sings, "Praise God from whom all blessings flow, praise Him all creatures here below. Praise Him above ye heavenly hosts. Praise Father, Son and Holy Ghost. Amen." As the last note dies out, Reverend Wright proclaims: "The church is called for many reasons. The church is called for church conference. The church is called for funeral services. The church is called for board meetings, and the church is called for civic meetings. But this is a service different from every other gathering. This is a worship service. And because it is a worship service, we will now have the Call to Worship."

Hold it! Let's pause the action right there. What does Reverend Wright mean by that statement? How is a worship service "different from every other gathering?" Different in what respect? According to whom? How does this difference, whatever it is, affect the experience of the participants? These simple questions, so seemingly straightforward, lead to some rather complex issues having to do with the slippery concept of religious ritual.

Ritual as an academic concept has been around a relatively long time in the social sciences. Emile Durkheim was the first to give it sociological legs in his classic work *The Elementary Forms of the Religious Life*, originally published in 1912 (Durkheim 1995). His functional treatment of ritual as a mechanism that reinforces social solidarity was so persuasive that his approach continues to dominate the literature ninety years later (Roth 1995)—so much so in fact, that the integrative function of religious ritual quickly became a kind of sociological cliché, repeated as a commonplace to generations of undergraduate sociology students. And like most clichés, the core idea has not really been refined or deepened—merely extended in several new directions. It has been extended to civic and national forms of ritual, most notably in the writings of W. Lloyd Warner and Robert Bellah, to sporting events, and to virtually any other kind of organized gathering. Because disciplinary consensus concerning the function of ritual seemed to set and harden so quickly, sociologists of religion who followed Durkheim channeled their theoretical energies in other directions and worked on other issues that seemed to offer more of a conceptual challenge. So scholarly debates about belief (the conversion process, correlation of beliefs and sociopolitical attitudes), institution (church-sect typologies, denominational growth or decline), and the relationship between religion and society as a whole (secularization, fundamentalism) have flourished for the past century. Meanwhile, sociological writings about ritual have been relatively scarce, and those that do not use Durkheim's functional perspective have been almost unheard of.

Though retired from active duty fairly early within sociology, the concept of ritual has nevertheless continued to enjoy a longer and more varied career in anthropology and religious studies. The issue for practitioners in these disciplines has always been trying to agree on precisely what ritual is. Some kinds of activities clearly and unambiguously come under the conceptual umbrella—a Native American rain dance or a Roman Catholic mass for example—while some clearly do not, like walking the family dog. But attempts to define exactly what it *is* about rain dancing or Eucharist-taking that sets it apart from dog walking invariably run into problems. Theorists have typically chosen between two conceptual strategies for distinguishing activities that are ritual and those that are not-ritual.

The first approach points to elements of formality and repetitiveness as hallmarks of ritual behavior (Nadel 1954; Rappaport 1979). These are certainly apparent in the Native American rain dance and in the Catholic mass, as both involve certain stylistically prescribed actions undertaken at set intervals. However, as skeptics of this approach are fond of pointing out, every type of action is at least somewhat repetitive (particularly, in fact, dog walking, as any canine owner can attest), and has at least some prescribed, formal element to it (the "ritual" of attaching the leash, visiting particular spots on the daily route, etc.). The second strategy has been to identify ritual as primarily an expressive as opposed to purposive form of action (Bocock 1974; Crocker 1974; Driver 1991; Firth 1951; Grimes 1982;

Leach 1968; Turner 1982; Wuthnow 1987). There is a communicative component to ritual that is absent—or at least minimal—in nonritual activities, so this argument goes, and both the rain dance and the Catholic mass communicate or express certain values and ideas important to their cultures. Critics of this strategy point out that *everything* we do in life expresses something, whether that expression is intentional or not. Even walking the dog communicates that one is a responsible dog owner who cares for the well-being of one's pet animals. Besides, others say, who decides whether an action is purposive or expressive? The rain-dancers are sincerely trying to make rain, which is a very rational, purposive act in an agrarian society after all. Likewise, communicants receiving the Body and Blood of Christ believe that it is efficacious for their salvation, which is certainly a goal-directed activity even though oriented toward a very otherworldly end. What these groups are not *primarily* setting out to do by dancing or taking communion is to communicate something about their culture, either to themselves or to any outside observer. And so the expressive/purposive distinction ultimately breaks down to an irrational/rational one in which the academic observers (who of course know how the world *really* works) judge the actions of the dancing Native Americans and wafer-ingesting Catholics (who obviously don't) and find them wanting. One can get around this problem by abandoning the attempt to classify actions as either ritual or not-ritual and talk about ritual as the symbolic dimension of social behavior (and so Robert Wuthnow can analyze the ritual elements of such mundane acts as driving a car). But then what's the point of having a special concept called "ritual" at all?

These kinds of frustrations and analytic dead ends have led at least one anthropologist to throw up his hands and declare that the concept of ritual is more trouble than it is worth (Goody 1961, 1977). Yet before we throw the baby out with the baptismal water, there is another approach that just might work. This third way is appealing not only because it avoids the pitfalls of the first two, but also because it shifts the definitional burden from the analyst/observer onto the shoulders of the people being analyzed and observed. Rather than asking how I, as a social theorist, should define ritual, I can simply ask how they—the Native Americans and Catholics and other ritual-performing peoples of the world—define it. This definitional sleight of hand diverts the eye from the act itself to the cultural discourse surrounding the act and changes the question from "what is ritual?" to "how are rituals successfully constructed in particular times and particular places?" (Bell 1992).

Now there is still a bit of analytic work for the social theorist to do, so it is not quite the easy way out that it may at first seem. First, one must identify what it is about these particular actions and events that the social group itself sees as qualitatively different from other, ordinary modes of action in their society. If rituals are culturally privileged actions and events, set apart from everyday behavior, then one must ask how it is that they are set apart, and who, exactly, is empowered to do this? There is a parallel here to the distinction between "art" on the one hand and "crafts," "hobbies," and other forms of human creativity on the other. One can try to develop a sociological definition of art—which turns out to be a very challenging task with difficulties very similar to defining ritual (Lewis 1980)—or one can simply look to see what is successfully classified as art by people with the power to apply that culturally honorific label (Becker 1982).

The first task of the analyst then is to identify the ritual "frame," or mode of interpreting the action or occasion, that sets it apart from ordinary social events (Goffman 1974). But it doesn't stop there, as one has to identify how people signify to one another that this particular mode of interpretation is the one currently in play. For example, we learn from anthropologist Gilbert Lewis that the men of the Gnau tribe of New Guinea will sometimes spit into the air to attract the attention of a spirit (1980: 25). But they (like males of the species everywhere it seems) often just like to spit. How, then, is "ritual" spitting differentiated from its "regular" or "nonritual" forms? There must be some additional clues to signal that this action is imbued with spiritual expectation, and not just a matter of spittle expectoration.

This brings us back to the earlier questions raised for us by Reverend Wright. How is a worship service different from a funeral or a political rally to members of Eastside Chapel? The difference lies both in the *intent* imbedded in the worship service, and in the *identity* of the participants. Put simply, a worship service is an occasion in which participants worship God, and the people gathered there do not come as mourners, as citizens, or as officers in the church bureaucracy (as they would in Reverend Wright's other examples) but as God's children. Finally, and this is the most important thing, God shows up too—and not simply as an omnipresent supreme being (after all, he travels everywhere like that)—but as an active, specially present agent who manifests his Spirit in the service, often in powerful and dramatic ways.

The special nature of this occasion—the element that elevates it to the culturally privileged level of ritual—is predicated on this understanding that the worship ritual is a time and a place of intimate communion between an almighty all-powerful God and his devoted followers. This "specialness" is signaled in myriad ways: overtly in the language of prayers, liturgy, sermons, songs, and testimonies, but also symbolically through bodily actions (genuflecting, kneeling, bowing of the head, folding of the hands, etc.), through the clothing of participants ("Sunday best," ushers uniforms, the white outfits of the "church mothers," choir robes), and through the "props" associated with the service (the pulpit, communion cups, grape juice and wafers, Bibles, the lack of decorative elements other than spiritual slogans). All of these elements combine into an emphatic cultural statement that what is happening here is not part of the ordinary, mundane world of work, home, school, or street.

The following two chapters apply this concept of religious experience to Eastside Chapel, first to experiences attributed to the working of God, then in chapter 4 to the interference of Satan and his demons. Chapter 5 analyzes the worship service as the privileged occasion in which God is specially present to his people, and chapter 6 examines some of the dynamics related to experiencing the presence of God in the ritual.

✳ 3 ✳

"Do You Really Know Who God Is?"

God is not dead, He's still alive

God is not dead, He's still alive

God is not dead, He's still alive

I feel Him in my hands

I feel Him in my feet

I feel Him all over me

—African American spiritual

"He is real! God is real!" Sherline Singleton exclaimed, jumping to her feet and shaking her long braids for emphasis. It was the late afternoon of a warm spring day and Sherline was in our two-room apartment with her son Markis. I had the tape recorder on for what turned out to be a lengthy and mostly unstructured interview on a host of topics ranging from her childhood and high school experiences to her involvement in Eastside Chapel to general comments on African American life in Charleston. At four years of age, Markis was already used to sitting through long church services several times a week, and he remained quiet and mostly still through the three-hour conversation. At this moment, Sherline was telling me about the Saturday night prayer meeting at which she had been filled with the Holy Ghost. I had asked her to tell me about the experience, and at first she expressed surprise that I didn't already know the story: "I didn't tell you all this? Really? I tell *everybody* this!" Sitting back down on the couch and settling into her story with obvious relish, she began to relate the experience. It was just after Reverend Wright had come to Eastside Chapel and initiated the Saturday services and invited interested members to come and pray for the church and to "hear from the Lord." As a newly rededicated believer, Sherline was one of the five or six that began to show up on Saturday evenings, and she was surprised to hear one of the other women praying in tongues.

> And I'd never heard speaking in tongues before in my life. I just said "Woah." To me, she was speaking a language, but it was a language I didn't know. She wasn't just saying a whole lot of mixed-up stuff. It was like she was actually having a conversation. . . . So the next Saturday night I got up and I said "father, father, father," and I just kept calling and kept calling and kept calling and kept calling. And a few minutes later, there was a si-lence in the room. Not a real silence, it's just that it wasn't quite as lively— [the noise level had] come down a little bit. And then I heard a voice. And the voice said, "What is it that you want, my child?" I said, "Save me Lord, save me!" And he say, "You want the Holy Ghost?" And I said, "Fill me." . . . And then he gave me his blessing. He said, "First you have to deny yourself and then you have to humble yourself." And I said, "Yes, Lord, yes Lord." The deeper it got, my cheeks started trembling, [it went from] from my ankles to my legs to my knees to my thighs, all the way up [my body].

This powerful experience lasted for what seemed like quite some time, and the process was physically draining. "Afterwards I was tired, like I just had a baby or something," she said. Upon finishing her story, Sherline paused, looked at me for a few moments, and then reflected on the impor-tance of that relatively brief episode and its continuing meaning for her. "[You know] that song, 'He touched me, Oh, He touched me'? Now when I hear people sing that song, I can testify that I have had a physical touch [from God]." More emphatically, she went on to exclaim, "You *have* to have a supernatural experience. You have to have a supernatural experi-ence with the Lord, so you know that the Lord been working. And that's *my* supernatural experience. I *knew* that the Lord was real, knew he was real, knew he was *real!*"

On the third Sunday in January, the Missionary Board had the responsi-bility of presiding over the morning worship service, as was the custom on the third Sunday of each month at Eastside Chapel. On this particular morning, the Board had invited Reverend Miriam Lesesne to deliver the sermon. Reverend Lesesne was a New Yorker, born and raised in the Fire Baptized Holiness Church, then widowed and retired before moving to

Charleston and joining the pastoral staff at Eastside. Moving to the pulpit and taking the hand-held cordless microphone, Reverend Lesesne announced that her primary text would be Revelation 19:6. She read aloud: "And I heard as it were the voice of a great multitude, and as a voice of many waters, and as a voice of mighty thunderings, saying, 'Hallelujah! For the Lord God omnipotent reigneth! Hallelujah! For the Lord God omnipotent reigneth.'"

Closing her Bible, Reverend Lesesne declared, "The subject this morning: 'Do You Really Know Who God Is?'" After a few scattered cries of "amen," she continued:

> To Abraham he was Jehovah-Jireh
> "The Lord will provide"
> Do you know him this morning as a Lord that will provide?
> To Moses he was Jehovah-Raffa
> "The Lord that healeth Thee"
> Do you know him this morning as a healer?
> To Joshua, he was Jehovah-Nissi
> "The Lord our banner"
> Do you know him this morning to parade in front of you?
> To go in front of you?
> To let folks know who you are?
> To Gideon he was "the Lord our peace"
> Jehovah-Shama
> To David he was Jehovah-Rohi
> "The Lord is my shepherd"
> Is he your shepherd this morning?
> To Jeremiah he was Jehovah-Tsidkenu
> "The Lord our righteousness"
> To the twelve tribes he was Jehovah Shammah
> "The Lord is ever present"
> Is he ever present with you?
> To Abraham again he was Elohim which means "God, God, God"
> To Paul he was El-Shaddai
> "The Lord sufficient"
> To Melchizadek the high priest he was El-Elyon
> "The most High God"
> Who is he to you this morning?
> "Do you really know who he is?

With this exhortation, Reverend Lesesne echoed the words of Sherline Singleton and reminded the congregation that belief in God, though essential, is not sufficient. It is not enough simply to take an intellectual stance and agree with the writer of Revelation that the Lord is omnipotent and reigns over heaven and earth; the issue is whether one has given God power in one's *own experience,* whether he reigns in one's *own life.* Thus, the question that Eastsiders must answer is not merely the theological one of "Who is God?" but the personal and experiential one of "Who is God *to you*?" At Eastside Chapel, God is not simply an object of belief and abstract reflection, but a living being—a person with whom one could and should interact in everyday life.

More than a simple reminder of the necessity of the experiential dimension, however, Reverend Lesesne's sermon points out a fundamental aspect of the Christian tradition: that these experiences are structured within the concept of a *relationship* between believers and their god. As Eastsiders encounter God and his actions in their lives, they do not conceive of them as random events, initiated by a powerful but inscrutable and forever unknowable deity. Rather, individual incidents that believers attribute to God are situated within a personal and collective history of such events. Likewise, experiences that Eastsiders attribute to Satan or to the work of angels or demons are also nested within explicit and implicit theological understandings about these particular spiritual beings and their modes of agency within human history. Thus, the relationship with God and the battle with Satan serve as both the overarching metaphors and the narratives within which individual religious experiences are placed.

A Relationship with God

The concept of relationship lies at the core of orthodox Christian theology. This concept is rooted in the belief that humanity was originally created by God specifically to be in relationship to him. This relationship was destroyed in the Garden of Eden as Eve and then Adam listened to the lies of Satan and disobeyed the command not to eat from the Tree of the Knowledge of Good and Evil. Jesus Christ, the Son of God (the triune nature of God also expressed in relational terms) came to earth and was allowed to die as a sacrifice that would restore humanity to a right relationship with God. Although those who accept Christ in this life have regained their relational position that was nullified by Adam's sin, the relationship will not be fully realized until they die and go to heaven or until the great communal feast at the end of time. It is within this grand narrative of God's relationship with humanity that Eastsiders situate their individual stories and their own personal experiences of God.

Reverend Lesesne's sermon is particularly interesting in the way it links Biblical characters with those names of God that best characterized their relationship to him, then challenges the congregation to pursue that same type of relationship with God in their own lives. Through this rhetorical structure, she invokes such figures as Abraham, Mosesm and Paul not simply as venerated heroes of the faith who should be honored, but as models for present-day believers to emulate in the pursuit of a closer relationship with God. This emphasis on *knowing* God, of building a relationship with him over time, permeates the religious discourse of Eastside Chapel.

Metaphors of Relationship

As important as it is, the concept of "relationship" can be a vague one. There are many different kinds of relationships possible between two entities, human or spiritual. What is the nature of this relationship between believers and their god? To answer this question, we must first realize that there are potentially two different objects of analysis here. First of all, there are the actual relationships of members to God, as perceived by themselves and others in the church, and then there is the idealized relationship that Eastsiders hold to be normative for all Christians. My analysis is of the latter, as it is this cultural standard that Eastside members strive to achieve, and it is the culture of this group that is my concern. Whether or not congregants live up to these standards (or whether it is indeed *possible* to live up to these standards) would be the subject of a very different kind of analysis.

Eastsiders, like other religiously conservative Christians, place great emphasis on the necessity of a personal relationship between believers and God and the nature of this relationship is built upon metaphorical extensions of human social relationships. These metaphors, taken primarily from the Bible, are used throughout the entire range of congregational discourse in hymns, sermons, prayers, and testimonies. Because they are rooted in Biblical language, the metaphors themselves are based upon social roles and relationships found in ancient Middle Eastern society (although many of them have ready counterparts in twenty-first-century America). There are two primary relational themes highlighted by these images: hierarchy and intimacy.

The metaphors that cluster toward the hierarchical end of the spectrum include the images of God's relationship to believers as king to subjects, commander to troops, master to slave, lender to borrower, shepherd to sheep, and parent to child. For example, one of Reverend Wright's sermons was centered on the theme of submission to God's control. In the beginning of this sermon, after preparing his audience with the statement that his message was about "ownership and servitude," Reverend Wright asked the congregation, "Are there any free people on the earth?" Several people answered affirmatively before he announced that the title of his sermon was "To Whom Do You Belong?" He went on to tell the congregation, "I'm not free. I'm owned by somebody." Reading from Webster's dictionary, he continued:

What does it mean to be a slave? "A servile or submissive follower" — that's what it means to be a slave, "a servile or submissive follower." . . . There's some people here today who are anti-slavery. I am pro-slavery myself. . . . For Jesus said, "Come and work for me for I have a yoke of slavery, but my yoke is easy. I have a bondage, but my burden, my bondage, is light."

Although this direct reference to slavery was somewhat daring on Reverend Wright's part, given the emotionally sensitive nature of the topic for his listeners, it was not uncommon for Eastsiders to refer to God as "Lord and Master," particularly during public prayers. Later in this same sermon, Wright switched relational metaphors several different times, all to bring home the same theme of God's power and authority.

> The scripture says, "The rich ruleth over the poor and the borrower is servant to the lender." God lent life to all of us, and he gave all of us a chance to live it to the fullest. But the life belongs to the giver. We are borrowers; he is the lender. And we ought to pay back the lender while we have a chance.
>
> Beloveds, soldiers are servants of the government, and we are the Lord's soldiers. Paul said to the church, "You are like a military force." He says, "Therefore, put on the whole armor of God." And beloveds, if the military can be subject to the government, how is the church complying to its government, which is the Lord Jesus Christ?

Some of these hierarchical metaphors temper the emphasis on power and control with allusions to tenderness and protective care on the part of God toward his people. The image of a shepherd with a flock, for example, taken from both the Gospels and from the Psalms, suggests a relationship in which God will comfort and nurture believers, providing them with good things and watching over their safety. This metaphor was one of Reverend Wright's favorites, and he would sometimes dwell on it at length. Consider the following passage from a different sermon:

> We rest in the Lord when we in his pasture. . . . We graze off of faith. We graze off of patience. We graze off of peace. We always eating joy. We graze off of long-suffering and patience. And we are not weary in well doing, because we are in the Lord's pasture. No matter what happens, we stay in the Lord's pasture and graze there because we know that whatever the Lord feeds us will sustain us.

While these relational metaphors imply certain behavioral obligations on the part of Christian believers (one *should* submit to God's power and authority and, at the same time one *should* develop and maintain an intimate relationship with God), I want to emphasize a somewhat different point: the obligations and expectations run both ways in a relational metaphor. Although the term "father" can have many connotations (disciplinarian, progenitor, final authority, etc.), the aspect of fatherhood that Eastsiders most emphasized was that of nurturing provision, as in the following passage from Reverend Wright's Father's Day sermon:

> There are many types of fathers, such as a father to the poor, a father to the hungry, and a father to the lost. And we know God our Father this morning to be a father to the lost, because when we were lost in sin, Jesus reached down and took us in. We know that he is a father to the hungry because he keeps feeding us and providing for us. We know that he is a father to the poor because most of us in here are poor and he keeps sustaining us in the midst of it all.

If this image of God as father combines aspects of hierarchy with nurturing provision, there are several other metaphors that emphasize the intimate nature of the relationship between the deity and his believers. For example, one metaphor drawn from the New Testament speaks of the church as the Bride of Christ, who will return one day to claim her as his own. Others portray Jesus as a friend and counselor, one who, in the words of Scripture "sticketh closer than a brother."

Of these relational metaphors, those that emphasize hierarchy and provision apply not only to those who have experienced salvation, but to nonbelievers as well. For Eastsiders, God does have the ultimate power and authority, even over those who do not recognize it, just as he is the ultimate source of every good thing, even if those who reject him enjoy them. Yet only those who have acknowledged his authority and have submitted themselves to his control can experience intimacy with God as a lover and a friend. This dual aspect of God's relationship to humanity is brought out in the following set of metaphors excerpted from another of Reverend Wright's sermons:

> His name is Jesus. Ahh, he is a lion. And he is a lamb. He is a lion today because he is the king of the jungle. My God from Zion—when you see the lion come, he is walking in his own power. By God he roars and everybody in the jungle gets silent. . . . But beloveds, before the children of God, he was a meek and humble lamb.

Norms of Intimacy

This type of intimate relationship that Christians may have with God is not only possible—it is expected. Jesus is supposed to be one's closest confidant and counselor, and the discourses of prayer, liturgy, songs, sermons, and testimonies abound with references to the standard of intimacy that should exist between believers and God. He is seen as a close friend, for example in the hymn "I've Found a Friend in Jesus," one who will "never, never leave me, nor yet forsake me here." In one traditional spiritual, the singer pleads with God to "Hold my hand, while I run this race," and in other verses to "stand by me," reminding God, "I'm Your child" ("Guide My Feet," African Methodist Episcopal Church Hymnal, 1984, #386).

One powerful and recurrent theme in the hymns that speaks to the standard of intimacy is that of God as a special confidant with whom one can share doubts, fears, and heartaches of life:

> I may have doubts and fears, my eyes be filled with tears
> But Jesus is a friend who watches day and night
> I go to Him in prayer, He knows my every care

> And just a little talk with Jesus makes it right
> ("I Once Was Lost in Sin," #351)

> Through this world of toils and snares
> If I falter, Lord, who cares?
> Who with me my burden shares?
> None but Thee, dear Lord, none but Thee
> ("Just a Closer Walk with Thee," #387)

> I must tell Jesus all of my trials
> I can not bear these burdens alone
> In my distress He kindly will help me
> He ever loves and cares for His own
> ("I Must Tell Jesus," #388)

The idea of God as a comforter also has a mother-like quality to its sheltering intimacy:

> Other refuge have I none, Hangs my helpless soul on Thee
> Leave, ah! Leave me not alone, Still support and comfort me
> All my trust on Thee is stayed, All my help from Thee I bring
> Cover my defenseless head, With the shadow of Thy wing

Sometimes the relationship between the believer and God is depicted as so intense and consuming that it is the only relationship in the believer's life. As one hymn declares,

> Thou spring of all my comfort,
> More than life for me;
> Whom have I on earth beside Thee?
> Whom in heaven but Thee?
> ("Pass Me Not O Gentle Savior," #272)

This almost desperate yearning and need for God also comes through in hymns such as #327:

> I need Thee every hour, in joy or pain;
> Come quickly and abide, or life is vain,

and #318:

> Father, I stretch my hands to Thee;
> No other help I know;
> If Thou withdraw Thyself from me,
> Ah! wither shall I go?

Although it is normative, it is not assumed that such trust and intimacy is automatically achieved or maintained. In fact, the hymns "Just a Closer Walk with Thee" and "My Everlasting Portion" both implore God to grant a greater closeness in the relationship.

Where do these high standards of intimacy come from? In part they derive from an Evangelical and Pentecostal tradition that places great weight on the personal relationship with Jesus as the cornerstone of salvation.[1] The hymns cited above are part of that tradition and are still widely sung by both black and white congregations within that part of the theological spectrum. There may be more to it than that, however. Although I don't have any real evidence, it was my impression—and understand that I am making comparisons to my own background in the white middle-class Evangelical Church—that there was a greater sense of emotional intensity surrounding the relationship with Jesus. The fragile nature of social ties among Eastsiders, which I explore in more depth in chapter 6 and elsewhere (Nelson 1997), might have contributed to this intensity, because the spiritual relationship with Jesus was often portrayed as a *substitute* for friendship, kin, and even marital relations.

This emphasis on intimacy with God may seem paradoxical when we realize that Eastsiders place an equally strong emphasis on the fundamental gulf that divides God and humanity. For God is held to be so far above humanity that he declares, in the words of Isaiah 55:9, "As far as the heavens are from the earth are my thoughts higher than yours." Thus while members strive for a close relationship with God, this intimacy is always qualified by the fact that it is a partnership forged between God and humanity, and thus of purity, power, and majesty joined with weakness, dependence, and a propensity to sin. The emotions of Christian life—love, joy, and peace as well as humility, gratitude, and repentance—spring from this tension of finite humans' being bound to the infinite "Wholly Other" in a tight embrace. Reverend Wright addressed this tension one evening at a revival service:

How many people know the Lord tonight? How many people know that you know him? I know what you all mean, but I'm gonna set the record straight. Nobody in here knows him. He's past our finding out. We are simply learning of him, but we don't know him. Job thought he knew him, 'til he set Job straight [when he] said, "Job where were you when I laid the foundations of the world?" Oh, we don't know him tonight. We're simply learning of him. But the Scripture says, "Take My yoke upon you and learn of Me." We don't know him. A lot of [people say], "Oh, I know the Lord!" Beloveds, we don't know him. Enoch walked with him for how many years? All you Bible scholars—Enoch walk with the Lord for how many years? Three hundred. Then he walk right off the face of the Earth with God. But if anybody knew God it was Enoch. You walk with somebody for three hundred years, that's a long time to get to know somebody. And there was still things about him that Enoch didn't know. And beloveds, we've been here less than, some of us, less than fifty years, and we says, "We know the Lord." But we're simply learning of him, learning of him. 'Cause his ways—his ways are past our finding out. There's too much to God for us to know all about him. But we're learning of him. Will you all buy that? I didn't hurt nobody feelings by saying that?

If this type of intimacy is the norm, how is it achieved? If believers are commanded to "know God," how do they go about it? How does one develop a close personal relationship with an invisible spiritual being? The answer, it seems, is that a relationship with God is cultivated in the same way as human relationships are—by a process of individual encounters over time. It comes, in short, by way of experience.

Encountering God

In the previous section I argued that individual experiences of God are seen in terms of a relationship with God, a relationship characterized by both submission and intimacy. Like human social ties, which tend to follow a particular cultural logic and "natural history," a spiritual relationship with God also moves along a recognized trajectory. This journey begins with an initial encounter with God known as salvation.

Salvation

For Eastsiders, as for many other evangelical Christians, the salvation experience serves as the cornerstone of faith. As a consequence, they literally divide the world into two groups—those who have been "saved" and those who haven't. Because it is seen as so essential, I want to examine the nature of this experience in some depth. Why is this experience so important? How does one become saved? What do Eastsiders believe happens in the salvation experience? How does it affect the new convert's life? And, finally, how can you tell those who are saved from those who aren't? I will take each of these questions in turn.

First of all, the salvation experience is so important because it is the only way to establish a right relationship with God. According to the evangelical theology shared by Eastside, humanity was created by God specifically to be in relationship to him. Adam's sin destroyed this relationship, and ever since that time God has been working to restore the connection, first through the chosen nation of Israel, and then through the death and resurrection of his son, Jesus Christ. Although Jesus took the full punishment for humanity's sins through his death on the cross, thus reconciling the entire world to God, Eastsiders believe that it is up to each individual to activate this forgiveness in his or her own life. The process of salvation, then, is really a joint process on the part of both God and humanity; God has accomplished his part, and now it is up to every individual to cooperate with his efforts.

The actual experience of salvation at the individual level occurs when persons acknowledge that they are indeed cut off from God by their own sin, accept the sacrifice of Jesus as payment for that sin, and promise to live their lives in submission to his leading. Thus for Eastsiders, salvation is a very simple process—one simply accepts the reality of one's own sin and the fact that God has done all that is necessary to deal with that sin. The hard part—hard in the sense that it goes against humanity's pride and willfulness—is finding the humility to ask for forgiveness and to turn over the control of one's life to God.

Although the theology behind salvation is relatively simple, and the experience itself can often seem quite mundane, Eastsiders believe that in the spiritual realm it is nothing short of a revolution—a complete and total transformation of the individual from one who was spiritually dead and cut off from God to one who is alive and truly a child of God. On Easter Sunday, Reverend Wright told the story of how Jesus raised Lazarus from the dead. Then, equating death to the state of original sin, he spoke of the salvation experience as a kind of resurrection:

> We came in the world dying. We had a carnal mind, and the Bible says, "To be carnally minded is death." But the day you hear the Word of God and open your heart, . . . when the words of eternal life come on the inside of you, you quit dying. [Jesus] is alive, and he not only raised Lazarus, but he raised me too. For I was dead one day, but he gave me life!

One phrase, familiar to most Americans since the 1970s, that Eastsiders use to talk about this radical transformation is to be "born again." This metaphor not only signifies that one is now born into a new spiritual family, but also points to the spiritual metamorphosis that takes place within the new believer. According to this theology, salvation completely transforms the mind and heart, the desires, and the actions of converts.

Not only does salvation move one from spiritual death to life and reestablish the relationship with God that was severed by Adam's sin, but God actually "moves in" and begins to inhabit the "heart" of the new believer. In the same Easter sermon quoted above, Reverend Wright likened this habitation of God in the believer's heart to an unborn baby inside an expectant mother. Like the fetus who makes its presence known to the mother, God also makes his presence felt within the believer.

> Women ought to understand [this], because when a woman is pregnant with child, and carryin' that child, she knows that there is life in her belly, because she can feel that child movin'. She can feel that child in the midnight hour, when the father is over there snorin' and sleepin'—'cause he can't feel that life. But she can feel that baby kickin' and scratchin'. The mama says, "I tried to sleep but this baby kept me awake all night long. I tried to sit down and eat, but this baby said, 'Mama, I don't want you to eat now.'" . . . Because there was life on the inside, and the life on the inside had a mind of its own. And when Jesus is on the inside of your life, I declare you'll feel that life kickin'. I declare sometimes you want to sleep, but you can feel that life keepin' you awake all night long. Sometimes you want to sit down and eat a bologna sandwich, but the life says, "No, no eatin' today." Oh, beloveds, have you got him on the inside?

The last few lines allude to an important fact. Such a radical transformation as that from spiritual death to life, from a position of separation from God to one of having God live on the inside of one's heart ought to result in a corresponding change in the convert's external behavior. As Reverend Wright once said, "Beloveds, how can you tell a child of God? When you see the child of God, you see the attributes of godliness and holiness in their lives." In concrete terms, these attributes seem to involve both refraining from certain activities, like smoking, drinking alcohol, listening to secular music, engaging in adultery, stealing, lying, and gossiping, as well as performing other behaviors, like attending church and doing good works for others. Thus, although salvation does not come about by simply living a moral life, morality will be the inevitable result of a true salvation experience. It stands to reason, then, that if someone does not exhibit this morality in his or her life, then that person must not be saved.

Although belief is essential to the salvation experience in that one must profess the reality of sin, the need for atonement and other core doctrines of the church in order to be saved, belief by itself is not sufficient to effect this transformation. The movement from spiritual death to life and the movement of God into the believer's heart comes about not simply because of a change of mind (which is perhaps why I never heard the more intellectually oriented word "conversion" used as a synonym for salvation at Eastside Chapel), but because of a personal encounter with God. The change in belief is a mere prerequisite to the initial meeting with God; it is the asking for forgiveness and surrender of control that takes place that is the heart of the salvation experience. In fact, Reverend Wright would sometimes mock mere statements of belief as "repeat-after-me salvation."

> I ain't never seen no repeat-after-me salvation in all my life. I've tried that stuff; that stuff don't work. That repeat-after-me salvation don't give no deliverance. Somebody is confused. They said the old folk were crazy—they didn't have good sense, goin' out there in the wilderness . . . seeking God. But at least those folk had to come back with some kind of testimony. . . . "I heard chains draggin' and I heard somebody growlin'. About that time I was gettin' ready to run for home. But another voice said, 'No, stay right there. That's the Devil.' And I stayed there and began to call on the name of Jesus. And I just kept prayin' and I kept prayin' and after a while my body began to feel strangely warm. And after a while it felt like I was walking on cotton, and after a while my hand began to tingle all over. But after a while it seemed like the whole world lit up all

around me. And I declare that the things I used to do, I don't want to do them no more."

This idea that belief is not enough, that a personal transformation is required for salvation is one that appears to be widely accepted in the community, even by those who do not attend church or profess to be Christians themselves. In fact, it was surprising to me that many of the unchurched that I encountered around the neighborhood professed to believe all of the same essential doctrine as Eastside Chapel, yet did not consider themselves to be saved. Judging themselves by the same Christian standards, they freely acknowledged that they were spiritually "lost." For example, Darryl Lawson told me that he had been talking to his brother for many years, trying to convince him to "give himself to the Lord." According to Darryl's account, his brother accepted the basic doctrines of Christianity, and even admitted that if he died right then he would go to hell, because he "knew right from wrong." Nevertheless, he was not willing to take the next steps of asking God's forgiveness and committing himself to "follow Jesus."

In fact, many of those who are "out on the streets" (a general phrase that indicates a lifestyle of drug or alcohol abuse, sexual immorality, and lack of legal employment) not only grew up in the church, but also still believe the doctrine they learned there, even if they are not currently living in obedience to it. Lenard Singleton told me that when he was selling and using cocaine he would sometimes come to church high and even get up to give a testimony now and then, even though he knew at the time that he was not "saved." I saw this phenomenon firsthand when Edward Cooper, the long-lost husband of one of the church members, a man who had been literally living out on the streets for months while he was using drugs, suddenly showed up at a "tarrying" meeting that some of the young men were holding. Despite the fact that it had only been a matter of hours since he had come home to his wife and children, Edward was full of religious fervor, even to the point of preaching at the other men who were there.

Lenard and I were discussing this incident one day when he told me, "Basically, the average wino or drug addict out there came up in the church, and some of them know the Bible better than me and you." When I asked him to elaborate, he told me, "See, the generation when we was coming up, our parents took us to church and taught us about God, so we had that seed planted within us. Even though we strayed away, that seed was still there. All it needed was some type of watering."

One might think, then, that the line between the "unsaved" and "saved" would coincide with that drawn between those who are "on the streets" and those in the church. This, however, is far from the case. In fact, many core members whom I interviewed told me explicitly that not everyone in the church was saved. Mary Jefferson, a long-time member and respected elder in the church put it this way: "There's a lot of folks in the church who are not saved. They just went up and give the pastor they hand, and got inducted in the church that way. . . . And [Reverend Wright] trying to get everybody saved. And that really put a lot of strain on folks who really think that they already saved."

People who attend church but are seen by others as not saved are derided as "churchgoers" or "church worshippers," and are accused of acting out of "form and fashion"—that is, simply out of habit or from a desire for social respectability in the community. Reverend Wright preached regularly and emphatically on this topic and openly assumed that many of his parishioners were themselves not saved. In fact, his entire sermon, "Do You Know Who Your Father Is?" delivered on Father's Day, was a bold challenge to the unsaved churchgoers in the Eastside Chapel. In the following excerpt he makes it very clear that such outward behaviors as church attendance cannot be used as indicators of anyone's spiritual status, then brings it very close to home for members of this congregation by using the metaphor of paternity establishment.

> Are we the children of God? That's a question for you. Are we the children of God? Well, beloveds, perhaps someone is confused because they're a member of the church. That don't make you a child of God. Because you get up and say you're a child of God, don't make you a child of God. Some people ball up their fist, "I'm a child of God and I dare anybody to tell me that I'm not!" Well, that don't make you a child of God either. Beloveds, if you a child of God, first of all you got to have a birth certificate with his name on it as Father. I know I'm sayin' something. And beloveds, if you're the child of God, you got to have his blood type. Hallelujah! Because I want you to know the blood will be tested to tell who the real Father really is.

Those who consider themselves to be saved at Eastside Chapel have no sympathy for those in their midst whom they consider unsaved, and in fact reserve more scorn for them than for those openly living lives of dis-solution "out in the world." In the eyes of the saved, these "churchgoers" are pretending or playing at Christianity—they are not "for real."

Those who consider themselves truly saved are a bit more lenient on those they consider unsaved within *other* congregations, reasoning that many times these people have the misfortune to sit under pastors who themselves have no personal knowledge of salvation. Sister Gadsden told me, "We [in the larger African American community] got a lot of minis-ters who aren't even saved! A lot of 'em! And that's what's damaging the members. . . . Half of them are not even called of God—half of 'em go to seminaries just to become a minister just like another job. But it's not helping the members."

"Filled with the Holy Ghost"

Once someone is saved and adopted into the family of God, there is an-other experience that is normative for the believer—receiving the "bap-tism of the Holy Ghost." Although this experience is commonly associated with Pentecostal and Holiness churches, it also seems widespread among more mainline African American congregations in the Charleston area.

In several respects, being filled with the Holy Ghost is similar to salva-tion. First, it is a one-time experience that separates those who have had it from those who haven't. Second, it is also relational in essence: those who have been "filled" say that they experience a more intimate relationship with God than they did before. And finally, the result is to bring the be-liever's heart and mind in further harmony with the purposes and desires of God. In this way, the filling experience is a further step that builds upon the initial work of salvation.

However, the experiential dynamics of the two experiences appear to be quite different. While salvation necessarily involves a decision on the part of the convert and so remains at least somewhat within his or her control, being filled with the Holy Ghost is seen as something that God has com-plete control over. Thus, one never knows when it is going to happen. When I asked Mary Jefferson when she had undergone these two experi-ences, she told me,

Well, I am saved, but I am not filled with the Holy Ghost. . . .
Q: And then what will happen after that—after you get filled?

Only time will tell.
Q: Now is that something that you pray for?
Yes.
Q: And it can just happen at any time?
Any time.

Several members told me that they were still praying to receive the Holy
Ghost. However, they made it clear that such prayers were not a prerequisite for the experience. Mother Pinckney told me, "I didn't pray for the
Holy Ghost—he just fill me. I didn't pray for it. I was praying now—I always pray—but I didn't ask [for that]." The relative passivity of simply
waiting to be filled at Eastside Chapel can be contrasted to other techniques for receiving the Holy Ghost practiced in other congregations, primarily those from Holiness and Pentecostal traditions. Darryl Lawson recounted the following story, which I quote at length because it illustrates
something of the perceived need for the experience as well as his own encounter with another congregation's means of attaining it:

> More or less, some people when they accept the Lord into their life,
> truly accept him, yielding everything, giving total submission to him, and
> their minds are on him totally. Then, yes, sometimes [the Holy Ghost]
> comes in right then. But some people have to pray and find out what it
> may be that would hinder them from really serving the Lord in fullness.
> Because the Scripture says that God is a spirit, and they that worship him
> must worship him in spirit and in truth. And there may be some thing,
> some obstacle in your life that could cause you not to give yourself over to
> the Lord. That's where tarrying comes in. Tarrying simply means to wait.
> A lot of the Pentecostal Holiness churches and Pentecostal Apostolic, their
> tarry is like—you're on your knees praying, and there's somebody right—
> I went through that too—God know. And I promise, I said, "If I ever have
> to go through that again, I guess I'm never getting the Holy Ghost." And
> um—they were around me, probin', punchin', shakin', just yellin' in my
> ear, and all of this good stuff. And it was a cousin of mine and I, we sang
> in the choir, and we went to this church . . . on Columbus St. And we were
> all in the church—I mean a bunch of young people—on our knees pray-
> ing, calling on the name of Jesus. And I mean, they were yelling in our
> ears, pushing us, shaking us, saying, "Come on now!" and I mean, yelling
> in my ears. So my cousin, she was on her knees, and I was on my knees,
> and I looked at her, and she looked at me, and she said, "Man, I'm tired." I

said, "Me too." She said, "I ought to fall out² just to get some rest." I said, "Go ahead." And when she did, I laughed. When that experience was over, I promised myself, I said, "If I ever, ever have to go through that again, no way!" . . .

[Some time after that], I went to Louisiana and . . . I was laying in my bed in Louisiana at my cousin's house. I just felt the urge to pray. I was listening to Aretha Franklin's *Amazing Grace* album, and the song came on "Precious Memories," the specific portion, "In the still of the midnight, God's sacred secret he'll unfold." And it was like twenty minutes to twelve or a quarter to twelve, and the song "God Will Take Care of You" came on, and I began to shake in the bed and to cry. Nobody had done anything to me, I just wanted to pray. . . . I laid in the bed, and the Lord spoke to me and he said, you know, "Get on your knees and pray for yourself because there's gonna be a time that nobody [will be able] to pray [for you], but I'm always there." Tim, I got on my knees and I began to pray and I began to tell the Lord I love him, I serve him, I magnify him, I adore him—I just began to praise him, and at that particular point, I knew what I was saying but it came out differently, it came out differently. And after that experience was over, I got in my bed, I got up happy. . . . And it didn't take all of that probing and punching and yelling in your ear, beating up on you. It was just me and the Lord. One on one.

As in Darryl's case, the direct result of the infilling experience is most often an impartation of the "gift" of "speaking in tongues." Yet this is not the result that those who have had the experience emphasize. Instead, they point to what they see as a qualitative change in how closely their own desires and actions, their "life living," conform to what they perceive as God's will. This in turn goes back to what they believe about the nature and function of the Holy Ghost. Darryl Lawson explained it this way:

The Holy Ghost is what the Bible teaches. It's a comforter, it's a guide, it's a keeper, it's more than three in one. And the Holy Ghost is something that—say for instance that you make me mad, real mad. Ordinarily, if I didn't have the Holy Ghost, I'd jump on you and kill you. But because of the Holy Ghost teaching, it would teach me, "Vengeance is not yours." It would bring the Word back to your remembrance to keep you from getting in trouble. Even with a male-female relationship, which I've been in—gotten into a lot of hot water with—the Holy Ghost has spoken to me, and in some cases I did not listen. And I paid dearly for that. But it will bring back to you the Word of God, telling you that "that's a sin, and you don't do that." If you're—even with a job, if you've been offered a job, you pray and ask the Lord to show you, "Is that the job?" The Holy Ghost will be a teacher or a guide to tell you [God's will].

Ronald Manigault, another young man in the congregation, gave support to this picture. Here he discusses the Holy Spirit as the internal voice of conscience, but also, like Darryl Lawson, emphasizes that the Spirit doesn't override the believer's free will—one has to choose to follow the Holy Ghost's leading.

[A]fter you [become saved], then you receive the Holy Ghost. The Holy Ghost basically come to lead and guide you, will speak to you and tell you what to do. Holy Ghost might tell you—[a woman] might come to church one time with a dress on, and the Holy Ghost [will] tell her, "That's too tight. You can't wear that to church." You might get out there, and you might go in the mall, and you might be looking at women, "No, you don't look at women like that now." He talk to you, [he's] your conscience. He lead and guide you. . . . When you ask the Holy Ghost to tell you—he will warn you before it happens that what you are getting into is wrong. Now you got to opt to do. Now he already said that what you about to do is wrong. But you got the option whether you gonna listen or override that. You got the power to override that. When you become one with the Father, you will listen. If you really a child of God, you will listen. You know that's wrong, and even if your flesh wants to do that, you can't.

Prophetic Words

While salvation and being filled with the Holy Ghost are one-time occurrences, there are several other kinds of experiences that are continual and recurring. One of these types of experiences is what I will call "words of knowledge," or prophecy, because it involves a special revelation of insight that members attribute to supernatural origins. This type of experience is extremely important in the lives of members. In fact, several people first joined Eastside Chapel because they saw Reverend Wright operate within this spiritual gifting.

Lenard, the former drug dealer and addict I mentioned earlier, encountered this prophetic aspect of Wright's ministry in a very direct way. While still continuing his drug habit, he started coming to church with Sherline, his common-law wife who had grown up in the congregation. Here, Lenard recounts one of the major factors that helped him overcome his addiction.

> At one point [Reverend Wright] just prophesied and picked me out of the congregation. He told me to stand up and said, "I got a word for you." . . . He told me that my time was up, whatever I was doing, my time was up. And basically, it scared me. He said, "I'm not trying to scare you. It's just a word from the Lord." I believed it, because I knew he was a man of God. And that turned me around right then. It really turned me around. I started getting my life in order, said I wasn't going to do any more drugs.

One of the tests that a word of knowledge concerning a future event is indeed from God is that it turns out to be true. Ronald Manigault told me about an evangelist he encountered while staying in Hilton Head:

> When she started prophesying over me, she started telling me some things that the Lord said not to do. And at that time when I receive that, I said I'm not going to do it. But the same exact thing that she told me, everything that she had told me, came to pass. I know, I know that was the Lord. I know that.

One unique thing about a prophetic word is that there are actually two discrete parts to it, the prophecy and its fulfillment. When I asked Mother Pinckney how she first got involved at Eastside Chapel, she told me that before she had even gone to the church she had a prophetic dream about Eastside. When she actually visited Eastside for the first time, she experienced what she perceived as the fulfillment of that dream:

> Before I went to [Eastside Chapel] I had a dream about the church. [I dreamt that] this man send me there, tell me to go to the church. And I said, "I don't know nobody in there! I ain't going in there, I don't know nobody in that church." And the man say, "There's a man in there I want you to go see." I said, "But I don't know nobody." He said, "You'll know him, 'cause he got the teeth out in the front." [Some time later] I went to Eastside with [my friend], and I sit down there. And let me tell you the fun of it, when church over, and everybody hugging each other and talking to each other, [laughs] this man come to talk to me . . . and that man

say, "So glad to see you! Come again!" And then he grinned, and—no teeth! And I say, "Oh God, this is the man, this the man!" So I know I had to go in that church. I mean—so real! So real! Just like how I saw it in my dream, that's how it happened.

Dreams and Visions

Although God imparts words of knowledge directly to persons, he also communicates with them through dreams and visions. One of the most striking things to me as I conducted this research was how frequently people seemed to have spiritual dreams. In fact, many times as I interviewed people about other topics, they began to spontaneously give me a history of the significant spiritual dreams they had experienced, often going back many years and even into their childhood. It is almost impossible to overstate the importance of spiritual dreams as an integral part of the religious life of Eastside Chapel, and it is this feature, along with shouting, that was the farthest from my own experiences in the white churches of my youth.

Members view spiritual dreams as communications from God. Sometimes these communications are rather straightforward and involve answers to prayer about specific decisions. Darryl Lawson, for example, had an important position as lay leader at a Reformed Episcopal church several blocks from Eastside Chapel when he began visiting the church regularly. He became increasingly restless and dissatisfied with what he felt was the lack of spiritual fervor in his church, and at this time he had several very pointed dreams about that congregation:

The first dream I had, we were in church, and I got up to praise the Lord. And the pastor jumped up from where he was in the pulpit and said, "That's enough out of you!" He said, "We're not having that!" And I jumped up and said, "That's enough out of you too! I don't have to stay here and take this." So I got up to walk out, and one of the ladies said, "I know you are going to Eastside Chapel." I said, "Well, wherever my soul redeemer says [to go], that's where I want to be." I was not even thinking about joining Eastside at this particular point, and as I walked out the door and got in the vestibule, I looked back—the entire church crumbled.

Mother Pinckney prefaced her account of the following dream by saying, "I know I been converted, because I go in Hell and get myself out. The [dream] was about a blouse, but I know it was my soul." In fact, she presented this dream to me as unimpeachable evidence of her salvation experience, a tradition that goes back many years in the religious history of African Americans.

See, I found myself in this place and it been hot and stinkin', smelly. Oooh! And the people been naked, both men and women. And I been walkin' through the place, and the heat had me hot, and my clothes been like stick to me. I don't know why I been walkin' through there, but I been walkin' on this thing, it was like a grate, and it was [made of] iron. And it been hot. I could see the fire down there under the hole. And the noise, some kind of noise like a great motor been grinding away. And I saw this tall woman and she been tall and shapely. She had a long waist, and her butt stick out and her thigh, like something you see on an art wall. And she had these two big vials on her shoulder full of blood. Yeah! And she was walking around toting those vials, look like she got to carry them. That must have been her task to walk and tote that, maybe [because of] blood she done spill from somebody or something, I don't know. But I walk along in that place, and oh Lord, I didn't want to be there. I don't know why I been in there. And I could hear this noise. It seemed like people had to be weighed in the balance on this huge scale thing. And if you didn't weigh what you supposed to weigh, they knock that thing back, and down you go! Yeah! And then I been running through the place. And I get to this deep, dark hole that's in the heart of the place. But I mean I know it been Hell, because fire been everywhere and stuff. And people been moaning and groaning—it was terrible. And somehow I had this long pole, and I let it down, and I been down there fishing in the dark. And nobody bother me. Everybody been mean and ugly, and I hook [something] on the wire to pull it up, and I pull that thing up. And when I get 'em to the top, I reach over and grab the thing, and it was a white blouse that belongs to me. And I mean it been *white*. I grab that blouse and look all around, and I feel them staring at me, and I run, I start running uphill. Hell's slippery and slidy, and you slide down and then you go back up, and the briar been hooking on your clothes, and I could feel them tearing my skin while I been running. And I mean the hounds of Hell been behind me. I could hear them growling and barking and there's people and all, everybody been behind me. And it was this straight place I had to run up. And I look back and I see the frogs and snakes and all the things I am afraid of—all that been behind me. And I run and I run, but I couldn't

get nowhere, like it was like a tunnel. And I mean it was dark—you could-
n't see your hand before your face. Then I started singing something, and
when I started singing I saw a light way down to the end of that tunnel.
And that light was like the sun or the world, and I know I been home safe.
And I run up, and then I run up. I don't know what happen, if the hole
close up or what. But I ain't hear 'em no more. But when I stand up and
look around, there was a white tree, I mean white. Almost look like these
white Christmas trees. And when I got to the tree, the blood been coming
down, just raining down, and I fell down, and oh my Jesus, I ain't never
seen nothing like that. I mean a big old white tree and the blood been just
trickling down. I fell down and that blood just washed me.

I am retelling Mother Pinckney's rather lengthy dream, not only for its
intrinsic interest and vivid imagery, but because of something I happened
to read much later after I left the field. In an old article on the "Religious
Folk-Beliefs of Whites and Negroes" (Puckett 1931), I came across the following example concerning the place of dreams and visions among the
slaves: "On the Sea Islands of South Carolina the [spiritual] neophyte
most commonly goes to hell, is given a bundle representing his soul, and
goes up (via wings or ladder) to Heaven" (p. 23). Mother Pinckney's dream
thus exemplifies a tradition in African American religious experience that
goes back at least a hundred years. In fact, Mechal Sobel has analyzed the
language of spiritual dreams preserved in the historical record, including
those of the ex-slaves collected in the volume *God Struck Me Dead* (Johnson 1993), and one of the most common themes she identifies is that of
"the detailed journey or travels of the soul from Hell to Heaven" (Sobel
1979). The crossing of a river is also a traditional African American symbol
imbued with spiritual meaning (Puckett 1931; Johnson 1996), and I
recorded several dreams in which river crossing plays a prominent role.

Not all dreams that members consider communications from God are
clear in their meaning. Often the dreams are full of symbolic imagery that
is not so transparent, and if this happens the members will tell the dreams
to the pastor so that he can interpret them. Deborah Watson told me:

The dreams that I've had! It's been so spiritual it had me coming out of
the dreams like I'd come out of an operation. You know, it's like a total reaction or a different physical change, you know. And I've not been able to
cope with it until the Lord showed me one night the spiritual dreams that
I would have, and I relates it to my pastor and tells him about the dreams

. . . and he relates and teaches me. That's how I was taught on how to deal with your dreams.

Given the frequency with which congregants seem to have these dreams, Reverend Wright spends a good deal of his time trying to interpret them for members. One time I arrived in his office for an interview and he was poring over a large Bible dictionary. Sandra Davis had called him earlier that morning and told him of a dream in which she had a guardian angel with a strange name, and he was looking it up in the dictionary for her. Not surprisingly, he sometimes tired of this role. At one Saturday night prayer meeting, after Sherline told a dream that she had during the previous week that she didn't know the meaning of, Wright exhorted the group to start asking God directly for interpretations rather than depending upon him.

Although dreams are usually considered a medium of communication, however oblique they may sometimes be in their meaning, Mary Jefferson told me how a dream broke her addiction to cigarettes. A heavy two-pack-a-day smoker for much of her sixty or so years, she had been hospitalized for possible cancer of the kidneys several years before I interviewed her. While in the hospital she had tried very hard to quit smoking, but found she was unable to do it.

Sometime while I was in the hospital [I dreamed that] an angel came. . . . I always think of an angel as a woman, you know, but this [was] a huge [man]—the most gorgeous thing you ever seen—and he came in that hospital room and he lift me out of the bed, and he took me across the Ashley [River] to the street Lilly Jackson lives on. I was so mixed up; I didn't know what I was supposed to do. I just went down the street to get the 51—to get the bus and go on home. And when I got to the corner, this woman from our church, she was standing there. She sent me to [where there was] a box with arms and legs and wings [inside]—and they were alive. No other parts of the body—just those things in there. And I went to the box, and I look in there, said "Ooooh." And this other angel in the box snatched me in, and he start beating on me. I [managed to get] out, and I just stretched my arms out and said, "Lord, what do I do now?" And this voice came from above me. And it was a strong voice that said, "Fight!—Fight with all your might!" And I went back in there—and before I knew it, everything was beat up to a pulp—it was like Jell-O, and I put my hand in there, it started oozing around my fingers. And then I smelled it—it was nicotine. I went back to get a bus from there to go home, not knowing that the first angel was there waiting for me at the crossroads. He pick me up and put me back to the hospital. And I didn't smoke any cigarettes from then on.

Visions are similar to dreams except that they occur while awake and fully conscious rather than while asleep. While most members reported having dreams, only a few talked about experiencing visions. Mother Pinckney was one of these:

One night I came out of K-Mart and this beautiful rainbow was right in front of the door. And I was so excited about this beautiful rainbow. Nobody seen the rainbow! I saw this big huge rainbow. People said, "I don't see no rainbow." But I know I saw the rainbow. Rev say that rainbow is a sign of promise. After Noah. That's a promise.

She also related a peculiar type of visual experience, which some people referred to as "seeing colors." I had heard allusions to this experience during one Saturday night prayer service when Reverend Wright referred to several people in the congregation who "saw colors." I didn't know what that meant until my interview with Mother Pinckney. She was telling me a story about Liz, one of Reverend Simmons's daughters who had moved to New York City. When Liz came back to Charleston many years later, she decided that she wanted to rejoin the church. At that time Mother Pinckney and Liz's sister, Reverend Nazarene, had been traveling all over Charleston visiting revival services. After hearing their stories, Liz also became interested in receiving the Holy Ghost. One night, she asked her sister and Mother Pinckney if she could accompany them to a service.

We been on the corner of Reid and King Street, to this church, and Liz is praying for the Holy Ghost, and I was praying for Liz to get the Holy Ghost, and the thing jump on me! Yeah! I was praying for Liz, and this thing happen to me. And I opened my eyes and everything was pink. The whole church, the room, the people, me, my hand, my feet, everything been pink. Everything was pink. And I know the church had red carpet. And I know that the church had white walls, but everything was pink.

Although "seeing colors" is similar to other spiritual visions in that it involves a transformation of the sense of sight during a state of consciousness, it appears to be different in the sense that it does not mean anything. And those who experience it do not seem to require it to mean anything. When I asked Mother Pinckney if the color pink had any symbolic significance, she said, "I don't know—it was just a new color to me. Everything looked that way to me." Thus, in contrast to the deep significance of dreams as vehicles of spiritual affirmation, communication, and direction, seeing colors is simply experience with no cognitive content beyond the fact that one's sensory stimuli have been transformed by the power of God. I have also not been able to find any account of this kind of experience in the historical or anthropological literature on African American religion.

While such "direct" experiences of God as salvation, being filled with the spirit, receiving words of prophecy, and experiencing dreams were commonplace occurrences at Eastside Chapel, members also attributed many of their everyday experiences to the working of God's supernatural power. The story of Lenard Singleton and his journey from selling (and using) drugs to selling cars at one of the area's largest Ford dealerships offers a good example of this. Lenard has a more middle-class background than many of the Eastside members. His father was a successful businessman, and Lenard grew up attending an integrated Catholic parish church on Broad Street in downtown Charleston. In his thirties, Lenard met his future wife Sherline when he was a street-level crack dealer and she was just trying to break a drug habit. Their relationship pulled Sherline into a deeper dependency at the same time that Lenard "became his own best customer"—began to use his product as well as sell it. Then Sherline got pregnant. Neither Lenard nor Sherline felt that they were prepared for this: she already had a fourteen-year-old son from a prior relationship, and Lenard had a daughter about the same age who was being raised by her mother. Sherline considered abortion and asked Lenard about it. He didn't agree with abortion, but said that he considered it her decision to make. Sherline decided to have the baby and "turn it over to the Lord," which meant putting her drug habit behind her. Through her influence, Lenard also determined to try and "walk the straight and narrow."

Sherline had grown up in Eastside Chapel and still went periodically, even when she was "out in the world." After learning of the pregnancy she attended the church regularly and most Sunday mornings even convinced Lenard to come with her. This was during the tenure of Reverend Galliard, the pastor who immediately preceded Reverend Wright. Although Sherline and Lenard came faithfully to church, he was still dealing cocaine and struggling with his addiction. Then Reverend Wright came to Eastside Chapel, and with his arrival, something dramatic happened that changed both of their lives. Lenard recounted the experience for me:

> When I first started going [to Eastside Chapel], I didn't really get nothin' out of [the service], you know. You can feel the spirit of a person in the church, and it was not under the leadership that it should be. And I didn't feel nothin', but I still would go, you know. And when Pastor Wright came, I mean I really felt the Spirit of God, and I knew this was a man of God.

Lenard went on to relate how Reverend Wright had singled him out and told him his "time was up." At this point in our interview, I asked Lenard if it had been difficult for him to break his addiction. He responded:

> Well, it was hard in the sense that, when I was doing it, it was a pleasure— it felt good. But the Lord really helped me because he inflicted pain on me at one point. Every time I used to do it, it was a bad experience—either pain came along with it, or [it was] just a bad experience. So, you know, I knew that he was trying to tell me something, and he was helping me to let go of it. . . . So I just praise the Lord for that, because that really helped me then, and I knew that when the word was prophesied to me that my time was up, every time that I did it, I could feel like I was dying, like I was dying from it, you know. [I knew that] the Lord was really behind me in helping me to let go of it. So it was easy when it came to that point.

Lenard could have explained the pain he experienced in a number of different ways—as the psychic effects of the drug itself (a "bad trip") or as some kind of chemical reaction in his body—but instead he attributed it to God as his way of weaning him from a habit that would, he feared, eventually destroy him. What is particularly interesting in Lenard's account is the mutually reinforcing combination of direct and indirect religious experience. He first receives a prophetic word that his "time is up"— itself an ambiguous message which could have been interpreted in a number of ways. Given his situation though, he sees it as directed toward his drug habit, of which Reverend Wright himself knew nothing. Then when he experiences pain while using drugs, he connects these experiences to the prophetic word and attributes them to God's discipline. This two-step attribution not only helped him to actually kick his habit, but also profoundly shaped his perception of God as a father who cares enough to dispense "tough love" to his children.

Stories like this—of deliverance from drug and alcohol addiction, of healing from all manner of illnesses and physical deformities, of miraculous financial provision in times of hardship—make up the bulk of the testimonies told during midweek and Saturday night prayer services. These accounts of divine intervention into every aspect of ordinary life, down to the commonly heard prayer of thanks to God for "waking me up" each morning, "clothed in my right mind" with the "blood still running warm in my veins" attests to how completely intertwined the spiritual, physical, and social forces are for Eastsiders. Like dreams, this kind of indirect religious experience also has a long tenure among African Americans. In his review of the historical record, Henry Mitchell concludes that "this tendency to see the providence of God in every good experience was virtually universal among slave believers, and very common among all blacks. Narrative after narrative relates some straw of good fortune in a haystack of adversity, and celebrates it as evidence of the care and concern of the Creator of the universe" (1975: 132).

Unfortunately, spiritual entities are not always positive forces working for the interests of Christians. Satan and his demons are also seen as quite active in the world and working to tear down whatever God tries to build up. These evil forces work in many insidiously subtle ways to tempt, deceive and discourage believers. They can also work in some not so subtle ways like actively possessing individuals, as we see in the beginning of the next chapter.

∗ 4 ∗

"On the Battlefield"

The months of September and October are busy ones for the African American church community in Charleston, as this is the season of the annual week-long harvest revival meetings. Because of his weekly radio broadcast, "Pastor's Prayer Time," Reverend Wright was a popular speaker on these occasions, and was often asked by other area congregations to preside over their revival services. One Thursday evening in mid-September, Reverend Wright was preaching at a small Missionary Baptist congregation in nearby Mt. Pleasant. It was the fourth night of a Monday-through-Friday series, and the size of the audience had grown larger with each service. Although I did not attend this particular service, which I regret given what happened that night, the whole event is captured on audiotape, and the following account is taken from that recording.

After a somewhat lengthy introduction to his sermon, Reverend Wright asked the assembled crowd the question that served as the title for his sermon: "Does the church know first aid?" Seeing that the congregation was puzzled by this somewhat cryptic question, Reverend Wright continued by reading from the Gospel of Luke 4:18:

And Jesus said, "the Spirit of the Lord is upon me because he has anointed me to preach the gospel to the poor. He has sent me to heal the broken-hearted, to preach deliverance to the captive and recovery of sight to the blind, to set at liberty them that are bruised, to preach the acceptable year of the Lord."

After pausing for a moment, Reverend Wright expanded on the text:

The subject tonight is, "Does the church knows first aid?" Jesus' ministry was about aiding people who were bruised and broken hearted, wounded and left desolate and poor. . . . Beloveds, in many churches people are sittin' up in the pews—beat up, boxed up, slapped up, kicked up, bleeding, deranged, poor—and the church must learn how to give first aid.

These injuries, Reverend Wright went on to tell the audience, are war wounds, sustained in battle with Satan, the avowed enemy of all professing Christians. Drawing on his own past experience as a new military recruit, Reverend Wright recounted in some detail the instruction in first aid given him by the army during basic training.

They taught us all of that to aid one another. Because when you on the battlefield, you need the help of one another. Because you don't know when you are going to be wounded. And I declare when you wounded, you need somebody to come to your aid, when you catch a bullet in the leg. The Bible say, "Beware of Satan's fiery darts." And see we don't realize that we are fightin' a spiritual war. Satan got a M-16, [but some] folk go walkin' around here and think that they can take all the shots the devil can fire.

The reality of this spiritual war was brought forcefully home to Reverend Wright and the congregation at the end of this same service. After a closing song, Reverend Wright extended an invitation for those who felt they had been wounded in some manner to come down to the front to receive prayer. Two women responded to this call, and as he prayed over them, his words revealed that he had come to consider one of them plagued by evil spirits:

Father, I come against the devil in her home, and I come against the enemy coming against your life. And Devil, you know that I don't take no junk and mess off of you, and I curse you out tonight. In the name of Jesus, I bind your powers. I bind your influences. I plead the blood of Jesus over her life tonight. I plead the blood. Victory in the name of Jesus! Deliverance in her soul and mind!

As Reverend Wright prayed this, she became more and more agitated until it became clear that he thought she was actually possessed by a demon, and that he would have to cast it out of her. After commanding the spirit to come out for several minutes, he addressed the congregation again:

Beloveds, the [Holy] Spirit revealed to me that this is a witchcraft spirit that had this woman possessed. She wasn't like this, but six months ago, she came in this state. As I prayed for her just now, I could see her personality. It surfaces for a moment and it flees because this is a strong spirit of witchcraft. This is why Jesus said that the church has got to fast and pray when it encounters witchcraft spirits like this. Because these spirits—if you have not fast and prayed, you have to wrestle with them to get them out.

After continuing to command the inhabiting demon to leave for about ten more minutes, Reverend Wright dismissed the congregation with a warning that only the spiritually strong should stay and help him with the exorcism:

For those of you who are leaving, we ask that as you leave the sanctuary try not to hold conversations. We going to work on this spirit some. This spirit don't want to come out tonight. This young lady tried to dig a hole in my hand. That's a spirit on the inside, fighting. In the name of Jesus. For these kinds of spirits you need some prayed-up souls. Because this kind of spirit is very strong—very strong. And weak people with no anointing don't need to be tackling these kinds of spirits. Persons who are going home, will you please exit the church and fast and pray for this young woman.

As this dramatic incident reveals, Satan and his demons are an important part of Eastside Chapel's conception of spiritual reality and are considered to be quite active in the experiential world. While this type of possession is considered very rare by Eastsiders, the devil and his actions are often alluded to in conversations, testimonies, prayers, and sermons, and many pointed to incidents in their lives which they felt to be of demonic origin.

Belief in the existence of a fallen angel who opposes God and his people—known variously as Satan, Lucifer, the devil, or by more exotic names like Beelzebub—has been an integral part of Christian belief since the founding of the faith (Russell 1981). In more contemporary times many Christians still believe in the existence of the devil. Reporting the results of a survey of northern California church members taken in 1963, Stark and Glock (1968) show that, on average, 38 percent of Protestants and 66 percent of Catholics agreed to the statement, "the devil actually exists." This represents a range of, at the low end, 6 percent for Congregationalists to a high of 92 percent among Southern Baptists. What kind of a devil is this that modern Christians believe in? In a national study conducted in 1978 and 1979, Hunter (1983) found that 66.8 percent of Evangelical Protestants surveyed affirmed their belief that the devil was "a personal being who directs evil forces and influences people to do wrong," while 28.4 percent of the same group thought that the devil was an impersonal force. Only five percent thought the devil did not exist at all.

At Eastside Chapel the reality of Satan as a personal being was something that was simply taken for granted, and vivid dreams about Satan were almost as common as those about God. Mother Pinckney related the following dream to me in our interview:

> There was some terrible beast—seem like he was on the other side of the world. The head part was over there, but the tail part was in America—that's how huge the thing been. And anybody he touch with that tail, they broke out in leprosy. And ooh, the people was . . . the people that that thing done touch was in terrible condition. I never saw the thing, but I hear him roar! Oh! It was some monster from the deep, or somethin'. But somebody say it was a snake. And that thing had to have been big to cover this whole world. He half over here and half over here! That's Satan you know. You see, 'cause when Christ died, Christ chain 'em in Hell for 1,000 years. And he had these seals open, the things that John saw on the Island of Patmos. And every time he open a seal, you know, he get nearer and nearer! And now he's loose! He's loose and he's walking on the land. And he trying to devour everybody he can.

In this chapter I am not so much interested in abstracting Eastsiders' beliefs about the devil as in showing how they perceive his actions in their everyday lives and in the world at large. The words of Neil Forsyth apply here:

> One may best understand [Satan] not by examining his character or the beliefs about his nature according to some elaborate . . . metaphysical system, but rather by putting him back into history, into the narrative contexts in which he begins and never really leaves. That is, we must try to see him as an actor . . . with a role to play in a plot, or *mythos*. (Forsyth 1987: 4)

The narrative contexts in which Eastsiders spoke about Satan were grounded in one fundamental root metaphor—that of combat or spiritual battle. As I noted earlier, Eastsiders subscribe to a fundamentally dualist conception of the spiritual world. There are no neutral spiritual beings in this worldview: on one side stands God and his angelic hosts, on the other the demonic forces led by Satan. Consequently, every religious experience—every event seen to be at least in part due to nonhuman and nonphysical sources—could be attributed only to either godly or Satanic origins. There is no middle ground for humanity either. There are only two choices: light or darkness, truth or falsehood, eternal salvation or eternal damnation, and those who have not explicitly aligned themselves with God through salvation are not only outsiders but also unwitting agents of Satan and enemies of God and his people.

Referring to himself and his own spiritual status before he became saved, Reverend Wright once declared at a Men's Auxiliary prayer breakfast:

> People that oppose me, don't oppose me, they oppose God. Because I'm only doing what the Lord's will is. People say, "I don't like Reverend Wright," but they don't even know me. I knew Roger Wright when he was young, and he was a liar and a thief, and a womanizer. I could go get [the old] Roger Wright, and if they say, "I like this man," then I know that they oppose God, because I was an enemy of God.

As this statement implies, each individual action can be evaluated according to this binary distinction between good and evil; one's actions are either pro-God or anti-God. Darryl Lawson once remarked to me: "No matter what you do in life, either you doing it unto one or the other, unto God or unto Satan." In metaphoric terms, either God or Satan is one's master and father—there is no third choice. One is either a servant of God or a servant of the devil, a child of heaven or a child of hell. Two of Reverend Wright's sermons, "To Whom Do You Belong?" and "Do You Know Who Your Father Is?" are structured around these oppositions.

> Beloveds, there are many who claim to be children of God. But some are in error. According to John 8:43, there many people in error who say that they are children of God. The only way to be a child of God is if Christ dwells on the inside of you, and you dwell on the inside of Christ.

But we've come to straighten this thing out. "Why do you not under-stand," said Jesus, "my speech? Even because ye cannot hear my words, ye are of your father the devil. That's why you can't hear me." Jesus said, "That's why you can't receive the Gospel that I bring. That's why you can't agree with the works that the Father is doing to my life, you discount it and you say it's not of God." Jesus said, "The reason why is because you are of your father the devil. You don't love God." See but Jesus was a bold man. Now you see why they hung him on the cross. And he said, "You are of your father the devil, and the lust of your father you will do. Whatever is in your father," Jesus says, "is in you." And the devil is a liar, the devil is a hypocrite, the devil is all those things ungodly. And Jesus said, "The rea-son why you fightin' me is because you're just like your daddy. Your daddy is against God. You go to church, yeah, you sit on boards, but you yanked up with your daddy—you got your daddy ways."

Given the either/or nature of this spiritual world and the necessity of making a choice between serving God or Satan, to Eastsiders the correct decision is self-evident. What rational person would choose hell over heaven, or select eternal punishment over eternal joy and peace? In his ser-mon "To Whom Do You Belong?" Reverend Wright makes this point abundantly clear:

I crossed over to serve this master [God]. Because this master has given me promises that the other master couldn't give me. The other master told me steal, drink, party, hang out, do whatever I want, and I look at the end of life and says, "Master, Satan what can you offer me?" And the an-swer was "Nothing." "Satan, why can't you offer me anything for serving you?" "Because," Satan says, "I'm not a creator of anything but a lie. That's the only thing I ever created. That's why I'm the father of a lie." "But," Satan said, "the God who I'm trying to get you not to serve, he is the cre-ator of the heavens and the Earth." Even the devil knows the word of truth. When I looked at that I said, "But, Devil, you mean to tell me I can feel good today but I got to feel bad tomorrow?" The devil says, "I'm afraid that's it." "Well, well, Devil, I don't think I wanta, I don't want to be your servant no more. I don't think I want to go to your juke joints no more. I don't think I want to go hang out in your speakeasy no more. I don't think I wanta lie down with your dogs anymore. I don't think that I want to be in your company anymore, Devil, because you out to destroy me. But I'm gonna look over here at that man that tells me that if I just lay down my sin, if I just come out of my sin, He'll forgive me, Devil. I think that's the man that I want to serve. The one that tells me that if I work until my day is done, if I hold out, if I hold on, then somebody will say, "Servant of God, well done. The battle is fought, the victory is won."

Because this duality of warring opposites constitutes Eastsiders' basic worldview, it is not surprising that the primary metaphor they use in constructing their experience of Satan is that of a war or battle. Like the relational metaphors used in construing their experience of God, Eastsiders take this imagery directly from Biblical passages, and particularly from the New Testament. For example, the author of I Peter 5:8 admonishes the recipients of his letter to "be sober, be vigilant, because your adversary, the devil, like a roaring lion walketh about, seeking whom he may devour" (King James Version). The most popular and extensive use of this metaphor is Paul's exhortation to the Ephesians: "Put on the whole armor of God, that ye may be able to stand the wiles of the devil. For we wrestle not against flesh and blood, but against principalities and powers, against the rulers of the darkness of this world, against wickedness in high places." After reminding the Ephesians that, despite appearances, their real enemy is their spiritual adversary the devil, Paul develops the metaphor to include specific pieces of "spiritual armor": the "breastplate of righteousness," the "shield of faith, "the "helmet of salvation," and the "sword of the Spirit." This collective identity as warriors against the devil is reflected in several popular spirituals: "I'm on the Battlefield for My Lord," "I'm a Soldier in the Army of the Lord," and the chorus of the song "Climbing Jacob's Ladder" is the phrase "soldiers of the cross." In keeping with this metaphor of war, Eastsiders often refer to Satan simply as "the enemy." This designation echoes the etymology of the devil's most common Biblical names, as the Hebrew word "*Stn*" ("*Satanas*" in its vocalized form) and the Greek "*diabolos*" both have root meanings similar to the English word "opponent" (Forsyth 1987: 4).

This image of war and battle constitutes the fundamental backdrop of Eastsiders' worldview, but it raises several additional questions: What are the stakes in this ongoing battle between God and Satan? Exactly what weapons and strategies does the devil use—and against whom? And how do ordinary Christians fight back? The following paragraphs explore each of these questions in turn.

The Stakes

Simply put, the most important and most immediate stake in the spiritual battle between God and Satan is nothing less than the eternal destiny of every individual man and woman. Because of their rebellion against God, the fate of Satan and his demons is already sealed: they will be thrown into the eternal fire of hell that was created especially for them. In the meantime, however, they are loose in the world and their main objective is to convince as many people as they can to join with them in their rebellion. The most fateful of these acts is the rejection of the salvation offered in the death and resurrection of Jesus Christ, and those who follow this path will share the eternal punishment of Satan and his demons. This is why the issue of salvation is so important, and why it is so emphasized in the church.

Although the salvation or damnation of individual human beings is the ultimate stake in the war between God and Satan, there are more temporal issues as well. In the theological worldview of Eastside Chapel, the entire world—including the human race and human society—was created by God to be subject to him. When Satan and his followers rejected God out of pride and then tempted Adam and Eve to sin, humanity and the world were lost to God. In modern political terms, Satan staged a successful military coup and humanity is now under his authority and control. The actions of God recorded in the Bible, and in particular the selection of Israel as a chosen nation, and the birth, death, and resurrection of Christ, and the foundation and growth of the Christian church, all represent one long campaign to wrest control of the world and of humanity back from Satan's dominion.

At the most personal level, the war between God and Satan plays out within each human being, and not just within his or her psyche, but within his or her physical human form as well. When a person becomes "saved" he or she is radically transformed not only in mind and soul but also in his or her body, which becomes an actual "vessel" of the Holy Spirit. Eastsiders hold that, although not generally apparent to others or even always to the individual believer himself or herself, every Christian is in a sense "possessed" with the Holy Spirit all of the time. When Christians "get the Spirit" and shout during the worship service, it is actually just an *intensification* of an already indwelling spirit rather than a temporary invasion from outside the body, a sudden fanning of the embers into flame rather than a purely spontaneous combustion. Because of this belief that the Holy Spirit dwells inside the mind, soul, and body of believers, the lines of attribution for individual actions sometimes become blurred. For example, when Eastsiders recount some past action of theirs that showed unusual devotion by committing a particularly selfless act or correcting someone whom they felt was straying from the truth, they often disallow responsibility for the action with this phrase: "Well, I thank God that it was not me, but the God *in* me."

This understanding that spiritual beings actually inhabit individual minds and bodies is carried over to Satan and the demonic as well. This does not mean that Eastsiders believe that every non-Christian is possessed by the devil or a demon. However, they do believe that the "natural man," the human nature that we are born with, is ultimately under the dominion of Satan. While Christians can still activate this "dark side" of themselves by indulging their sinful desires rather than the will of God, non-Christians are wholly dominated by it; not knowing God or possessing the Holy Spirit, non-Christians have no "light" to counter the "darkness" of human nature. This is how Eastsiders understand ordinary, run-of-the mill evil committed by both Christians and non-Christians—the influence of human nature that is stained by original sin and therefore under the authority of Satan.

However, some behavior is so reprehensible, so outside the boundaries of "ordinary" sin and evil, that a stronger cause seems necessary to explain it. In some of these cases, believers can draw upon the idea of demonic possession as an explanation. The four books of the Gospels offer a ready template for this type of attribution. In his sermon "Do You Believe in Ghosts?" Reverend Wright refers to the famous story of Jesus, the demons, and the herd of swine, and then relates it to a serial rapist who was terrorizing the Charleston area at the time.

> Jesus said there are some ghosts in the world that are unholy ghosts. And these unholy ghost haunt the minds of men. And when Jesus came along, Jesus cast out these ghosts. He cast it out of the man in the graveyard. He was out there cutting himself because these ghosts was haunting his mind. And Jesus went out there and Jesus told those ghosts, he said, "Come out of the man." He cast the ghost out and the ghosts talked, and the ghosts said to Jesus, "Lord will you allow us to go in the hogs?" But the hogs say, "We don't want to be haunted by no ghosts, especially unholy ghosts." My God! And beloveds, there are a lot of human beings today walking around haunted by ghosts. Their minds are haunted by ghosts.

They hear ghosts talking to them. They hear ghosts telling them to shoot this person, hurt this person, rob this person, rape this person. Beloveds, they're looking for the serial rapist. But I got news for the police department—it is not the man that is doing the raping. It's those spirits on the inside of the man. You can kill the man, but those raping ghosts will come out of the man and go into somebody else. . . .

And beloveds, we ought to know something about ghosts. Hallelujah! Oh, I got some more to tell today! I want you to know what ghosts do in people's bodies. Ghosts alters behavior. I don't know if you realize that, but ghosts alters people behavior. Beloveds, when you got a ghost on the inside of you, a wicked ghost, a evil ghost, that ghost will alter your behavior. And beloveds, you can see some folk that appear to be natural and normal people, and then they can get in the midst of a situation that transform them. And all of a sudden they look evil. They talk evil. They act evil. They even smell evil. And beloveds, they got a evil ghost. And sometimes ghosts don't only come in one, sometimes they come in bunches like bananas. A whole bunch of 'em move on the inside. Because beloveds, these bodies are temples. That's what the Bible says they are, and ghosts want to haunt houses.

The spiritual war between God and Satan, then, is one that is waged for and through the hearts, minds, and even the bodies of human beings. But there is also a social and collective aspect to the battle as well, a contested front that includes institutions and communities, and it can extend to whole metropolitan areas and even to whole cultures and societies.

In these cases, the term "battlefield" can take on a more literal meaning and refers to actual geographic territory. Besides church buildings, other types of property that are associated with God's actions can also qualify; one elderly Eastsider told me that when she visited the Bakkers' "Praise the Lord Club's" facility in Charlotte, North Carolina, she was aware of a "special sense of consecration."

While sanctuaries and other religious facilities represent God's beachheads, all other territory is ceded to Satan and his demons—the "rulers of the darkness of this world" in the Apostle Paul's words. This does not mean, however, that the geography of sin is a flat and featureless terrain. Just as there are church buildings and campuses that signify the presence of God, there are also "strongholds" of Satan, which signify the hold he has over humanity. To Eastsiders, these are the bars, liquor stores, nightclubs, "juke joints," and drug corners known collectively as "the street."

This opposition between "the church" and "the street" is a metaphoric representation of all the other polarities—belief and unbelief, holiness and sin, salvation and damnation—that ultimately derive from the opposition between God and Satan.

The territorial nature of the spiritual battle between church and street was brought home one particular night during the midnight prayer meeting when Reverend Wright announced that, starting the following week, we were going to meet over at Bayside Manor. Despite its innocuous name and bland two-story, 1970s "townhouse" architecture, Bayside Manor is the most notorious public housing project in the Charleston area, possibly because it is so physically isolated from the rest of the city (behind a dump and a graveyard and adjacent to the marshy ground on the Eastern edge of the peninsula's neck). Reverend Wright explained to the group that, just as Gideon marched around the walled city of Jericho seven times, we were going to meet for seven consecutive weeks in Bayside Manor, marching through the housing project and doing spiritual battle. The clear assumption behind this identification of Bayside Manor with Jericho is that it was a stronghold of the enemy and contained a more fully realized vision of hell than did other pieces of local real estate.

This took me by surprise. I had been to Bayside Manor on several occasions—I had even been inside a couple of the units—and from my perspective, it wasn't any scarier than the Eastside neighborhood that we were sitting in at that very moment. In fact, it seemed a lot less scary because it was completely residential and there were no abandoned buildings, bars, or corner liquor stores where groups of young men could hang out. It seemed to me that church members weren't a whole lot better off than those behind the stenciled "No Trespassing" signs on the housing project walls. Of course, my own white middle-classness had distorted my perspective, truncating the lower end of the social spectrum, and I did not yet realize the very important distinctions that they made between themselves and others they felt were in quite a different social category.

In any case, we did not go to Bayside Manor that next Saturday evening because it rained. There was a smaller turnout for midnight prayer service that particular Saturday—whether because of the rain or the scheduled visit to Bayside Manor, I am not sure. There was a feeling of relief, though, at the news of postponing the trip for another week. One of the men later admitted to me that he had a "spirit of fear" about going there. Brother Anthony, a lay leader who was studying to be a pastor, talked with me for a bit that evening, and said that he felt God had kept us from going because we weren't "spiritually ready" for the trip. He said that if we had gone, we would have been "beaten up" by "the enemy" and that while we had been praying in the church, he had a vision of us walking through the housing complex while demons were throwing things at us and hurting us. Next week we would go, he concluded, and this time we would be prepared with the whole armor of God to defend us.

The following Saturday we met at the church at about 10:30. After a few preliminaries, we split up into groups and carpooled over to one of the parking lots at Bayside Manor. When everyone had arrived, Reverend Wright gave us our instructions:

> As we walk through here, everybody stay together and pay attention to what you are doing. Some people don't seem to be able to pray and walk at the same time, but you are going to have to manage it. There are a lot of spirits over this place, so we are going to have to rebuke these spirits by name. For example, say, "Spirit of incest, I rebuke you in the name of Jesus!" and then renounce its impact on people's lives.

With this bit of guidance, the whole group of about fourteen started marching along the sidewalks that threaded through the townhouses, led by Reverend Wright. Despite the late hour (it was about 11:30 by this time), there were quite a few people about, including many young people talking in clusters around the stairwells and next to cars in the parking lot. I felt a sense of relief at the inadequate lighting that barely illuminated our path between the buildings. This was an unusual feeling, especially considering I was in a notoriously dangerous housing project at night, but I was feeling very visible and very white, and the low light offered at least some sense of invisibility. Mostly, I was concerned that the residents would take offense at the presence of our little band of marchers, so I kept my voice low and decided to concentrate on sending out blessings over the people rather than addressing any demons directly, let alone by name. However, this "low-profile" strategy didn't really work too well, as Reverend Wright was striding briskly at the front of the group, arms raised, loudly decrying the spirits of poverty and drug addiction and of all sorts of other personal and social ills.

To my surprise, however, nobody yelled anything back at us or expressed any hostility. In fact, we even picked up a few additional marchers along the way for a time—some older women who definitely responded favorably to our presence and seemed to approve of what we were doing. Most of the younger people simply ignored us, and we didn't address them directly either. Several young men did seem to run in the opposite direction from us, something that Sherline Singleton noticed and commented upon to me later. She believed that these men were running away because they were oppressed by evil spirits, and so fled when confronted with an invasion by the Holy Spirit in the form of our little parade.

When we reassembled back in the parking lot after about fifteen minutes, Reverend Wright announced that next Saturday we would come back and spend several hours going door-to-door and talking to the residents, "just like the Jehovah's Witnesses." Although I was out of town that weekend and thus not present for that foray, the following Saturday, I arrived late to find the group in the parking lot, having already marched through the housing project. Everyone was in a high state of excitement and praying loudly. Several women seemed quite agitated and were jumping up and down in place as the others prayed. Reverend Wright told everyone to open their eyes and look around. We did and saw that several residents stood and watched us from the doorways of their units. They didn't say anything to us, and we didn't say anything back, and I couldn't tell if they were offended, amused, or sympathetic. After the group was dismissed, I gave Lenard Singleton a ride home. As we drove out of the housing complex and back downtown, he reported seeing a black cat strutting down the railroad tracks that partially enclose Bayside Manor and seal it off from the rest of Charleston. The cat, Lenard said, was a sign that Satan still asserted his authority over the housing project, although he was sure that the devil was mad about all of the praying that we had done on "his territory." Although we never knew what, if anything, resulted from our weeks in Bayside Manor, all the participants felt that they had done their duty as good soldiers. They had gone into the heart of the enemy's stronghold and had at least loosened Satan's grip a bit over that piece of territory.

This idea that spiritual beings can occupy or dominate a community, which motivated our foray into Bayside Manor, also operates on a larger geographic scale. Whole cities, regions, and even nations can be seen as under the controlling influence of different types of spirits, just as Bayside Manor was under the sway of particular types of spirits. Reverend Wright once alluded to a "spirit of slavery" that still operated in Charleston. When I asked him in an interview what he meant by that, he gave me a detailed answer:

When God spoke to Cain, he said "Cain, the blood of thy brother cryeth out from the earth." There was murder in the land. In Revelation, it said, the souls under the altar were crying out "How long before thou will avenge our blood?" [These are those] who have been persecuted. This city of Charleston was a strong slave port. Much domination and control was here—mind control. A lot of people were killed here. There was a great uprising here—Denmark Vesey. All those people were hung here and killed for simply plotting to get their freedom. A lot of children were killed here. A lot of people were drowned off of Charleston harbor. They were mistreated and their souls are crying out for justice. And in the same hand, the spirits that dominated Charleston—those old racist spirits of the Confederacy—are still here. And they still have that domineering, controlling mentality hovering over this city. You can leave out of Charleston and go to a city like Atlanta or go up north to Washington, DC, you can feel a liberation of the mind. When you come back to Charleston, you feel that mental bondage again—because it's all spiritual. See, whatever the land was consecrated for, the spirit of that consecration lingers there for generations and generations. And it's just like America— there are certain spirits in America that are going to be here until America ends. There's a spirit of rivalry in America, because America was founded on rivalry. There's a spirit of division and hatred in America, and that's always going to be here. It was against the Europeans and Indians, then it was the North against the South, it was against slavery and freedom. That rivalry, warring spirit will always linger over America. And it can't die, I mean once it tries to die, it keeps resurfacing. So that spirit is definitely here, [and] those kinds of spirits inter-react with the inhabitants of the land—people fall under the domination or influence of [these] spirits.

There seems to be kind of a dialectic here concerning the relationship between spiritual and geographic territory, one that is mediated by human behavior. In this scheme, people's actions can actually create or at least influence the spiritual climate of a community. However, once created, these forces then influence succeeding generations and their actions.

Weapons and Strategies

One Saturday evening at the midnight prayer service, Lenard Singleton relayed a message he felt that God had given him to tell the church. It was a warning that Christians need to be aware of Satan's "battle plans" and that to effectively counter his schemes, believers needed to be as obedient and as disciplined as an army. Reverend Wright affirmed this prophetic word and continued with a lengthy discourse of his own concerning the need for all armies, physical and spiritual, to take into account their enemy's strategies and tactics. He concluded by emphasizing that this warning should be taken seriously by the whole church. What, then, are Satan's "battle plans" as Eastsiders see them? How do they experience this in their own lives or in the lives of their friends, family, and neighbors? There are several main tactics that Satan uses, and each relates directly to how Eastsiders perceive the character of the devil and his ultimate objective of persuading humanity to join in his rebellion against God.

Probably the most common experience that Eastsiders attribute to Satan or the demonic is that of temptation to sin. This type of attribution is widespread among evangelical Christians and, according to some older surveys, is about as common as experiences of salvation (Stark and Glock 1968: 138). There are many models for this type of attribution in the Bible, the most famous of which is Jesus' own temptation in the wilderness recorded in the Gospels. Temptation can be experienced in two ways: internally and circumstantially. First, one can attribute one's own sinful thoughts and desires to the seductive voice of Satan, trying to entice the believer to disregard God's commands. For example, when I asked Lenard Singleton if it was hard to give up his cocaine habit when he got saved, he told me, "I really had a battle with it, because Satan was trying to tempt me [by saying], 'You know you can go back out there and do your little bit—maybe every two weeks or once a month, just a little.'" Second, one can attribute the actions of others or certain situations one happens to find oneself in to the manipulations of Satan, who tries to prey upon believers' weaknesses.

No matter which type of temptation, internal or external, Eastsiders believe that Satan will work much harder to tempt Christians to sin than non-Christians. Therefore, the newly saved are particularly likely to be targets of attack. As Mother Pinckney explained to me: "As long as you been deceived that's where the devil got you, he ain't gonna bother you, because he already got you. But you try to get out of that mess, he really going to get on your trail. And then he's gonna have all his armies to get you."

Satan will also try harder to tempt those who are successfully advancing God's kingdom. This is the explanation Lenard gave for the fall of some prominent Christian leaders:

I mean, you can just look at—my God, look at all these evangelists, Jim Bakker and Swaggart and all of them. . . . These people you know, they really start out serving the Lord. Well, what happens in a situation like that, you know, it opens more vents for Satan to come in. He's got more things to come against you with, bringing lots more money, and then your ministry, then in your congregation you've got a bunch of beautiful women, and the devil's gonna work through people, and he's gonna work through money to get to you. And if you're not strong—he's got you.

Even in the midst of a church service, the devil can work to distract members from focusing on God. Ronald Manigault said that he always sat in the front of the church for this reason. "I don't look back once I'm in the church. [The devil will] have you start looking back, he'll start having you look at women. All kind of thoughts go through your mind."

Aside from temptation, the most powerful weapon in Satan's arsenal is that of deception. Of all of "the enemy's" tactics mentioned in interviews, sermons, prayers and other forms of discourse, by far the most common is that of deceit. In fact, Satan is often referred to as the "Father of Lies," a title taken from several of Jesus' statements in the New Testament.

One of the devil's primary deceptions is to convince people that the only important thing in life is worldly success and happiness. After several men in their twenties had left the church within a period of several weeks, I asked Darryl Lawson if he was ever tempted to leave, and if he could see what was drawing them back out into "the world." He replied:

I don't see anything. It's temporary, and that's what I try to tell anybody I talk to. Anything of this world is temporary. You get married, it's temporary. And I don't mean in divorce, but I mean it's temporary because either you or your spouse will die. You know, we're not promised to be here forever. Your children, they're temporary. Your home—even more temporary than your marriage. . . . So everything is temporary, but everything that God has planned for us is eternal. Take sex for instance. And I don't mean to be carnal, but we all know that once the thrill of the moment is over, it's gone! And you can't recap—you can think about it, but you can't recapture that feeling. But Jesus Christ, he'll give you that joy over and over and over and over. So the world has nothing really to offer. It's just like a mirage. It paints a beautiful picture but once you get out there it's different, it's cruel. . . . I don't see where the world has anything to offer. It looks good from a distance, but you know, you got to read the reality of the world.

This sentiment was echoed by many in the church. Reflecting on his career as a drug dealer before getting saved, Lenard Singleton told me about the constant anxiety of trying to satisfy both his suppliers and customers while all the time worrying about eluding the police. I remarked that it sounded like a very stressful way to live and that it must have been a relief to get out of it. He replied:

> The thing about it, when you out there in the world, the devil will keep you going. He'll keep you to the point where [you think] everything is going fine—you think you on top of the world. You got money in your pocket, you got drugs, you got pleasure, women around you, and you think you living the life. But then it's destruction, because it will all blow over in one snap of the finger. The devil keeps you blindfolded, but the victory is in the Lord.

The fundamental attitude that Eastsiders had toward unbelievers is that they are deceived and kept ignorant of God's truth by the devil. Although the phrase "false consciousness" had no place in their vocabulary, it would be an accurate term to describe how Eastsiders feel about the unsaved and applies equally to those who are in "the world" and to the "churchgoers" and "church worshippers" who are not "really saved." The latter are the ones that the devil has really blindfolded, because they are exposed to the truth every week in church and outwardly profess to believe it, although inwardly they oppose God and his purposes. In fact, the main point of Reverend Wright's sermon "Do You Know Who Your Father Is?" was to directly challenge the unsaved in his own congregation in the same way that Jesus challenged the pharisaical religious leaders of his own day.

One of the implications of emphasizing the deceptive tactics of Satan is one must recognize that not everything is as it seems and that not every event can be taken at face value. For example, one of Satan's tricks to pull on Christians is to make them feel as if they were physically ill, thereby keeping them sidelined from the battle and incapacitated from doing God's work. Mother Gadsden told me about one of these incidents and how she finally managed to "break the lie" by going to church anyway.

> I just felt so bad, I thought I had the flu. But the devil put those on you, you know—you're not really sick. You go to the doctor and the doctor say that there's really nothing wrong with you. This been years back. He didn't find nothing wrong, nothing wrong. I mean I had—I don't know what

kind of medicine I had, [but] nothing did no good. Go back every week, the doctor said he just didn't find nothing wrong. And you know, it didn't even register to me at this time. Even here a couple of weeks ago, I had these um—a touch of the flu or something. And I had it for like five weeks, you know. And staying home, you know, you won't [ever] feel good, [because] you got to go and get under the anointing of the Word. And now I feel better. And I thank the Lord I feel much better, 'cause you got to go and get under the anointing. The anointing break the yoke. Ooooh! Jesus! And the yoke is all these things Satan put on you.

Even after they become saved, Eastsiders believed that Satan could still try to deceive them. Ronald Manigault told me that the devil often tries to manipulate people into not going forward to receive special prayer at the end of the service, telling them that everyone in the congregation will think badly of them for going up.

That's the way the enemy can trick them. What he does, he tells them that the people are going to talk about them, but yet he blinded their minds and don't let them see that some of those people are really saved. Takes a whole lot of faith to [come forward and get special prayer]. What it is, I think—you got to block out within your mind, because the devil, he be telling you, "Boy, you better not go up there, boy, they gonna be looking at you."

Satan especially tries to attack the truth of God and make believers doubt that their own spiritual experiences are valid and real. After describing his experience of being filled with the Holy Ghost, Darryl Lawson described how the devil tried to take it away from him: "And after that experience [of receiving the Holy Ghost] was over, I got in my bed—I got up happy. Got in my bed and as soon as I laid back in the bed the devil came to me, he said, 'You ain't got nothing, so you ain't got nothing to [tell anybody about].'"

Fighting Back

With Satan constantly trying to tempt and deceive believers, how do they fight back? What weapons do Eastsiders feel that God has equipped them with in this fierce spiritual battle? The primary weapons used to combat both temptation and deception are twofold: addressing Satan directly by rebuking him in the name of Jesus, or simply speaking the "Word of truth."

When Darryl Lawson felt that the Devil was trying to steal his experience of being filled with the Holy Ghost, he addressed Satan directly and said (in his mind, not out loud): "I bind and rebuke you in the name of Jesus!" On a few occasions when Reverend Wright was preaching and there was a lack of congregational response, he attributed this resistance to Satan's influence through one or more people in attendance. During these incidents he would stop his sermon in mid-delivery to address the interfering spirit:

> Somebody tryin' to bind me today, but you can't bind me because God is with me. Hallelujah! I rebuke the devil! I rebuke him in you. I rebuke him in your heart. I rebuke him in your mind. You low down snake devil! Get outta here! Hallelujah! I been washed in the blood of the Lamb, and no devil in hell, no devil in hell is gonna stop me! But I'm gonna preach the Word!

When Eastsiders experienced ordinary troubles in the material realm that they attributed to Satan, such as mechanical problems with their car or physical sensations of illness, they would often address him directly and say, "Satan, you are a liar!" In the testimonials I heard, Eastsiders felt that the use of this phrase was often effective in treating the problem at hand.

On other occasions merely declaring the spiritual truth about a situation will cause Satan's schemes of deception to fall apart. Mother Pinckney told me the story of how she joined Eastside Chapel when Reverend Simmons, the founding pastor, was still in residence. A friend of hers, Clara Jones, had brought her to church. When the service was almost over and Reverend Simmons was giving the invitation to join the church, Mother Pinckney wanted to go up but was suddenly gripped with indecisiveness.

> Clara said, "Why don't you go up there and join the church?" So I get up, and then I sit back down. And she said, "The devil got you geeing and hawing like this." And when she said that, something snapped. And I got up and I went up there, and I give Reverend Simmons my hand, and when I touch his hand, something hit me on the top of my head and went on through me like that! Just like electricity! That's right! And I join that church that night.

Most often, speaking the truth to Satan in order to foil his plans involves quoting passages from the Bible, a strategy modeled on the Gospel accounts of Jesus' own use of Scripture in dealing with his temptation by Satan in the wilderness. As Reverend Wright notes in the following sermon excerpt, the Holy Spirit will help those in the midst of temptation by supplying the appropriate passage of text—which is one reason why all believers should know their Bibles.

> When we fall into a situation, the Holy Ghost brings the Word back to us. It's just like when Jesus was in the wilderness and the devil came to him and tried to tempt him. The Holy Ghost on the inside of Jesus brought the Word back to him, and he spoke the Word back to the devil. And beloveds, we are no good today unless we learn how to stand in God's Word. For the Bible said, "Heaven and earth will pass away, but God's Word shall never fail." We won't fail if we stand in his Word.

Although each of the above strategies involves a statement directed at Satan—either a rebuke, a declaration of truth, or a quotation of Scripture—there are times when such articulations are not effective. During one of our interviews, Mother Pinckney and I were discussing her former husband, a violent man who had been physically abusive to her and her children when they were younger (he had long since abandoned the family and had not lived with them for many years at the time of my research). During that period, Mother Pinckney felt that Satan had gotten hold of her husband and she was struggling to find a way to resist his abuse. She told me a story that I quote at length because it not only illustrates a particular method for resisting the devil's attacks, but also reveals Eastsiders' perceptions of the limits of satanic power.

> See, God would do things that would eliminate the use of fighting back or hitting back or whatever. He will take care of it. I come from church one Sunday evening, and I always cook before I go, and the kids eat all the food. I had stewed meat for dinner. And there was some gravy in the pot, and the crust in the bottom of the pot. So what I did, I scrape all the gravy out in the crust, then I set it on low, and then I was stirring it, because when the heat come, it start soaking it up, to make a meal. And [my husband] come in. Now he ain't been there, 'cause he didn't come home [the night before]. He must

have come in during the day, and see when he come home, there was no food, 'cause the kids tear the pot up. Well I was stirring the pot, he come in [and said], "Hey, it's too burnt, you been gone all day, blah, blah, blah." I was still stirring the pot you know. That nigger grab a fork and hold 'em right to my throat, and I stir the pot. I still stirring the pot now, I didn't say a word, now, I just stirring the pot. And all at once, a song get in my mind, and I start hummin' [hums]. That joker set the fork on the table and said, "You know one thing? You are a cool so-and-so. Here I come to kill your so-and-so, and you hummin' a song!" I said, [hums again]. Yeah! Yes Lord! [claps] And then I said, "Thank God, I know how to get rid of the devil. And anytime he come and start raising hell, I start hummin', and he can't stay in there, he got to go.

Q: Is it a hymn?

It's just a hum, sometimes I don't know what it is, no words, just a feeling, and he got to go. Just a feeling, no song, no words, no nothing, just something that God know. He knows, I mean, 'cause when you hum, the devil don't know what you singing. When you singing a song, he know you singing a song, and he know you singing it to the Lord, and he would put something there in your mind to take the song away. But when you hum, he don't know what you doing. That's between you and God. So sometime a moan will get you where a long prayer wouldn't get you—'cause see, your whole soul in that. Just pour your heart out and then God know, you know what I mean, He'll just take control.

One concern of Reverend Wright and other congregational leaders was that some Eastsiders might too quickly attribute accidents and other mishaps to the interference of Satan. One Sunday morning during the middle of a sermon, Reverend Wright's cordless, hand-held microphone suddenly cut out. After asking the congregation to "raise a song," he strode off of the dais and to his study. This was the only time I ever witnessed a microphone going dead in the middle of any service, and given that the interrupted sermon dealt with the supernatural power of God and of Satan ("Do You Believe in Ghosts?"), it would have been quite easy for Reverend Wright to blame Satan's interference for the incident. Although I do not know for sure, this possible interpretation on the part of the congregation must have occurred to him, because when he returned after several minutes with a newly restored microphone, he commented to the congregation, "One thing about using microphones with batteries in them—they just go dead when they go dead. Now, getting back to the sermon ..."

Reverend Wright's concern for over-spiritualization among Eastside members was more unambiguously illustrated during the worship service one Sunday morning when the leg on the drummer's stool suddenly broke, sending the drummer crashing to the ground. Immediately, assistant pastor Reverend Jackson, who was sitting on the platform this particular Sunday, jumped up and yelled, "Satan, you are a liar!" On this occasion, Reverend Wright ignored both the incident itself and Reverend Jackson's exclamation and calmly continued with the service. At the next meeting of the Saturday night prayer group, he told those assembled:

> Reverend Jackson's got to learn that not everything is the devil. Some things just happen. If you drive your car long enough, you're bound to get a flat tire. If you drive on the streets long enough, you're bound to have an accident. Now one thing about that drummer's stool, I sold it to Brother Green, and it had a crack in it—it was already broken when I sold it to him. He tried to fix it with glue, but the glue didn't hold. Now I talked to Reverend Jackson about this, and he has been in here crying his heart out to God about it. He knows what he did was wrong, and he wants to only hear from God.

This story illustrates several key points. First, the availability of an alternative "natural" explanation does influence which events will receive a spiritual interpretation. Because Reverend Wright knew about the stool's cracked leg he was able to dismiss the drummer's fall as an unfortunate accident. More importantly, however, this incident shows the important role institutional authority has in shaping the attribution process. In this case, the assistant pastor deferred to the authority of his superior and changed his own initial interpretation of the experience.

Reverend Wright's sanctioning of Reverend Jackson may seem somewhat extreme, but the potential for problems in belief systems that allow for members to experience a wide range of spiritual activity is enormous. For example, should the illness of a member's child be attributed to God's test of the family's faith, or is it an attack of Satan? The choice between these alternatives influences not only how this particular situation will be dealt with by members of the church, but also has potentially divisive theological implications concerning the nature and character of God and his relationship to believers. Because of this dilemma, pressure exists for a collective standard which can be used to interpret particular events, and the institutional authority and reputation of the pastor presents a useful solution to this problem.

* 5 *

"In Spirit and in Truth"

Minister: I was glad when they said to me, "Let us go to the house of the Lord!" Our feet have been standing within your gates, O Jerusalem!

People: For a day in your courts is better than a thousand elsewhere. I would rather be a doorkeeper in the house of my God than dwell in the tents of wickedness.

Minister: O Lord, I love the habitation of your house, and the place where your glory dwells.

People: But the Lord is in his holy temple; let all the earth keep silence before him.

—From the African Methodist Episcopal Call to Worship

It was the second Sunday in March, and Reverend Wright had just stepped behind the pulpit to deliver his sermon. He began with this prayer:

Lord because you are God, we thank you for creating us in thy image and after thy likeness. We thank you for this marvelous opportunity to enter into your house. Lord, there is no better house on earth then your house. And Lord, our fathers have built this house that we might come and worship you in spirit and in truth. And now Lord because we are assembled in thy house and because we have come to worship you, will you come and abide among your people? Will you speak to us out of thy word? Will you encourage our heart? Will you make us brand new again? Somebody needs to be revived; will you revive today? Somebody needs to be found who is lost; Lord, will you find today? Lord, somebody needs to be mended because they're broken. Somebody needs to be healed because they're sick. Somebody needs to be fed because they're hungry. You're a great deliverer, a mighty God, a Wonderful Counselor, a Prince of Peace. You're our bridge, our shelter, our bright and morning star, our bread, our shoes, our clothes-our everything, God. And we're in thy house because we love to praise thy name. And our Lord will you come and walk through the temple just a little while? Will you let your angels come in and camp around? And Father if there be any enemy amongst us Lord, we'll rebuke him and drive him out in Jesus' name. Let the people say Amen.

With this short prayer, Reverend Wright touched on each of the five essential elements of the worship service at Eastside Chapel. *Will you come and abide?* The worship service is first of all a face-to-face encounter between God and his people, a time and a place where the deity may "walk among" them for a while. *Will you speak to us?* When God is present, He will speak words of encouragement and instruction to the congregation. *Will you make us brand new again?* God will also act with power to touch and transform individuals; he will heal the sick, mend the brokenhearted, and save the lost. *We're in thy house because we love to praise thy name.* There is a powerful emotional undercurrent to the worship service, an understanding that this is the proper time and place to express praise, love, and gratitude toward God for what he has done throughout the week. *If there be any enemy amongst us, we'll rebuke him and drive him out.* Not everyone in the congregation is a true child of God. These unsaved church members are unwitting tools of the devil and their presence can hinder both God's voice and his transforming power.

The Presence of God

Worship is a time and a place set aside for the communion of God and his people, an occasion in which the deity is especially present to those who have gathered. The idea that God is present in the worship service is so basic to the understanding that Eastsiders have of this occasion that it usually remains implicit. Yet it can be glimpsed here and there in songs or the liturgy, and in some off-hand statements from the pulpit. For example, Reverend Wright would sometimes say in the introductory remarks to his sermon, "Our hearts are glad to be in the presence of the Living God," or somebody will "raise" the popular spiritual which proclaims that "Jesus is already here / all you have to do is open up your heart / Jesus is already here."

At first this emphasis on the presence of God during worship may seem to contradict the standard Christian doctrine of God's omnipresence. In fact, Eastsiders often rejoice that "the Lord is always near" and in their ability to "call on the name of the Lord" at any time and place. Yet while they do believe that God is present everywhere, they also believe that he is more intensely present and manifest in some times, places, entities, and actions than in others—what Ninian Smart calls the doctrine of the "multipresence" of God (1972: 11–12). So while God is always present and available to believers, he is *more* present and *more* available during the worship service. This is true for several reasons.

The first reason is that the worship service takes place in the church sanctuary—a sacred space set aside for the special habitation of God. In fact, Eastsiders often referred to the church in terms of the Biblical metaphor as the "house of the Lord." Almost every prayer and testimony begins with an expression of thanks to God for being, "in the house of the Lord one more time." The words of a popular chorus sung during Sunday morning worship services, revival meetings, and other kinds of services offer an invitation to "come and go with me, to my father's house, to my father's house, to my father's house."

This perception of the sanctuary as a place in which the presence of God is particularly manifest makes many worshippers feel that upon entering the room they have crossed a boundary between the profane and sacred worlds. Because of this, they don't simply file in, stand around and talk with friends and then find a seat as they would if it were merely a lecture hall or an auditorium. Instead, they proceed immediately either to the pews or to the mourner's bench to kneel down and pray anywhere from several seconds to almost half a minute, and then quietly assume their seats. This act not only marks the transition from the everyday world outside the sanctuary to entering God's house, it also serves as a kind of purification rite before entering into the presence of a holy God. This ritual is not limited to worship services or other official events; the pastor of another Eastside congregation went through these same motions when I met him in the church's sanctuary for an interview.

Sanctuaries and other buildings used repeatedly for collective worship can become associated with powerful manifestations of God's presence. Because of this association, they retain a kind of spiritual charge that retains potency even when not in use, and parts of the building most closely associated with God's presence retain the most power. I once overheard a member of Eastside Chapel remark that when he was crossing the church platform one Sunday after service he could "feel the power" radiating from behind the pulpit.

Even though the sanctuary is the Lord's house, the experienced presence of God within the worship service is not simply a matter of sacred space. The occasion of the worship service itself also acts to call forth the presence of God. There are several often-heard phrases taken from the Bible which speak to this issue: "Where two or three are gathered in his name, he will be in the midst" or "The Lord inhabits the praises of his people."

Because God is present in the sanctuary during collective worship, there is an understanding that one's effort to attend services regularly and to show proper respect and reverence while in the service is an accurate reflection of one's true spiritual attitudes. As a result, one of the most basic understandings that Eastsiders have of worship is that it is an obligation—a work done out of the recognition of God's superior status and as an expression of gratitude for what he has done in their lives. According to this understanding, the worship service is an arena for the display of religious commitment and devotion, and attendance on Sunday mornings is not simply an option but a minimum requirement—a service that Eastsiders owe to God for who he is and what he has done in their lives. This understanding seems to echo that of the first-century Christians in that the Greek word "*latreia*" used in the New Testament can be translated into English as "worship," but also as "service" or "duty" (White 1990: 33).

In English usage, worship is a declaration of inferiority before a superior being, an act that not only expresses submission, but is itself a manifestation of that submission (Smart 1972: 17). Not attending worship (or even coming late) is not simply a failure to express one's devotion—it is itself an act of anti-devotion. In this area and others, Reverend Wright consistently equated visible effort (or the lack of it) with the state of a person's inner commitments and motivations. To drive this point home, he often remarked on what he interpreted as the reluctance of some Eastsiders to attend church and compared this to their behavior in other aspects of their lives:

Lord, why is it that you look so sad and filled with melancholy sitting upon your throne? God said, "Because the creatures that I have created with my hands have gone away from my laws." God says, "When it's time for them to enter in my house," God said, "they won't even come on time." God said, "They go to their jobs at seven o'clock in the morning, but when it comes to my house they come in any old time."

At one of the monthly men's prayer breakfasts at a nearby steak house, the discussion turned to Brother Ivory, a recent migrant from New Orleans who had started to "get clean" from drugs. He had even started coming to Eastside services for several weeks, but then began drifting back to the streets. Several of the lay leaders were speculating on the reason Brother Ivory stopped coming—could it be that he didn't feel welcomed by the church, or that younger men such as Ivory were ignored by the older men in the congregation? At this point Reverend Wright became somewhat impatient. Interrupting the discussion, he declared:

> You are all looking for the answers outside of yourself, but the answer is on the inside. Why do *you* come to church? What makes *you* stick with it week after week? See, if their heart is in the world they will fall away, and there's nothing you can do, no matter how many times you talk to them and encourage them. If Brother Ivory had to get up to go pick up a thousand dollar check, you better believe he wouldn't have any trouble getting up in the morning to pick it up!

While attendance at the worship service was itself an act of devotion, simply showing up regularly (even on time) was not enough. Worship, Eastsiders felt, involved effort—and just as one went to one's job in the morning ready and willing to work hard, one should attend the worship service with a similar "mind to work." Reverend Wright once admonished the congregation, "When you come to the Lord's house, you ought to come with a praise in your heart, you ought to come with a sound in your mouth, you ought to come with a dance in your feet." Another time, he asked rhetorically,

> Why won't you work for him today? Why do you tire so easily? You know how we get—we tire out real easily. Especially during preachin' time. We get real tired—even before the preachin' starts, we're tired. Devotional services—if they don't cut off in fifteen minutes, we're tired. You got to beg folk to sing a song. "Can I get another song? I'm begging, somebody will you testify?" And nobody will testify. "Let me see if I can find five dol-

lars, if I pay somebody will you get up and say something good about the Lord?" We tire so easily.

At a fundamental level then, worship is work. It requires effort and commitment, not only to show up regularly for services but, once there, to put one's heart into it and expend physical and mental energy praising God—often for an extended period of time. This is seen as God's rightful due as one's creator, savior and sustainer, a work of gratitude for all he has done. Attending worship joyfully and gratefully as a response to God's blessings underlies a remark of Reverend Wright's at one revival meeting when he described praying for a young boy with cancer. After informing the congregation that the child had to be connected to a machine twelve hours a day, he exclaimed, "Twelve hours! And folk come to church with life, health, and strength, and act like they doing God a favor."

The idea that worship is an obligation, and one that should be taken seriously, was particularly impressed upon me by an incident that happened late in the year. At the end of April I was invited by preacher-in-training Anthony Scott to hear him speak at a special program one weeknight. Besides me, Anthony had invited Lenard Singleton, Leroy Wigfall, and Sherman Davis to accompany him. Although Sherman couldn't make it because the Israelite Prayer Band that he belonged to was scheduled to appear at a different revival service, the rest of us met Brother Anthony after his seminary class. I drove the group up to the host church, a small congregation off of the interstate between Charleston and Orangeburg.

The service was a Seven Speakers Program, in which the host church invites seven ministers from other congregations to speak. As I mentioned earlier, such a service is structured as a kind of preaching contest, with each speaker bringing a handful of supporters to cheer him or her on, much like school sports teams' bringing a small contingent of the faithful with them on "away" games. There was a small folding table set up just in front of the pulpit, behind which sat two men, a "master of ceremonies" to introduce the speakers, and a secretary to keep track of donations. The practice is for each speaker to get ten minutes to preach, after which he or she makes a contribution to the offering basket, followed by those from his or her home church. A particularly inspiring sermon can elicit donations from others as well, who want to show their approval for a good performance, and a few older women came up after every sermon to contribute their loose change, dribbling maybe thirty-five to seventy-five cents in the basket each time. At the end of the service, the amount donated by each church is announced, along with a grand total. It is an effective way to raise money, and the church took in a total of over $200 with only about thirty people in attendance. It also gives opportunities for novice ministers like Anthony to gain experience behind the pulpit.

The interesting thing about this particular service, and the reason I am including an account of it here, is that during the course of the service some members of the host church made it a little too obvious that, for them, the purpose of the service was financial rather than spiritual. This attitude, openly displayed, deeply offended my earnest friends from Eastside Chapel, and was the subject of much indignant conversation on the ride back to Charleston. The trouble began early on when the master of ceremonies stood up to open the service by saying, "Well, let's get this started, because the purpose of this speaking program is to raise money." As each of the six speakers came up (the seventh was a no-show but did send an envelope of money), it became apparent to me that only Anthony and one other speaker, a young woman from a Church of God in Christ in the nearby community of Strawberry, were really making a serious effort to preach. The other four simply stood up and gave rambling discourses that seemed to have been made up on the spot, comprised of religious catch-phrases loosely stitched together and delivered without energy or enthusiasm. At one point, a deacon from a Baptist church said "amen" from his seat and let out a huge yawn at the same time, eliciting some chuckles from him and the crowd (except of course from our contingent—we frowned disapprovingly in his direction).

At the end of the service, people made jokes about how they could have been watching TV instead of spending the evening in church. The sanctuary was cleared out within minutes as people sped home, their duty done. My friends were livid. Anthony shook his head in disgust and said, "If [our] pastor had been there, he would have put those people in check." Leroy was particularly upset by the master of ceremonies' statement that the purpose of the service was to raise money. "The real purpose," he spoke for all of us, "should have been to hear the Word."

The Word

"To hear the Word" is a term that I heard many times during my year at Eastside Chapel. This phrase refers to any and all communications believed to come from God and includes, but is not limited to, the Old and New Testaments of the Bible. In fact, the most popular use of the term was in reference to a sermon. Not just any sermon though, only one preached by a pastor with the "true anointing" of the Holy Ghost. This emphasis on direct communication from God flows directly from the understanding that God is present in the service. When worshippers are in God's house, they want to hear—no, more emphatically, they *expect* to hear—something from him. In the warm-up to one of his sermons, Reverend Wright declared, "We are blessed to be in [God's] house and blessed to be called his people. And I don't know about you but when I come into the house of the Lord I want to hear something from God. Since I'm in his house I like to hear something from him."

Although worshippers do expect to hear something from God, this is never seen as simply a given. God is still God, and neither his presence in the service nor his Word to the congregation is held to be automatic or taken for granted. But when God's Spirit is present in the service, tremendous spiritual power is unleashed—power to reveal hidden spiritual truth and predict future events, power to transform lives and remove whatever hinders participants from reaching their full spiritual potential—even power to heal physical and emotional ailments. Perhaps the most important of these capacities is that of revelation, for it is through the spoken Word that many of these other powers are activated within the worship service.

Revelation

Although Eastsiders like to assert the simplicity of God's truth as revealed in the Bible, they also acknowledge that there are deeper mysteries and complexities to this spiritual reality. Studying the Bible individually (or in the Thursday night Bible study) is seen as necessary for guiding the Christian to a better understanding of God's ways and purposes. However, members also feel that purely human and intellectual effort is not enough to penetrate the deep spiritual truths contained in God's Word; these deeper meanings can only be revealed by the power of the Holy Ghost. One night in Bible study, Reverend Wright asked the group to ponder why it was Moses and Elijah that appeared with Jesus on the Mount of Transfiguration. When Sherline Singleton began to answer, Reverend Wright stopped her in mid-sentence to ask, "Did the Spirit reveal that to you or the flesh?" Somewhat taken aback, she hesitantly answered that she was "trying to think about it with her mind." Reverend Wright immediately dismissed her answer and told those present that they should always let the Spirit reveal answers to them and not their minds. Later, in a sermon about the Holy Spirit, Reverend Wright informed the congregation that one of the Spirit's main tasks is to bring insight and understanding to believers as they read the Bible:

> Jesus said [the Holy Ghost] is going to teach you. The word "teach" means to instruct, and you know, whenever we can't receive instructions, we are lost. That's what the word "teach" means. It means to bring the wisdom of the Word to us in reality. And beloveds, you can't read the Word of God and understand it unless the Holy Spirit is living on the inside of you. And I know I'm telling the truth.

Because the Holy Spirit is the one who reveals truth, when the Spirit is present in the worship service, he communicates these spiritual truths to the gathered worshippers. Usually this happens in the sermon, for of all the segments of the worship service, it is the sermon that is specially set apart for God to speak to the congregation through the preacher. This is apparent in much of the discourse of prayers and sermons:

Lord, will you speak a Word tonight—speak a Word to this congregation?

We have come to have a good time, but we also came to hear what "thus sayeth the Lord."

The revelation of God's Word through the sermon actually begins days and even weeks prior to the actual worship event when the preacher gets a sudden divine inspiration for his or her message. This can happen at any time and through many different mediums. Reverend Wright explained this process to me:

> Sometimes I'll get the Word when I'm on my knees. There are other times when I'll say, "OK, it's going to come," and I'll go through that day and somebody will speak to me about something. And in the midst of that conversation, boom [snaps fingers], I say, "that's my Word." Other times I'll be driving along in my car on the interstate or—the Lord will drop a Word in my spirit. And whenever I get it [snaps fingers], I know. That's it. Whether it comes from somebody

in a phone conversation, or, wherever it is, I know, that's the word for Sunday.

Q: So it could come from many different places?

Sometimes. Some comes from me being on my knees in meditation; sometimes the Lord will drop a Word in my spirit. And sometimes I'll be watching television, and the Word [snaps fingers], I say, "That's the Word." Like I was in my bedroom last week and some-body on the TV mentioned "friendly mergers, hostile takeovers" [the theme of the previous Sunday morning's sermon]. And I said [snaps fingers], "That's the Word." I wrote it down. And um, but the Spirit—the Holy Spirit—when I was in Columbia I think, last week, spoke to me about "Designed for Performance." That was the word for Sunday evening—and that was the second message, but I got the second message before I got the first message. I knew that was for Sunday evening when I got it.

Q: So once you get that initial Word, then what do you do with it?

I get the Word, and then I start researching the Word in Scripture— seeing how it compares [with Biblical texts], and what revelations are in it. Because revelation is always in a Word that you get.

These same "Words" often serve as the "subject" or title of the message. These are always announced at the beginning of the sermon in a standard form, such as, "taking for my subject tonight 'Don't Cheat on the Test'" (which was actually the title of Anthony Scott's sermon at the seven speakers program). Sometimes the subject is announced in a rather oblique and indirect way: "If I were to take a subject tonight, it would be 'Take the Bypass.'" As is clear in the above examples, many of these "Words" are stock expressions drawn from everyday speech about ordi-nary objects and events. The revelation lies in how these mundane words and phrases illuminate deeper spiritual truths. Much of the sermon then, consists of a thorough and systematic exploration of these metaphoric re-lationships, often relying on a dictionary as much or more than any schol-arly Bible commentary (although these are sometimes used). For example, in Reverend Wright's sermon, "Do You Know Who Your Father Is?" he first dissected the phrase "child of God" with particular attention to the word "of." With the help of Webster's dictionary, he identified several us-ages of the word and their Christian implications: "The word 'of' today is 'used to indicate qualities or attributes.' And if we are children of God, we are supposed to have the attributes of God in our life." Definitions of the word "father" were brought in next and also mined for their spiritual parallels:

> "A father is any man who exercises parental care over another or others," and that means that a father—somebody who has a fathering spirit—can be a father to anybody that they take under their care. That's what the word "father" means. And that's also what the Bible says—that we are adopted in the royal family through Christ Jesus.

A discourse structured around Biblical texts and dictionary definitions may sound like a fairly scholastic and dull affair, but the genius of the black church sermon is that its content—though drawn from these more abstract and intellectual sources—is "brought home" in a vivid and compelling way. Sometimes this is done by relating Christian teaching to provocative issues within the black community. In Reverend Wright's sermon "Do You Know Who Your Father Is?" he deliberately took the issue of spiritual parentage and drew out the parallels to a close-to-home issue among low-income African Americans — paternity identification: "Beloveds, if you are a child of God, first of all you got to have a birth certificate with his name on it as Father. And if you're the child of God, you got to have his blood type. Hallelujah! Because I want you to know the blood will be tested to tell who the real Father really is." In another example, Reverend Wright read several verses from the second chapter of Jeremiah. When he reached the verse "I see great armies marching on Jerusalem with mighty shouts," he then left the text and inserted, "Armies of alcoholics, armies of crack, armies of cocaine, armies of profane language, armies of disowned babies, armies of Michael Jacksons, armies of Bobby Browns, armies of Mike Tysons, armies of Magic Tragic Johnsons." And back to the text—"coming to destroy her."

Sometimes a preacher can sharpen a sermon's impact through the process of translation, or code switching—taking a Biblical account or theological concept and putting it in the vernacular of the street. The resulting juxtaposition of sacred and slang breathes fresh life into ancient stories and gives them relevance to the congregation, as the next two sermon excerpts show. This vernacular can be more "country" in origin— "But you know Jesus said, 'I didn't come to feed you no corn bread and black-eyed peas,' but Jesus said, 'I have come to feed this food which is from God out of heaven.'" Or it can be a translation into black slang—

"God came down and said, 'Adam, where forth art thou?' In street language that would be, 'Say, Adam, where you at?'"

Bringing It Home

Once these revelations from God have been delivered to the pastor, it is his or her duty to communicate them effectively through the sermon, often using some of the techniques outlined above. However, speakers do not depend on their ability and preparation alone. At some point in the sermon the Holy Spirit becomes manifest in the preacher's words and bodily actions, charging the message with spiritual power. At this point, the Spirit takes a more active part in the delivery of the message. Reverend Wright discussed this traditional aspect of the African American sermon with me at some length:

> It is all done—it is orchestrated by the Holy Spirit. It can be duplicated, but it won't be an original. You can fake it, you can act it out, but there will be no anointing there. Whenever I'm teaching, or explaining to a black congregation—a black congregation looks for a message subject, so they can kind of see where you are going. And once you lay out the subject of your sermon, and they can see where you are going, they want you to "take them home" with emotionalism—to drive it home. And they'll do good—they'll stay with you for fifteen minutes if you have a good delivery, they stay with you, but after that fifteen minutes, they gonna grow a little weary. Fifteen or twenty minutes, thirty minutes if you real good at presenting it. But [you've got to] have a climax—and that's what we call the "great climax"—where you become emotional and the anointing sets in. And this is all inspiration, because now you are saying things that you didn't plan on paper. It's kinda ad libbing. Once you do that, they'll go along with you, but once the anointing leaves you—sit down. Because if you don't, then you can run back into flesh—the imitation—and then you start losing the people.
>
> Q: How can you tell when you are getting that anointing, and how do you know when it stops?
>
> The anointing is an inspiration, it is something—whenever it comes, you know it. I can tell in a very carnal way, so you'll understand [laughs]. It's kinda like when you're making love, when you get ready

to climax, you know it—you feel it. All right. But when it's gone, you know it's gone! That's it! Hey, it's over. I mean, you wish it would last sometimes a little longer, but you know, it's there and it's gone. Spiritually, it is the same kind of experience—you feel it, you sense it. . . . Now you can be a good, gifted presenter and not have any anointing, and I mean just have the people jumping up out of their seats. But that's just gifting, that's just ability. But the anointing goes beyond that—anointing will take you into a realm of information that you hadn't even—you got no forethought of, no foreknowledge. No pre-thought, let me put it that way. And you preach, and these things just coming out, I mean you didn't plan it. You know it feels good, but um—you know it is the Holy Spirit taking over. Because we allow ourselves to be used by him in that way.

There are usually very marked verbal and bodily indicators that a preacher has come under the anointing as he or she delivers a sermon. Albert Raboteau offers a good summary of the audible signals of this transformation: "The preacher's harsh vocal sound, the constriction of voice, the audible gasp at the end of each line, [and] the tonal quality" (1995: 150). There are many physical clues as well, such as jerking, bobbing, pacing, and other rhythmic movements of the body. These aural and visual signals indicate that the preacher's footing has shifted. His or her words are no longer mediated expressions of God's revelation—they are now a direct communication from the Holy Spirit. The preacher's status has changed from one of both author and animator of the verbal performance to simply that of animator (Goffman 1981: 144, 171).

The preacher's position of authority in the congregation rests solely upon the idea that he or she is the mouthpiece of God's Word, the medium of the divine message. As pastor Wright once exclaimed in the midst of a sermon, "I ain't nothin but a filthy rag saved by the grace of God. That's all! That's all we are! Sure the Bible says, 'Give honor where honor is due,' and I'm the pastor. [But] all I got is the Word of God, and when I run out of the Word, I run out."

Prophecy

While the sermon is the primary vehicle of spiritual revelation within the worship service, there are other possible—though much less common—

means of expressing God's voice to the congregation. Darryl Lawson, who had visited the congregation frequently even while he was still a lay leader in another church, decided to switch his membership to Eastside Chapel after he saw evidence of prophetic ministry during a Sunday morning worship service.

> [One Sunday] I was sitting there, and [Reverend Wright] was preaching—I think it was the altar call—he said that two members from the church, their time was up. They were going to die, 'cause the Lord had showed him that two persons were going to die. And he began to tell the church to pray, to reach God. And Reverend Ainslee, Sister Ainslee's husband, was standing right by Reverend Wright. And he just—he said, "Reverend Ainslee did you touch me?" Reverend Ainslee said, "No." He stopped, he said, "The Lord just spoke and said one of you are going to be spared." And I couldn't believe this—this was Sunday morning service! Tuesday, they went to church at Canaan Missionary Baptist in the North Area, and when I got back to work the next morning, they told me that Reverend Ainslee had passed away. He was one of the ones that they saw. They saw him—I think he was either sitting in a wheelchair or standing on the bank of the Ashley River, waiting to cross over. And at that point, I just—I know that the Lord is operating in this church. And um, I started visiting more and more. Because really, it takes that in order to make it in this world—to hear from the Lord.

Transformation

When God's Spirit is present in the worship ritual his truth will be revealed. Eastsiders feel that this truth goes beyond the intellectual clarification of complex doctrines or even the prediction of future events through prophecy; rather, they believe that these revelations contain spiritual power with the capacity to transform individual lives. For them the Word of God is "sharper than a two-edged sword," to use the Biblical phrase, and does not stay merely at the level of intellectual discourse. Eastsiders often speak of the preached Word almost as a physical entity that will provoke a reaction, the nature of which is a reliable indicator of the auditor's spiritual state. Those who are not saved or who are saved but not "living right" will feel uncomfortable with the incarnate truth of the preached Word;

"convicted" of their sin, they will shrink in fear and trembling. Reverend Wright once prefaced a sermon with these words:

> Now I want to warn some of you. The Word is going to do you great harm today, because some of you are standing in a danger zone. And I want to tell you that the Word is going to do you harm. But beloveds, the harm that it does to you—if you will harken, the harm will be turned around to good. I know I'm tellin' the truth here, because I know when I went to church, and the preachers preached the Word when I was living in sin, that Word used to cut my natural back. I used to feel so uncomfortable. And I used to wish that the preacher would hurry up and get through so I could get back to feeling like my old self again. And there's something about sitting under the Word when you know you're not living according to the standards of God. The Word makes you feel uncomfortable. The Word makes you feel scared. The Word makes you feel threatened. Beloveds, there's only one way to live, and that's to live God's way.

In contrast, those who are both saved and living right will react to revelations of spiritual truth by becoming even more closely conformed to "God's way" of living.

Eastsiders believe that the Word of God does not become an active, tangible presence in the sermon simply through the content of the spoken discourse. Only an "anointed" preacher—one specifically called by God for this task and not one who simply chose to become a pastor "like any other job" as Mother Gadsden put it—can truly preach the Word. Reverend Wright was careful to point out that some preachers may use tricks to stimulate congregational response, and that faking indicators of anointing was a relatively easy thing to do. He drew a clear distinction between response to the content of the Word and response to the style of its delivery, implying that it was a temptation for preachers to manipulate congregations into an emotional enthusiasm with no spiritual value: "Are people going to be moved? Let the Word move them, not how you turn your voice, how the music backs you up, not how much you jump up and down and stomp your feet and shake."

However, he was also careful to point out that the true anointing which many preachers copied was absolutely necessary to effect transformation in the lives of congregants. Simply laying out a logical exposition of the Word is not enough—the anointed preacher must "bring it home" through the direct inspiration of the Holy Spirit. Speaking of a more educated and status-conscious African American church where he had preached recently, Reverend Wright told me,

> Now I could stand before them and lecture for thirty to forty five minutes, and they're fine. They resent the whooping, singing, squalling kind of preaching. They feel that they are beyond that. "You don't have to yell at us and squall and work up this sweat, and all of this good stuff. You don't have to do this. We would rather hear the academic side of your message. We want to critique how well you deliver it, if you use the right verbiage. You know, we impressed by that. And if it makes sense, then we says, 'Thank you Reverend. Nice sermon today' [spoken meekly in an "educated" voice]. 'I really enjoyed that—very good point.'" But it's not going to change their lives. It simply makes a point mathematically to them.

So far I have been speaking of transformation in the sense that the content of the spoken Word operates on the conscience and will of individual auditors, prompting changes in their moral lives outside the confines of the worship service. While this type of transformation is considered miraculous and due solely to the action of the Holy Ghost, Eastsiders believe that there is another level of transformational power inherent in the spoken Word of God. The Word is, as I mentioned above, a special incarnation of God's presence. And where God is present there is power— power to heal, power to restore relationships, power to break addictions to drugs and alcohol, and power to revive those weighed down by the hopelessness and violence of life in the ghetto. Therefore, Eastsiders feel that when the Word is proclaimed, it has a direct power and a presence of its own, connected to but independent of the particular words used by the preacher.

Because the preached Word embodies the presence of God, Eastsiders believe that by simply being exposed to the preached Word of an anointed pastor, worshippers can come away spiritually, mentally, or even physically transformed. Reverend Wright once received a note from a congregant that said, "I want you to know that on Sunday, April the 5th, I was sitting in church and the Spirit spoke to me and said, 'Don't take any more of your heart pills,' and I haven't. I know that you are truly a man of God. He healed me through your ministry." Reverend Wright did not pray for healing on this particular Sunday, either for this individual specifically, or collectively for those assembled. Rather, this parishioner believed that it happened simply because she was sitting under a minister who was preaching the Word, and it was the power of the Word alone that effected the healing of her heart.

When Eastsiders talked about the transformative effects of sitting under a pastor who "preaches the Word," they would often say that, "the anointing breaks the yoke." That is, the anointing of God's Spirit upon the pastor flows through the Word that he or she preaches and over those assembled and frees them from the power of things in their lives that hinder them in their relationship with God. These hindrances might be physical, emotional, mental or spiritual, but all of them are "yokes" in the sense that they keep the believer from living the Christian life in its fullest sense. These yokes are ultimately those of Satan, and represent his attempts to stunt and stifle spiritual maturity and growth. While these yokes or "hindrances" as they are sometimes called, are the subject of much individual prayer, sitting in the worship service under the preaching of an anointed pastor was seen as an efficacious way of dealing with these problems. For it is "under the anointing of the Word" as the Spirit of God became manifest in the service that these yokes were broken. To this end, Reverend Wright once began a revival sermon with the following prayer: "Father, in Jesus' name. We thank you for this blessed privilege and opportunity tonight, to stand in this place. Now, Father, we call down the spirit of revival. We call down an anointing in this place. Let it break yokes and set people free. In Jesus' name."

Eastsiders believe that the power of God's presence, either through the Word, or through other aspects of the service, usually works over the long-term; it is a process that happens through repeated exposure to the Word of God and the presence of the Spirit in the worship service and is similar to the gradual effects of exercise or dieting on the physical body. However, sometimes God's presence is so overwhelming and the Spirit moves so powerfully that this process of transformation is condensed into one extraordinary experience. When this happens it is called getting "deliverance," or, more commonly, a "breakthrough." In the following two examples, Reverend Wright used the term during the Sunday morning worship service to describe for the congregation what had happened during the previous week:

And as we were here on Thursday night, as we came out of our Bible study and we entered into the sanctuary for our prayer service, the Lord did visit us. And there was a breakthrough in the midst of the church, and the pastor began to minister about people in the church and things that cause them to be bound up and spiritually constipated. And eyes were opened and people understood some things, and all of that helps the church to grow.

We had a marvelous revival at Oak Grove. I'm tellin' you the Lord gave a breakthrough in Oak Grove. A spirit of worship and praise came in that place, and my God, we had church in a serious way.

In these instances, the term "breakthrough" seems to refer to something experienced by all of the participants, a sort of collective step up onto a higher rung of Jacob's Ladder. It seems, however, that there can be both collective and individual breakthroughs. Individual breakthroughs are private experiences of transformation and deliverance undergone by individual worshippers, and although these may take place during a more general breakthrough, they might also happen in a service that others would not characterize as extraordinary. For example, Darryl Lawson mentioned in an off-hand remark during our interview that some people "got their breakthrough" at a particular worship service. I took the opportunity and asked him more about this:

Well, a breakthrough means that you're going through a certain situation, and it seems as if, just no matter where you turn, nothing helps. But you pray and pray and God, he hears you, and at that moment, he just . . . whatever have you bound up that you just can't seem to praise God or just let him have his way in your life, he breaks it up so that you can be free.

The opposite of a breakthrough meeting is one in which either the pastor or the congregation (or both) remain "bound up" and can't seem to feel the presence of God within the service.

Because a breakthrough is the most sought-after experience, earnest participants always arrive to the worship service with a hope that it might happen to them, either individually or collectively. Reverend Wright often made requests similar to the following in his prayers of invocation, in this case mixing his spiritual metaphors: "Will you just wet this place down with your spirit? Will you just let the fire burn? God, will you just *move* in this place today? Will you do a mighty work in this place today?"

The Role of Emotion

Adoration. Love. Hope. Joy. Gratitude. The worship service at Eastside Chapel is an emotionally charged affair. When I say "emotional" here, I don't simply mean it in the sense of overt action like shouting, dancing, clapping, and loud cries—which tends to be the way the term is traditionally used in describing African American worship. I mean that these five specific emotions are evoked by and displayed in the service. Putting it sociologically, these emotions are normative—people expect other worshippers (and themselves) to not only display them, but actually feel them.

A worship service, like a funeral, carries with it a proper definition of itself. According to Eastsiders' understanding, the worship service provides an occasion for God to meet with his people in a time of celebration and praise. It is a party that worshippers give in honor of God for who he is and in gratitude for what he has done in their lives. This definition of the situation carries with it implications for the particular emotions that congregants should feel throughout the service. Hochschild (1979) calls these emotional standards "feeling rules" and indicates that these rules not only pressure people into *displaying* the situationally "correct" emotion (what she calls "surface acting") but actually motivate them to try to *experience* appropriate emotions and suppress inappropriate ones (or "deep acting").

The fundamental emotion expected of congregants attending a Sunday morning service is worship, or praise. Indeed, the Sunday morning service at Eastside Chapel (and most other Christian churches) is called a "worship service," and those who attend are identified as "worshippers;" therefore, this particular emotion is built into the occasion itself. Lest those in attendance forget this, there are numerous "feeling reminders" throughout the service.

Hymns often serve as powerful reminders of this emotion norm. The Hymn of Worship is sung directly after the Call to Worship. One popular hymn for this segment is "We Praise Thee O God," with the words "All glory and praise to the Lamb that was slain." Other hymns of praise include "Praise Him" ("Hail Him! hail Him! highest archangels in glory / Strength and honor give to His holy name!") or "Down at the Cross" with the chorus, "Glory to His name, Glory to His name; / There to my heart was the blood applied; / Glory to His name!" After the scripture reading, the congregation always sings "From All That Dwell" ("From all that dwell below the skies, / Let the Creator's praise arise"). And during communion service they might sing "Let us praise God together on our knees" ("Let Us Break Bread Together").

The message that praise and adulation are the appropriate emotions during the ritual is also proclaimed from the pulpit in numerous ways. What follows are two examples, the first from a pastoral prayer and the second from a sermon, both by Reverend Wright:

> In Jesus' name we'll give you the glory, the honor and the praises, because all of it belong to you to start with.

> Oh he is a mighty God, and we should adore him. We should adore our God. We ought to sing hymns of adoration and praise to the living God.

The emotion of gratitude, or thankfulness, is also held up as a standard during the Eastside Chapel worship service. This feeling rule is often invoked during prayers, as it is almost a requirement for those approaching God on behalf of the congregation to thank him for the opportunity to "be in the house of the Lord one more time." This can be seen in the following two excerpts from Reverend Wright's pastoral prayers:

> Precious Father in Jesus' name. We are grateful for another day. We are thankful that you kept us all the night long. We're grateful that you allowed us to enter into the house of worship once again. Father in heaven. We thank you for this wonderful privilege to enter into thy house again. And Lord, we—we are just so grateful.

Love for God and for fellow Christians is also held as a normative standard during the worship service. This is particularly evident in the Eastside liturgy. In the traditional AME Call to Worship the minister proclaims: "Lord, I love the habitation of your house, and the place where your glory dwells." Another regular Sunday feature, the summary of the Decalogue, repeats Jesus' famous words: "You shall love the Lord your God with all your heart, and with all your soul and with all your mind. This is the great and first commandment. And the second is like it, you shall love your neighbor as yourself. On these two commandments depend all the law and the prophets."

The Benediction exhorts congregants to "keep your hearts and minds in the knowledge and love of God and of his son, Jesus Christ our Lord."

Finally, the words of hymns also remind worshippers of their duty of love toward God with such lines as "I will ever love and trust him" and "Fill me with thy love and power" ("I Surrender All"); "Lord, I want to be more loving in-a my heart, in-a my heart" ("Lord I Want to Be a Christian"); "But drops of grief can ne'er repay the debt of love I owe" ("Alas! And Did My Savior Bleed"); "Fling wide the portals of your heart . . . adorned with prayer and love and joy!" ("Lift Up Your Heads, Ye Mighty Gates").

Along with praise, joy was perhaps the most talked-of emotion within the service. The traditional AME Call to Worship contains several lines that speak of gladness and joy: ("I was glad when they said to me let us go unto the house of the Lord" and "Make a joyful noise unto the Lord, all the earth"), and many hymns also contain reference to this emotion: "O the joy of full salvation" ("I Surrender All"); "I am so glad I entered in" ("Down at the Cross"); "It makes me happy when I sing . . . to know that I have been born again" ("I Know I've Been Changed"); "It was there by faith I received my sight, and now I am happy all the day" ("Alas! And Did My Savior Bleed"); "Thee will I cherish, Thee will I honor, Thou my soul's glory, joy, and crown" ("Fairest Lord Jesus"); and "A joy I can't explain is filling my soul since the day I met Jesus my King" ("Learning to Lean").

Reverend Wright frequently mentioned joy in his sermons:

> He is a wonderful God. Somebody said, "This joy that I have. Crack didn't give it to me. Alcohol couldn't give me this kind of joy. Oooooh, beer couldn't give me this kind of joy!" [sings] "This joy that I have, the world didn't give it to me." But I declare I got it from my God. You ought to come to the altar and drink, get some of this jooooy down on the inside! Ah, I love to enter into my master's house. It's, it's a joy for me to come into his house.

The discourse of worship at Eastside Chapel also includes hope, though not as often as some of the other emotions. Hymns that speak of hope include "Jesus, Keep Me Near the Cross" ("Near the cross, I'll watch and wait, hoping, trusting ever, 'Til I reach the golden strand just beyond the river.") and "My Hope Is Built" ("My hope is built on nothing less than Jesus' blood and righteousness" and "When all around my soul give way, He then is all my hope and stay"). One of the Sunday School classes that I attended took as its theme "The Gift of Living Hope," based upon the New Testament passage "By [God's] great mercy we have been born anew to a living hope through the resurrection of Jesus Christ from the dead" (I Peter 1:3).

This particular list—adoration, gratitude, love, joy, and hope—are the individual feelings that make up Eastside Chapel's normative constellation of emotion, and the liturgical discourse constantly reminds worshippers of these feeling rules. Yet they not only remind congregants of the rules, they also work to evoke these same emotions, thereby helping worshippers to achieve these very standards. This works because emotion operates according to a specific logic (Proudfoot 1985; Ortony et al. 1988). Each individual emotion (take pride for an example) presupposes a cognitive structure that includes both an object to which it is directed (the self in this case) and one or more grounds, or supporting reasons, that make it culturally reasonable or plausible (in the example of pride, say accomplishing a difficult task well).

Emotions are reasonable then, even if they are based upon grounds that later prove to be false or are directed toward objects that turn out not to exist. Fear is an appropriate response to a shape that I initially take to be a bear, even if, upon taking a second look, it turns out to be nothing but a large stump. This is a crucial point when dealing with religious emotion, because these emotions are based upon a belief in the existence of the spiritual world and upon the attributions believers make concerning this realm. Because academics and other skeptics often dismiss belief in the supernatural as unimportant in understanding human behavior, they are often left casting about for the "real" object of religious emotions. Fear is indeed irrational to one who sees only the stump but never the bear.

Because of emotions' cognitive structure, invoking particular objects and grounds will arouse particular feelings. Within the context of the worship service, the object of the emotion of gratitude is God and the grounds include all of the good things that believers attribute to his action in their lives. The prayer that contains the lines "We are grateful for another day. We are thankful that You kept us all the night long" not only reminds Eastside worshippers that they should feel grateful to God, but also recalls to their consciousness some of the many good things God has given to them. The same is true of the other emotions. When the Eastside congregation sings the final stanza of "Amazing Grace," "When we've been there ten thousand years, bright shining as the sun; / There's no less days to sing God's praise / Than when we'd first begun," each congregant is reminded of his or her belief in God's provision for the future and the eternal life to follow, evoking hope within. When the choir sings, "A mighty fortress is our God, a bulwark never failing," those present are reminded of the power and majesty of God, an image that evokes feelings of praise and worship. When worshippers sing the words of the old spiritual "I know I've been changed, the angels in the heaven have changed my name," it may call to mind their own spiritual journey out of spiritual darkness and evoke joy and gratitude within.

The People of God

One of the central features of corporate worship is that the roles of partic-ipants are clearly delineated within the structure of the ritual itself. On the one hand there is God, whose presence within the service we have already discussed, and on the other hand, there is the "people of God," consisting of the actual humans present who have come to worship. According to Eastsiders, the people of God are those who have gone through the salva-tion experience—these are the only legitimate participants in the ritual. This does not mean that one has to be a member of Eastside Chapel to be included in this category. There are frequent visits among the African American congregations in the Charleston metropolitan area, and as long as they are from an approved denomination or congregation, such visitors are assumed to be "saved."

There are other complicating factors though. Like any other Evangelical congregation, Eastside Chapel encourages its members to bring "unsaved" friends and neighbors to church with the hope of evangelizing them and adding them to the membership rolls. This status of "unsaved visitor" is not officially recognized in the liturgy or structure of the worship service (although it is implicit during the altar call at the end of the sermon). Officially, the worship service assumes only the participation of the saved, and yet regular worshippers do acknowledge and accommodate such pre-sent-yet-not-officially-included visitors. What is far more troubling to some is the presence of persons who may think that they are saved when they are really not. There is a strong and widespread feeling among some members that others in the church (and these "others" vary according to to whom one talks) are not truly saved and attend simply from habit, to look respectable, for entertainment, or for other illegitimate reasons. This perception may be more common in African American congregations in the South, where norms of church attendance are stronger, than in other regions of the country (Welch 1978; Stump 1987; Taylor 1988). Because the worship service assumes that participants are truly "the people of God," many Eastsiders feel that the unsaved in their midst who remain week after week are interlopers—frauds, imposters, and hypocrites. Reverend Wright once stated this openly from the pulpit: "As a pastor I have to stand up and look in people's faces, and some of 'em are hypocrites. And I know that they are, and I have to preach to them and love them in spite of their hypocrisy."

Because the unsaved could not possibly have a true understanding of the spiritual significance of the worship service, Reverend Wright acknowledged that the transforming power of God's Word went completely over the heads of some of his parishioners. Rather than a communication from God, they saw the sermon simply as an amusing type of diversion. "Now you got a lot of carnal people who . . . look at [the sermon] as entertainment. They are not grasping the Word, and they gonna leave out of the church still lyin', whorehoppin', doing whatever they doing, because the Word didn't reach them—they were simply amused and entertained for twenty or thirty minutes."

But the presence of unsaved persons, who by definition are not, in Goffman's words, "ratified participants" in the worship service is more than simply a nuisance or distraction to saved congregants. Many Eastsiders believe that their presence in the service actually inhibits the effectiveness of their collective call to God and results in a diminished sense of his presence in the worship. Because God is sensitive to the unity of the worshippers, the more cohesive and single-minded they are in praising God, the more God makes his presence felt. Thus, the congregation has the collective power to draw out the presence of God by being in "one accord." Reverend Wright once admonished the congregation:

> When we come to the Lord's house on Sunday morning and there's no Spirit of God, that means that somebody has come without the Lord on their mind. They have created a division, they have created separation. And beloveds, if everybody that pushed those doors come into the house of the Lord with the Lord on their mind, the Spirit of the Lord will be present.

In another sermon, he went on at greater length:

There's some people in the church who are proud and above the Word. No matter what you preach, no matter what you tell some people, nothing will seem to affect them. Their conscience has been seared with a hot iron, and they can't hear the Word. They can't receive the Word. The Word don't move them. Their hearts are filled with contempt. And beloveds, that's the kind of stuff that's hindering God's church from being a triumphant church, from being a victorious church. And it is [because] people [are] living in the midst of the church with so much junk and malice on the inside.

The assumption that not everybody has come to the service with "the Lord on their mind" combined with the idea that lack of religious zeal and commitment of some may undermine the transforming power of God for the many has some far-reaching implications for worship at Eastside Chapel. Such a culture of suspicion regarding the spiritual status of fellow worshippers creates a pervasive sense of mistrust within the congregation. The problem for the individual worshipper, then, is how to convince others that he or she is "for real," because simply showing up is certainly no guarantee of a person's spiritual authenticity. There must be more overt displays of commitment within the service. Opportunities for such displays are numerous, as we will also see in the next chapter, yet other congregants always take them with at least a few tablespoons of salt.

One common strategy follows the logic that the best defense against accusations of hypocrisy or lack of commitment is a good offense. This leads to a rather unusual feature of many religious gatherings: the spiritual exhortation, which is delivered not by the pastor or any official church leader, but by one lay person to the entire assembly. These are often accompanied by strident assertions of spiritual authenticity, such as, "I don't know what *you* came to do, but *I* came to praise the Lord!" or "If *you* don't want to praise him, *I'll* praise him for you!" The following sermonette was delivered at a revival meeting by a female attendee and was prompted by the leader's request for someone to stand up and give a testimony:

Giving honor to God the father, Jesus the son, and the precious Holy Ghost. We came to lift up the name of Jesus tonight! I came in here to rejoice in the name of Jesus tonight! I see too many sad faces tonight! You know, Jesus is everything to me tonight! Hallelujah! We came to lift up the name of Jesus tonight! I come in here, and see some sittin' in the back, some sittin' over here waiting on the drums. You can't wait on the drums tonight! Receive the Holy Ghost and you will be rejoicing! Hallelujah!

As in this example, exhortations are often given when the leader of the service invites "testimonies" from the participants.

In the white Evangelical subculture of my youth, a "testimony" was a story of how God had worked in one's life, either to bring salvation or some other kind of transformation of the self. These were highly personal and revealing accounts, often laying bare particular weaknesses and sins before the audience. At Eastside, however, testimonies of this kind never revealed sins or shortcomings beyond the standard formula of, "When I was out in the world, doing whatever it was that I was doing," and several members told me directly that it was never a good idea to reveal one's weaknesses to others in the congregation.

The assertion of one's spiritual authenticity and exhortation of others was not limited to services at Eastside Chapel, but rather seemed to be a common feature of local religious life. Midweek prayer meetings, revival services, and "tarrying" services, because of their smaller size, more informal structure, and expectation of lay participation, were often the forums for this type of discourse. The most pointed example that I saw actually took place at a midweek service in a small nondenominational church in a different part of town. Several members of Eastside Chapel, including Mother Gadsden's daughter Theodosha and her fiancé, Pastor Bernard Jackson, regularly attended this service, which was led by former Eastside Chapel Sunday School teacher Dr. Alexander Palmer. Mona Lisa Scott, wife of minister-in-training Anthony Scott, brought me to the service. She was a follower of Dr. Palmer, who was a somewhat controversial figure in the church; several congregational leaders, including Mona Lisa's own husband, did not think that his teaching was "of God." In a conversation earlier that evening, Mona Lisa confided to me that she felt persecuted at Eastside Chapel, and complained that the women in the church didn't think that her shouting was "for real." She attributed this to jealousy on their part. First because she danced so often—at least once every week— while many of them did so rarely or not at all. Second, she had married Anthony, one of the few young marriageable men still in the church, while they remained single. She also felt "picked on" by Reverend Wright, and in this she was probably correct. Just the week before, during Sunday service, he had made a general request for someone from the congregation to come forward and pray for a woman who had responded to the altar call.

Mona Lisa had started to walk down the center aisle when Reverend Wright motioned for her to go back and then called on someone else by name. She was still smarting from that public humiliation, but had found some solace in her relationship with her spiritual mentor, Dr. Palmer.

About halfway through the meeting led by Dr. Palmer, a woman in the front row, about mid- to late thirties by her appearance, jumped up and announced that the Lord was moving her to speak. She said that the Lord had begun to show her that her coworker was her enemy, then told a long and rather confusing story about coming into work and seeing a penny lying on the floor. In past times when she saw a penny on the floor she would put ammonia on it (a folk belief or superstition, I surmised), "even though," she said, laughing at herself, "it was on the man's Oriental carpet." "Now," she asserted, "I just step right over that penny. I don't have time for that foolishness." After the service I asked Mona Lisa about the practice of putting ammonia on pennies. She replied, "I tell you, I don't know what she was talking about, but she was out of line. That's why I jumped up there and started talking—to put her in her place."

And that's just what happened. As soon as the penny woman sat down, Mona Lisa sprang to her feet and started denouncing the whole group for not listening to Dr. Palmer and not "receiving his teaching."

> You all are giggling and not taking this seriously. This is the Bible! It is God's Word and should be taken serious. I know that some of you are glad that I haven't been able to come to this class for a while. You have been glad that Mona Lisa Scott wasn't here. I know you and your minds! God has revealed your minds to me. My phone don't barely ring because you folk don't like me. I thank God for sending me the friends I do have, like Brother Tim and Reverend Jackson and Sister Theodosha. I've been through my persecutions, and now I'm just going through my mastery tests. You know how in school you have mastery tests? Well that's where I am at. I went through my persecution, and now I just get up in the morning and say, "Devil, you just get out of my way now!"

Mona Lisa went on in this manner for several minutes, and I grew more uncomfortable with each of them. But the most surprising thing to me was the response from the group. Instead of taking offense to Mona Lisa (and I was nervous about this, seeing as how I had come in with her) many people reacted as if it weren't directed at them but at some other group. Several people encouraged her by calling out, "Preach, now, girl!"

and "That's right." Theodosha got up a few times and did a little dance in front of her seat. Meanwhile, Dr. Palmer was talking with a frail woman in the front row. When Mona Lisa was finished addressing the group, he asked her to lead in a prayer for the healing of this woman, which seemed both a validation of her performance and a vindication for her humiliation at Eastside Chapel the week before.

Like Mona Lisa's exhortation, aggressive assertions of one's spiritual authenticity are often coupled with harsh words for others who are not perceived as living up to high standards of inner devotion and commitment, and it appears that this practice may be widespread throughout lower-class African American churches. In his excellent ethnography of African American gospel services in North Carolina, Glenn Hinson (2000) quotes several singers as introducing their performances by asserting, "We didn't come for no form or fashion." Hinson notes that these proclamations of motivation and intent, stated forcefully and almost challengingly in my experience at Eastside, "are almost as pervasive in gospel services as declarations of praise and ministry" (p. 232). Hinson devotes considerable space to discussing how "the saints" he studied discerned between who was "pretending" and who was "for real."

In chapter 7 I will return to the theme of mistrust and how it affects social relations within the church as well as the dynamics of ritual. The important point here is that individuals whom others identify as "not saved" and therefore participating in worship for the "wrong" reasons, or who don't attend to the occasion with sufficient devotion and seriousness of purpose, not only offend the devout sensibilities of the truly faithful, but they also impede and obstruct the manifestation of God's presence in the service. Because the experienced presence of God is the purpose of the event—the underlying rationale for the worship service in the first place—these spiritual interlopers are more than mere annoyances. They may block the breakthrough of God's anointing that worshippers have been waiting and praying for.

The Problem of the Presence

In the successful worship service, God is in the midst of his people. He is moving among the worshippers, speaking words of instruction and encouragement, healing sick bodies, repairing damaged hearts, and saving lost souls. Gathering for the worship service is a collective call to God, and

Eastsiders wait eagerly and expectantly for his Spirit to come. But God is not tame. His spirit does not automatically come with the proper recitation of the Call to Worship, like a genie summoned from a lamp. And when he does arrive, it is not always with the same intensity or power, which is why especially forceful manifestations of God's presence always received some comment from Reverend Wright and other members. And there is another issue as well: God is a spirit and cannot be perceived with ordinary human senses. This second problem is an epistemological one: *how does one know?* How does one know when the Spirit of the Lord is present? Reverend Wright alluded to this problem from the pulpit one Sunday morning:

> I wonder if you can tell me whether [God] is here this morning? How do you know that he is here? I don't see him sitting nowhere in the pews. But you are trying to make me believe that he is present. The only way he could be present is that he has to be a spirit. And if he is a spirit that means that you can't see him but you can sure enough *feel* him. I wonder if there is any one besides me that can feel his Spirit in the room? Oh yes. All right. Well, I'm glad I've got some witnesses who can sure enough feel his presence.

And yet, despite Reverend Wright's words, it appears that individual feelings are not enough—the Spirit must be manifest in more overt ways that demonstrate clearly to all that God is present in their midst. There is a twofold problem then—how to successfully invoke God's Spirit, and how to recognize the Spirit when he comes. The strategies used to address these problems take the form of the traditional "emotional" worship style among African American churches, which is the topic I turn to in the next chapter.

∗ 6 ∗

Sacrifice of Praise

One Sunday morning in mid-November, Reverend Rose Drayton, the assistant pastor at a nearby AME congregation, was invited to preach. A middle-aged, gray-haired woman in a floral-print dress, she approached the pulpit with confidence and began by reading a portion of Scripture from the Old Testament book of Daniel, in which the Babylonian king Belshazzar sees a disembodied hand writing on the wall during a banquet. When a Jewish captive named Daniel translates the writing, the king hears a prophecy regarding his impending demise. After reading this passage, Reverend Drayton closed the Bible, looked out over the congregation and announced that her theme was going to be "The Party's Over." The gist of the sermon, which was delivered in the traditional call-and-response style, was that people should start living right because pretty soon God was going to come back and announce that "the party's over." The congregation was very quiet during the Scripture reading and remained quite still for the several minutes it took Reverend Drayton to set out her general theme and establish her rhythm. Then she moved out from behind the pulpit and said, "Pray with me for a little while, now," and people started to come alive.

It happened gradually. At first one person in the choir stood up. Then after about half a minute, another choir member stood up. Then more choir members stood, and then people in the congregation started standing up, until after several minutes almost the whole choir and about half of the congregation were on their feet. The responses to her phrases became louder and more emphatic during this time. Several women choir members in the front started smiling and waving their arms at Reverend Drayton in a "go on now" motion. The drummer tossed a drumstick in the air and caught it again with a flourish. People began clapping and shouting back at her during the response time in the cadence. One young man in a black suit and red shoes started running to the front of the center aisle, pointing his finger, and shouting at her, then running back to his seat. He did this over and over. The organ and drums started chiming in during the response times, building in volume and emphasis until finally at the end of the sermon they took the congregation immediately into a song. As they started playing, several women began to "shout" in earnest, moving out to dance in the unconfined spaces of the aisles and in front of the pulpit. One woman in a green and white checked dress began jumping around on both feet, like a child on a pogo stick. Four or five women ushers ran to her and tried to put their arms around her, but she still jumped, the ushers struggling and hanging from her, and creating a sight like a prize fighter in the ring refusing to be restrained. After about half a minute she ended up prone on the floor with a white linen cloth covering her legs. Almost a dozen other men and women created similar scenes across the sanctuary for about ten minutes, then, just as things were finally getting quiet and under control, one woman sitting in the pew a few rows behind us all of a sudden went off like a firecracker. She seized up and started yelling in a strangled voice, like she was being electrocuted. The ushers came running over and escorted her to the back of the sanctuary. The energy level began to subside and the service continued with the hymn of meditation. Throughout the commotion and displays of religious athleticism I noticed Reverend Wright, seated behind the pulpit, observing the congregation with his hand over his mouth—almost, but not quite, concealing a happy and amused grin.

"Emotional" Religion

The scene described above is typical of the African American religious form known in both popular and scholarly vernacular as the "emotional" worship service. Though this is a rather misleading label because it concerns more expression than emotion per se, I will continue its usage here because of established tradition. This type of ritual has received much attention from observers over the past several hundred years, and northern travelers who visited black religious gatherings in antebellum times often described their own emotional reactions to these services. On the one hand, they were often "overcome" by the intense displays of emotion and almost hypnotized by the fervor of their coreligionists. On the other hand, the word "heathenish" does come up quite often in these accounts, and the "emotional" worship service was often seen as a holdover from "pagan" rituals with African roots. This question of the "emotional" service, and the "shout" in particular, as an African survival has been picked up and debated to some extent in historical and anthropological circles.

Sociological responses to the African American "emotional" service have been more consistent with the functionalist approach to ritual outlined by Durkheim. Yet instead of emphasizing the more general social functions of the ritual as a mechanism of solidarity, sociologists have tended to explain the particularly emotional form of ritual as serving individual psychological needs rising from poverty and racial oppression. I will reserve my criticism of this approach for the conclusion. Rather than emphasizing any latent social or psychological functions of the "emotional" worship service for its participants, the approach I develop here treats the ritual as an ideal form—a kind of cultural blueprint with a particular logic, structure, and interactional dynamic. This approach extends that of folklorist Gerald L. Davis (1985: 26) who has written about the African American sermon as a performance "guided by concepts of *ideal* forms and *ideal* standards" shared by both the preacher and the congregation.

The underlying cultural logic of the emotional service proceeds directly from its desired end—the experienced presence of God and the working of his transforming power. However, this emphasis is not unique to African American religion, but present to varying degrees in all forms of Evangelical Christianity—particularly in the charismatic and Pentecostal traditions. What *is* unique, and what underlies the structure and interactional dynamics of the "emotional" black worship service is its emphasis on particular forms of bodily movement and emotional expression as evidence of God's presence in the ritual. As a cultural blueprint, the "emotional" worship service is a standard that individual performances can be measured by. That is, particular worship services and the major units within them (the sermon, music, testifying, shouting, etc.) are thought to be more or less successful in conforming to an ideal standard, which varies somewhat by congregation and for different kinds of services.

The following pages offer a descriptive analysis of the "emotional" service as a collective cultural performance and some of the dynamics that distinguish it from "nonemotional" worship service. After considering the behavioral norms, interactional processes, and structural elements underlying this type of ritual, we can return to the explanatory question: How is it that the norms and standards of the "emotional" ritual survive and even thrive? What is appealing to Eastsiders about this particular style of worship? After all, they know very well that becoming "emotional" in church is looked down upon by the more middle-class and educated segments of the African American community, particularly among the more high-toned and sedate AME congregations in the same neighborhood. Several members came to Eastside Chapel from those very same churches, to the puzzlement and disapproval of their former pastors and fellow parishioners.

Behavioral Norms of "Emotional" Worship

Standards of appropriate behavior operate in all social situations, from casual encounters between friends to the more formal occasions like weddings and funerals. Worship rituals come with their own set of expectations, and these can differ quite markedly from one congregation to another. The account of Rose Drayton's sermon at the beginning of this chapter gives a graphic picture of the kind of behavior that was considered completely appropriate at Eastside Chapel but that would be out of place (to put it mildly) during, say, a high Episcopal service. A close examination of this scene reveals two generic types of behavior that, although apparently similar, reveal some interesting differences. First there is what I will call "response behavior" which includes both vocal and bodily reactions to the music, preaching, prayer, or whatever provides the current focus of attention and stimulus. The response behaviors in the above story included cries of "amen" and "hallelujah" as well as standing, running, pointing, and clapping. While shouting or ecstatic dancing might seem to be simply a more extreme type of response behavior, shouting operates on a different level than response and thus is guided by a somewhat different set of rules.

Response Behavior

In unemotional churches, the norms guiding response behavior are quite simple: no response is allowed, not even a polite smattering of applause at the conclusion of a performance such as characterizes secular occasions. Contrast those standards with the response behavior exhibited at Eastside Chapel, where those in highly visible positions (in the choir loft behind the pulpit) stood up and waved their arms, where a congregant ran down the aisle pointing and shouting at the preacher, where the musical instruments played loudly during the pauses in the preacher's delivery. If congregants in an "unemotional" service behaved in this overtly responsive manner they would immediately disrupt the proceedings; the situational order would be completely shattered and all such behavior would have to cease before the service could proceed.

However, in some important respects the norms of behavior at Eastside Chapel are not so different from standards operating in other types of gatherings. For example, the response behaviors at Eastside Chapel bear a resemblance to those at sporting events where it is expected that spectators will cheer a good performance by their team of choice. In fact, a visiting pastor once scolded the congregation for not responding to his point with sufficient enthusiasm by saying, "You should be on your feet and cheering about that. If you had just seen Michael Jordan slam-dunk the ball on the court, you would be up on your feet. Well, the Lord has slam-dunked your sins into the sea of forgetfulness, and that is something to cheer about!" On another occasion, just after an extended period of shouting and energetic dancing, Reverend Wright commented on the eruption of such "spontaneous" forms of enthusiasm:

> We bless the Lord for his spirit and his people who don't mind magnifying him. That's the way the Lord's house ought to be—a spontaneous house [full of] spontaneous combustion. That's right, I believe in being spontaneous. For those of us who are into the sports scene, whenever the person kicks a field goal, the whole crowd is spontaneous. Whenever a touchdown is run, they're spontaneous. When a home run is hit, they're spontaneous. And if people can be spontaneous about foolishness that won't heal the sick, raise the dead, or change the situations of the world, then the church ought to sure enough be spontaneous about the God who laid the foundations of the world.

Aside from sports, the other secular arena in which response behaviors parallel those of the "emotional" service is concerts by rock or rap musicians. Reverend Wright never tired of drawing unfavorable comparisons between the relative lethargy of worshippers in church and the frenetic energy of fans at a concert or couples at a dance club. "I don't know why is it we tire so easily when it comes to [praising God], and when I look at [rap musician] Bobby Brown, I see [his fans], and they jerking their shoulders all back, screaming, twistin' around, squattin' down on the ground, carryin' on—and they just got so much life and vitality." Speaking at a revival in a nearby Baptist church, Reverend Wright opened his remarks by saying that he had recently been flipping through the TV channels and had come across the show *Soul Train*. He commented on all the women who were "a-bucking and a-dancing," demonstrating with his body the kinds of moves they were doing and drawing smiles of recognition from the congregation. He said, "I like their spirit. I don't like the way they're dressed, and I don't like the music, but they gonna dance, and they don't care who's watching them. If the camera comes on them, they just start bucking even more. And that's the way the church should be."

In the "emotional" service these kinds of physical displays are not only allowed, but encouraged. The key here is that such overt actions as standing, clapping, and running demonstrate emotional involvement and spiritual commitment. Like applause after a solo during a jazz concert, these actions signal support and encouragement for the performers and, more significantly, the larger message they are communicating. According to the cultural ideal of the "emotional" service, this type of bodily movement is equated with the spiritual life and vitality of the congregation. Reverend Wright once commented on his radio show,

> I go in some churches and they are dead. The choirs don't move, the congregation don't move, the preachers buy a sermon, they don't move. There's no moving. About the only movement you see is when the undertakers roll the casket down the aisle, and you hear some crying and weeping, perhaps, and some movement then—but other than that [nobody moves].

Movement, then, delivers messages on several different levels: about one's spiritual vitality and authenticity (hence the crack about unmoving preachers who "buy a sermon" rather than receiving the "Word" directly from the Spirit the way they should), one's emotional involvement in the worship service (which in turn speaks to one's commitment to God), and one's stance toward the particular message being delivered. Lack of movement indicates a proud spirit and a hard heart, something Reverend Wright often commented on:

> There's some people in the Church who are proud and above the Word. No matter what you preach, no matter what you tell some people nothing will seem to affect them because their—their conscience has been seared

with a hot iron. And they can't hear the Word. And they can't receive the Word—the Word don't move them because their hearts are filled with contempt.

One fundamental difference, then, between "emotional" and "nonemotional" worship services is simply the set of rules governing congregational movement and response. The range of permitted and encouraged response behavior sometimes leads a naive observer who is used to "nonemotional" norms to the assumption that there are no holds barred concerning congregational activity. However, it was my observation that at Eastside Chapel and other "emotional" churches, the conduct of worshippers was very tightly monitored. Even the "shouting" or ecstatic dancing that some congregants engaged in was closely watched and subject to social controls, as I will show in the next section.

Shouting

Prior to my research in Charleston I had visited a black church exactly once, on the invitation of a good friend in Chicago. When I came to South Carolina, my first series of church visits on the Eastside were to a United Methodist church on the main street bordering the neighborhood. This congregation is very middle class and quite sedate in its worship style— nobody hollered amen or jumped out of their seat for the whole service. Thus, I was struck, as are most people the first time they encounter it, by the episodes of shouting that I witnessed on my first trip to Eastside Chapel. Because it is one of the most distinctive aspects of African American religion, shouting is frequently commented upon by observers, and it is a term that encompasses a wide range of behavior. To give the uninitiated reader some sense of what this behavior looks like, I quote from my field notes for the Sunday morning worship service on November 17:

> Today in the service there was a point during the hymn of praise in which the energy in the service was quite high. Most of the worshippers were on their feet clapping. Several people had taken out tambourines and beat them in time to the steady, churning rhythm of the organ and drums. Abruptly, a middle-aged woman right in front of us started dancing vigorously with her legs, all the time holding her arms straight down at her sides. She held her eyes squeezed shut and shook her head from side to

side, suddenly appearing oblivious to those around her and to the service in general. An usher came into the row and took her by the hands to draw her out into the center aisle. Once into that more open space, she began to jump and spin around at the same time—faster and faster until she was just a blur. Another usher joined the first and they linked arms, forming a protective enclosure around the spinning woman. She jumped and spun this way for over a minute, then collapsed and lay prostrate on the floor and seemed to be unconscious. The ushers brought over a white linen cloth and draped it over her legs. Nobody in the church seemed to pay it much mind. She was down there for about five minutes as the music continued. Suddenly, she sprang up and threw off the linen cloth. She took off running toward the front of the church then turned and ran over to the side aisle, cornered, and then ran to the back of the sanctuary. Then she came around the back and down the opposite side of the church. She kept this up for about five minutes. During this time, about three or four ushers were all in the front of the church craning their necks to follow her progress around the sanctuary. One of the ushers positioned herself at the front of one of the side aisles and stood there like a coach, hands planted on her hips, watching her runner perform laps.

Not all of the shouting at Eastside Chapel was this athletic. Kylon Jones, a high school student and leader of the Rainbow children's choir, had a much more subdued style. With his eyes closed and a grimace on his face, he would begin his shout by shaking his head slowly from side to side. After a few minutes, he would begin to shuffle his feet slowly and ease out into the center aisle. Once positioned there, he would shuffle, grimace and shake his head for several minutes before slowly easing back into the pew. Mona Lisa Scott, another frequent shouter, always danced in the front area of the church between the pews and the mourner's bench. She displayed more of a hopping and skipping style of dance, moving back and forth across the floor.

Because shouting is the most exotic and "foreign" aspect of African American religion to those who typically study it, the phenomenon has received the most attention in the academic literature.[1] Scholars have defined shouting variously as "ecstatic" or "paroxysmal" dancing (Lincoln and Mamiya 1990: 365), and though much has been written about shouting (particularly in terms of its historical origins in both European and African religious practices), I will not review those debates here.[2] My primary interest in shouting is how Eastsiders make attributions concerning particular instances of shouting, how those who have done it describe the experience, and how they connect the place of this form of behavior in the structure of the worship ritual.

Although shouting styles vary quite a bit, Eastsiders believe that the person in the midst of a shout has temporarily lost awareness of his surroundings and control over his actions. For this reason there is always a crew of five or six ushers stationed around the sanctuary on Sunday mornings whose job is to intercept shouting worshippers and bring them out into the aisle so that they will not accidentally bump into the pews or trample nearby children. Oftentimes the shouter will shake her head vigorously from side to side. If she wears glasses, one of the attending ushers will attempt to remove them before they go flying across the sanctuary. If the shouter is a woman and does "fall out" or faint, the ushers keep a white linen tablecloth handy to drape over her legs to protect her modesty. Because of the close physical contact between shouters and attending ushers, women ushers attend only to women, and men attend only to men.

Though shouting is a central feature of the Sunday morning service, it doesn't happen only during these times of collective worship. Eastside members sometimes mentioned how they had been alone at home praying or reading their Bibles and had started to shout. Reverend Wright mentioned such an episode in a sermon one Sunday: "I tell you I'm so happy! I wake up in the morning shoutin'. I woke up this morning, and I turned on some music. I was in the house, and I found myself cuttin' a little step. And I had to check myself out. I said, 'Man,' I said, 'you sure are happy this morning!'" In several of my interviews with a few of the older women, simply talking to me about their Christian faith and their experiences with God moved them to get up and go into a kind of mini-shout, pacing around the room in an agitated state exclaiming "Thank you, Jesus!" for several minutes while I paused the tape recorder and tried not to feel too awkward.

Because shouting often does happen during services, those who do it in the worship service are in full view of the rest of the congregation. This means that their shout invites comment and criticism from other worshippers, and such remarks and observations are frequently made between Eastside congregants. Shouting is a topic of intense interest to Eastsiders, and because it is a contested form of behavior in the African American church at large, there is a well-developed discourse that Eastsiders apply to particular instances of shouting and to individual members who frequently practice it.

Everyone I spoke with at Eastside Chapel believed that the phenomenon of shouting was genuine. That is, they believed that the Holy Ghost did sometimes "come upon" or "fill" a person with the impulse to dance "in the Spirit." However, they did not believe that every particular instance of shouting was a legitimate manifestation of spiritual impulse and control. More commonly expressed is the acknowledgement that, while shouting in general is "real" and does often happen, some people's expression of it is suspect and open to challenge. Scholars of African American religion have sometimes tried to "explain" shouting by speculating about some of the psychological functions that this behavior might serve for those who practice it. These alternative explanations have not escaped indigenous observers within black congregations.

Wendell Watson, a construction worker in his mid-thirties, had grown up attending Eastside Chapel and still sang in one of the choirs. While he approved of shouting in principle, he was rather cynical about many of those who actually practiced it, and told me that he thought many of them were acting simply out of a desire for status within the church.

> People want to be seen. It's like, we went to a church the other night where people were shouting and jumping up. [When the] music stopped [*snaps his fingers*], they stopped. It gets next to me—it's just music. It's the kind of thing like, "Well, I'm saved! I can shout and jump around and roll on the floor and cut a flip."
>
> Q: Do you think—like at Eastside Chapel a lot of people do shout. Do you think most of it is genuine?
>
> I think 70 percent is genuine. I think some people do it because it is expected that they will do it. It's just their way of saying, "I'm saved, you're not. I'm going to heaven and you're not." "I have title so I'll do this." "I'm in the pulpit, so I do that." "I'm sitting on the bench over here, and this is the amen corner, or whatever, so I'm gonna do it." Some people do it to hide their personal lives.

Sometimes a person's shouting is criticized not because it is thought to be disingenuous, but because it is thought to be done in ignorance. That is, people might shout simply because they thought they were supposed to without understanding its true significance and without waiting for the prompting of the Spirit. Wendell also used this explanation and pointed to Harold Memminger, a young man with a slight mental retardation who was often seen in his red suit and red shoes dancing in the service: "Maybe

one or two people might [shout] because they don't know no better. It's
like Harold doing his Chuck Berry duckwalks out there. You gotta over-
look him. He means well." Reverend Wright often alluded to this issue in
his sermons and in other more informal talks to the congregation. One
Sunday morning the following statement of his from the pulpit was received with much enthusiasm and applause:

> So many people in the house of God talking about they got the Holy
> Ghost and got no life. Man, later for that stuff. And beloveds, I want you
> to know for everything real there's a phony. There's a lot of pretenders.
> There are a lot of people shoutin' too, but it ain't got no Holy Ghost! I
> know I'm tellin' the truth!

Even when shouting is thought to be genuine and prompted by the
Holy Ghost, it is still not considered to be one of the more important aspects of the Spirit's work. Rather, it is seen as a simple expression of joy
and praise to God for what he is doing in the believer's life. When done in
the right spirit and a full appreciation of God's love, it can be a testimony
to others. While acknowledging that some people shout for reasons of status, Deborah Watson also pointed to the legitimate reasons for shouting
and noted that it may serve as a testimony to others about what God can
do:

> Now some people shout because they see someone else shouting. And
> then some other people shout just to get attention. Someone who wants
> to be seen can shout. But . . . shouting can also represent a testimony, be-
> cause if I've been burdened all week long and I done have a heavy load
> like a weight, and I mean to tell you the weight is got heavy enough to
> where I just got to let God have his way in my life, okay? And he lifts me
> up off of a walk that I couldn't dance, then that's something to shout for.
> And when he gets me off of that and then I get in that church and I hear
> the Word, I've got something to shout about. I've got something to give
> God the praise about.

Many of the accounts I heard about shouting experiences left me confused about the locus of control during these incidents. On the one hand,
some people spoke as if it were an immediate and involuntary physical response to an overpowering outside force—much like the way one would
react if burned by fire or touched by an electric charge. In fact the images

of fire and electric shock were common metaphors for the physical sensations experienced during shouting episodes. This imagery has a long tradition in the African American church. The following testimony of an ex-slave, recorded in the 1930s, could well have been spoken by any member of Eastside Chapel: "I used to wonder what made people shout but now I don't. There is a joy on the inside and it wells up so strong that we can't keep still. It is fire in the bones. Any time that fire touches a man, he will jump" (Johnson 1993).

This description as an involuntary response is certainly how it appears when observing people in church. In fact, like electricity, it can seem to travel from one person to the next by a touch, or even through the charged atmosphere around a shouting person. Here are some notes on one particularly active Sunday morning:

[After about fifteen minutes of shouting], just as things were starting to quiet down and become more subdued, one woman suddenly went off like a firecracker. I was standing in the aisle, so I had a good view of what happened next. She seized up in a contortion and started yelling in a strangled voice, like she was being electrocuted. While she was going through these spasms, she happened to touch the woman sitting next to her. Although her neighbor seemed not to be paying the shouter any particular mind, when she was touched by her, the second woman immediately started going into similar convulsions. I saw Sherline Singleton and several other ushers running toward both of them from different points in the sanctuary. Sherline was running down the center aisle from the back of the church and was almost there when she seized up in mid-stride. Snapping backward like she had been struck by a sniper from the front of the church, she cried out, and went into her own dancing frenzy.

According to these observations, shouting seems completely beyond one's control, and it seems that the Spirit is experienced as an irresistible force. Yet some accounts of shouting seem to indicate a greater sense of control and that one could resist promptings to shout or could engage in it as a purposive, voluntary action. Darryl Lawson, for example, related the following story to me:

I went to church with my aunt out on Younge's Island, and I had on [my best] white suit. I had on a white suit and a pink shirt, a burgundy tie.

Clean! We're at the church, and they sang this song, "Come Over Here." They sang, and I mean the Spirit was moving. My cousin—she jumped up and was kickin' loose over in the corner. And I started feelin' it, and I said, "Uh-uh, not in these people's church. No, no, no." And God just spoke to me and said, "Don't quench the Spirit." I said, "Lord, if it happens again, I have no choice but to let go." And as soon as I said that, it hit me sharp again. And my chewing gum flew out of my mouth, and I was just going. When I came to, my cousin had the chewing gum in her hand, saying, "You didn't have to step all over my toe like you did." And I was saying, "Calm down, calm down, calm down." But I learned that no matter what you have on, no matter who's sitting around you, forget. Forget that; just let the Lord have his way.

Reverend Wright spoke to this issue in the midst of castigating people who claimed to be "servants of God" but still engaged in worldly activities like drinking alcohol and dancing in clubs.

But how can you be a servant, if you still drinking out the Michelob bottle? Aaaaah I'm drinking from heaven's fountain! Somebody said, "I'm still a servant." But you're still out there on the devil's dance floor, and when you come to the house of God, you're glued to your pews. But somebody said, "He never gave me a shout. I don't know how to shout." But let me tell ya if you got life in your body, if you can still move your legs, if you can still wave your hand, [then you have a shout]. Everybody that's God children got a shout.

This seems to indicate that shouting is merely a matter of submission and volition—one simply decides whether or not to shout, and the true child of God will choose to do so as a matter of course.

After puzzling over this issue of control for some time, I asked Sherline Singleton if shouting was something one simply decided to do or if it was completely under the Spirit's control. In her reply, she said that the Holy Ghost did sometimes come upon a person in an overpowering way. However, in order for it to happen, one had to have given up control previously and that a person's attitude of receptivity is a prerequisite for such experiences. She went on to say that many of the younger women in the church in their teens and twenties did not shout because their vanity made them unwilling to "let go" and forget about their clothes and hair. "I see all those 'pretty girls' in church—that's what I call them—and they should be

grateful for their looks, but they don't want to shout and look undignified."

Both Sherline and Darryl discuss how shouting is somewhat embarrassing and makes the shouter look undignified. In fact, Darryl reported
that for many people, including himself, watching people shout could be a
great source of amusement.

> See, we was joking with each other about how we cut up in church and all
> that, [but] I've sort of gotten out of that. . . . Because I'd laugh and I
> found out that with me watching other people I was missing out on my
> blessing. So whenever I get caught up [in watching people shout] I close
> my eyes and begin to just wait on the Lord. [My friends would see me
> later and] say "Darryl, did you see so and so?" I said, "No." "You missed
> it!" Now some of them I do see and I like to sit back and laugh, but more
> or less I try to close my eyes so that I can get lost in the Spirit and let the
> Lord take control.

Reverend Wright commented in a sermon how it was good to "laugh
together in the Lord" and related with some amusement Darryl's humorous reenactment of the shouting styles of two other young men in the
church. "We were to revival the other night, and Brother Arnold was tearing up the floor, and Brother Darryl was showin' us [afterward] how
Brother Arnold was doin' all them steps, and how Brother Lenard was trying to be Samson pushing the wall down."

This humorous treatment of shouting—with Eastsiders characterizing
it as "cutting up" or "cutting a rug" and playfully mimicking others' shouting styles—can be seen as a way of dealing with the essential contradiction of shouting behavior. For on one hand, shouting is viewed as the
most intimate physical and emotional expression of a believer's relationship with God. As such it is very much parallel to the connection between
sexual intercourse and the marital relationship between husband and wife.
Because this intimate and intensely emotional experience of God is highly
prized, it is treated as a valuable and worthwhile thing to desire (hence the
concern that some merely do it for reasons of religious status). Yet when
shouting occurs in the worship service this intimacy and emotion become
a matter of open and public display. This emotional transparency, coupled
with the lack of control exhibited by shouters, conflicts with standards of
emotional and bodily control expected of adult members of society, particularly men. This contradiction creates an embarrassing situation for the

shouter, who is subject to the jokes of her friends and family after the service is over. This humor tends to be subdued, however, because the one who teases her friends one Sunday morning may be the same one who is shouting in the evening service or during the week's revival meeting and subject to the same treatment.

The humorous treatment of shouting raises another issue as well. One might expect that such displays of divine "possession" (as some scholars refer to shouting), would inspire awe and terror in those witnessing the transformation, or that it would at least be accorded some level of seriousness and formal respect. When any shouting begins in the worship service, one glance around the sanctuary reveals that most of those not busy shouting are busy watching the antics of those who are, and they display the same mixture of wry amusement and comic enjoyment on their faces that Darryl Lawson speaks of.

This attitude toward shouting speaks to the kind of God that Eastsiders feel they worship and to the kind of relationship they feel that they enjoy with him. By all indications, shouting is both an expression of joy and worship, and is itself a very intense emotional experience, the dual aspect of this is captured in the often-heard phrase "getting happy," which is used as a colloquialism for shouting.

On one hand, shouting may be seen as an extreme form of physical response—like clapping, only with the whole body rather than just the hands. Certainly this is true from a behavioral standpoint. One can watch congregants progress from clapping and verbal responses to more vigorous behaviors like swaying and stomping their feet and finally "cutting loose" into a full-blown shout, and from this perspective the transition from clapping to shouting seems to be simply a matter of degree.

Yet from the perspective of the individual undergoing this transition, there is a radical break between clapping and other response behavior and shouting. To get a sense of the internal state of the actor during a shout I interviewed several Eastside members in detail about their experiences while shouting. When a congregant engages in response behavior such as standing, clapping, pointing, waving, and the verbal counterparts of these, it involves the person more completely in the service. Indeed, this behavior is only possible for the congregant who is completely "tuned-in" to the sermon, prayer, song, or testimony that is providing the stimulus. (It's hard to clap to the rhythm when you're not listening to the music.) But a congregant who is shouting has entered another realm of consciousness; he or she has left the service far behind and is overcome by the awareness of the presence of God. I asked Darryl Lawson about his state of consciousness when he was shouting and if he was aware of his surroundings. He replied: "You would know what's going on—cause I remember bumping into a couple of benches. [But that's not where I am focused] . . . I don't try to figure out who's around me or anything, because I'm just enjoying my Jesus."

This withdrawal of consciousness is taken by Eastsiders as the sign of a genuine shout and is attributed to the work of the Holy Ghost. However, shouts that congregants suspect are simply responses to external stimuli are considered counterfeits. Because music provides such a powerful stimulus, and because much shouting occurs during musical selections, congregants may have reason to suspect that some dancers are simply responding to the music rather than undergoing a true shift of consciousness prompted by the Holy Ghost. Sherline Singleton told me that "it is a proven fact that every shouting doesn't have the Holy Ghost—they just shouting." When I asked her how congregants could shout without the prompting of the Spirit, she answered:

> Music. Cause when you were younger and you hear something you like even if you didn't get up and dance, you knew how to move to the music. What are they doing? You know how to dance already—and when you hear drums or hear a good beat on an organ that you can dance to [then you can do it].

When a worshipper is in the midst of what members consider a genuine shout, he or she is perceived by others to have stopped responding to external stimuli and to be acting solely upon the internal stimulus of the Holy Ghost. While in this state others treat the shouter as if she were not in control of her own behavior.

However, despite the apparent chaos that sometimes erupts when many people shout at the same time, the conduct of the shouters is highly structured and strictly monitored. Although it may appear to the uninitiated observer that "anything goes," particularly when one sees such behavior as congregants running laps around the church aisles or jumping up and down, there is actually a tightly defined range of permissible behavior in effect even during these shouting episodes. Mona Lisa Scott, a young woman who dances quite frequently told me, "People come up to me and say that they have never seen anybody dance [the way I dance] before, and that I'm not for real." Although her style may have been a bit unorthodox by Eastside Chapel standards, it was not so far from the norm that she was prohibited from shouting; most people simply ignored her. However, if someone were to exhibit behavior that fell far outside the acceptable domain, it would probably be interpreted as the influence of the demonic and thus would be subject to stronger sanctions. Reverend Wright once admonished the members of his Saturday night prayer group to be on their guard against such unholy influences and even suggested some possible symptoms for them to watch for: "Some of the folks that dance around on Sunday, they are not reacting to God but a familiar spirit.[3] When somebody is rolling around by the wall and fighting everybody who tries to help them, that's not God. . . . Our God is a God of order and discipline."

This order, which is so different from the order of "nonemotional" services, is enforced by the whole congregation through sanctioning (evidenced by the number of people who have censured Mona Lisa), but it is the particular duty of the ushers. These guardians of ritual order, with their uniforms and white gloves, stand at attention at their posts in the four corners of the sanctuary and constantly monitor the behavior of participants. When someone begins to shout, he or she is immediately surrounded by ushers of the same sex who will link arms around the dancing person. Officially this is because of the belief that the shouter has no consciousness of those around him and might inadvertently injure himself or others. But it is also a very effective form of surveillance and control, and ushers will remove someone who they feel is disrupting the service. Also, by not surrounding someone who begins to dance, ushers can withhold legitimacy from their shout, as often happened when Mona Lisa began to dance.

"Emotional" Worship as Collective Behavior

"The behavior of a rioting mob, a screaming audience, or an ecstatic religious congregation is markedly different from that of either an enduring informal group or a large, formal organization" (Turner and Killian 1957: 3).

Structural Facilitation

So far I have argued that a key difference between an "emotional" and "unemotional" service is simply that response behaviors and shouting are permitted in the former but not in the latter. There is more to the story, however. In fact, these "emotional" forms of participation are *required* of the congregation. In order to facilitate the realization of this norm, the "emotional" service has several unique features not found in "nonemotional" services.

Structural "Space"

One important facet of emotional services is how much room the service provides for extended displays of response behavior and shouting on the part of congregants. If the service is structured so that each segment simply marches from one thing to the next, there is no opening that can be filled by dancing, shouting, ecstatic utterances, or impromptu testimonies. A flexible approach that allows for, and even expects, these activities during the service as the Holy Spirit is manifested is thus essential. Kylon Jones, a teenager and leader of the children's Rainbow Choir made this explicit when he led the service on Youth Day: "Sometimes we have to give the Lord what's due unto him. Some of you want to be out of here by 12:00, but if it's not the will of God, we won't be out of here by 12:00. Praise the Lord!"

The service leader, who functions as the "master of ceremonies" from the beginning of the service until the sermon, along with the organist and the preacher are most important because they are the persons who actually set the pace of the service at any one point in time. The organist probably plays the most important role because most shouting occurs during musical selections by the choir or during congregational singing. James Ravenel, the main organist at Eastside Chapel, told me he was always very aware of the energy level of the congregation at every point in the service, and would often begin or continue to play to accommodate shouters. He had a repertoire of "shouting songs," which are upbeat and very danceable songs like "Lift Up Your Heads, Ye Mighty Gates," that he would begin to play when an episode of shouting broke out in the service. Reverend Wright and other preachers, both from Eastside and visiting from other churches, will pause in the delivery of their sermons, sometimes for as long as ten minutes, while the congregation shouts. These preachers make no attempt to subdue the congregation or continue their preaching during the shouting.

Duration

Emotional intensity and physical involvement in the worship service build over time. Because of this, time plays a crucial role in facilitating emotional involvement in the service. There must be enough time for congregants to become immersed in the service and the world generated by the ritual. Thus, one hallmark of emotional church services is simply the length of time that they last—generally from two to three hours every Sunday morning. This length of time is enough for worshippers to relax and focus on the activities at hand without worrying about what they are going to be doing after the service.

Long duration facilitates intense involvement within each segment of the service. The sermon, for example, usually lasts from forty-five minutes to an hour. Hymns and other songs can be sung for ten to fifteen minutes at a stretch. Prayers and testimonies can last this long as well.

Ambiguity, Reluctance, and the Evocation of Response Behavior

The norms pertaining to "emotional" response are not imposed in the same way as those that pertain to "nonemotional" activities like singing hymns or responsive liturgical readings. For example, in "nonemotional" services, responsive readings include cues for when congregants should begin and end participation, and there is an obligation upon every congregant to contribute verbally in a prescribed manner. Thus each person's role is scripted for these segments of the service, and there is no ambiguity about what one should be doing from one moment to the next. Things are not so simple in an "emotional" service because expectations of response are diffused throughout the entire congregation and are not assigned to particular individuals. For example, the preacher expects that *somebody,* or a handful of people perhaps, will say amen when the preacher makes a strong point, yet no person or group of persons is *designated* to respond in this way. In this type of situation, the involvement of each congregant is constantly ambiguous: at each point one may respond or not respond. There is no set script to follow, although each congregant knows the general story line.[4]

There is another factor at work also. In an "emotional" service, response behaviors are supposed to become more and more vigorous as the service progresses, culminating in shouting or, sometimes, speaking in tongues. This process was illustrated by the Eastside congregants' reactions to

Reverend Drayton's sermon. At first there were only vocal responses of "amen" and "that's right." Responses progressed to standing, then clapping, then pointing or waving, and then finally to shouting. This process is normative and it is expected that it will diffuse throughout the congregation. That is, no one is designated as the first one to bring congregational responses to the next level. Yet while this process is normative, from the perspective of the individual there is a certain cost to initiating a higher level of response in that the more vigorous responses make one more visible to other congregants, who are in a position to critically evaluate the genuineness of the response. For example, the first person to stand may stand alone for several minutes before someone else joins him or her, and shouting always makes one highly visible while in the midst of a somewhat embarrassing display of ecstatic behavior. Thus, congregants may be reluctant to initiate the response level to a higher pitch.

These factors of structural ambiguity and resistance to high visibility, both of which operate to inhibit congregational response, must be overcome. It is the task of those in performance roles to evoke congregational participation through the nature and quality of their performances, and in this they draw upon several resources. I will focus here upon two types of performances: music and spoken discourse.

Music

Music is a very important resource for drawing out congregational participation. The resources musicians draw upon include such elements as the number and type of instruments used (particularly drums), style (volume, use of beat, instrumental breaks, elaborate or simple structure), the proportion of the service dedicated to music as well as the length of each particular song, the expected participants (soloists generally evoke less fervor than choir and congregational singing), and finally, the lyrical content of the songs (emotional sentiments of praise or comfort in everyday language rather than abstract concepts or archaic words and phrases).

Discursive Strategies

Observers of African American religious ritual have often noted the use of stock phrases in prayers and testimonies (see Goldsmith 1989: 110 and Morland 1964: 107). Drake and Cayton (1945) reported that "there is a common stock of striking phrases and images which are combined and recombined throughout the Negro lower-class religious world." In fact many of the same phrases that Drake and Cayton recorded in Chicago over sixty years ago can be heard almost every Sunday at Eastside Chapel. Such phrases include the following: "I thank the Lord that he woke me up this morning in my right mind. He didn't have to do it but he did. I thank God that he allowed me to come to the house of worship one more time."

One might think that such lack of originality and repetition would lead to a loss of passion. Yet at Eastside the use of certain well-worn phrases invariably brings about an enthusiastic, emotional response, much more than a less formulaic statement with the same content would evoke. This fact was brought home to me one morning during the monthly men's prayer breakfast. When it was my turn to pray, I began to ask for safety on the road for my wife and myself as we were going to be driving a long distance on the following day. In my spontaneous prayer, I framed the request as if I were making ordinary conversation, making it up as I went along. While previous prayers had evoked heartfelt cries of "yes, Lord" from the other men, my prayer did not meet with the same agreement until Lenard Singleton interjected the phrase "we ask for your traveling mercies" over my own words. When this stock phrase was uttered, all of the men responded, "yes, Lord," in unison. Zora Neale Hurston recognized this same phenomenon in the "sanctified" black churches of Florida when she wrote, "The more familiar the expression, the more likely to evoke response. For instance, 'I am a soldier of the cross, a follower of the meek and lowly lamb. I want you to know that I am fighting under the blood-stained banner of King Jesus' is more likely to be amen-ed than any flourish a speaker might get off." (1981: 91)

While the use of certain stock phrases and verbal formulas seems to work during prayers and testimonies, sermons make much more use of metaphor to evoke a strong congregational response. The most effective metaphors appear to be those that subvert the worldly or everyday realm of meaning, include some element of wordplay, and appear to be spontaneously generated. For example, in the short section below, Reverend Wright was able to take the congregation into a peak of response and even stimulate about ten minutes of shouting at the very beginning of his sermon, all by utilizing metaphorical images and plays on words. (The congregational responses are indicated in the brackets.)

> And I'll tell you what—I'm excited about my Jesus! ["Yeah."]
> I'm gettin' more and more excited about him daily.

He's my bread you know.

That's right, if you come to my house, I got some bread there.

That's right, and I didn't get it from the Pig.[5] ["That's right."]

But I got it at the foot of the cross. ["Well."]

He is my Wonder Bread. ["Yeah."]

He is my Roman Meal. ["Oh yes."]

Oh yes, when you read Romans 8, I tell you, it will tell you about
    that Roman meal bread! [clapping, "Yes Lord!" someone starts
    shouting—organ starts playing]

He is my Galations bread! ["All right"—more vigorous response]

He is my Revelation bread!

Then, what I like about him—he is not only my bread, but he is
    meat in the middle of my bread. [clapping, shouting, organ]

And you can eat him alllllll the day long! [more shouting, organ,
    drum beat]

He is good for what ails yah!

Then, I I I I [stutters] can take you to my refrigerator.

Then I can take you to my faucet and I can turn it on.

And I've got water in my house. [drum/organ beat]

I'm not talking about the water that comes out of the ground.

But I'm talking about the Living Water that come down from
    God out of Heaven.

It's good for you if you're thirsty!

It'll quench your thirst!

And give you life on the inside!

My God, my God!

Oh yes! My God! Hallelujah! Oh yes! (Reverend Wright pauses
    here as many congregants are now shouting.)

In fact, many of Rev. Wright's sermons are built around extended
metaphors, some of which can be discerned by their titles alone, including
"Does the Church Know First Aid?" or "Does the Church Have Sugar?"

Call, Response, and "Circular Reaction"

At Eastside Chapel it is not entirely up to the preacher or choir to move
the congregation to higher levels of excitement; a good deal of the responsibility rests upon the congregation itself. In fact, it is impossible for a
preacher to fulfill his or her role without the active support and response

of the congregation. John Dollard, a white academic who, in the course of his research on "Southerntown," regularly attended an African American congregation in that community was asked several times by the preacher to "say a few words." He finally accepted the invitation and later described how congregational responses enhanced his speaking ability.

> Helped by appreciative murmurs which began slowly and softly and became louder and fuller as I went on, I felt a great sense of elation, an increased fluency, and a vastly expanded confidence in speaking. There was no doubt that the audience was with me, was determined to aid me in every way. . . . The little talk ended with a round of applause, which, of course, was permitted in this case; but more than that, the crowd had enabled me to talk to them much more sincerely than I thought I knew how to do; the continuous surge of affirmation was a highly elating experience. For once, I did not feel that I was merely beating a sodden audience with words or striving for cold intellectual communication. (Dollard 1957: 243)

The responsive feedback from the congregation increased Dollard's confidence and enabled him to give a better performance than he otherwise would have. Because his performance improved, it evoked more enthusiastic responses, which then further enhanced his abilities. When the congregation does not respond with sufficient enthusiasm at Eastside it severely hampers the ability of the preacher to maintain his or her performance. Because Reverend Wright and other preachers depend so heavily on congregational response, they will make sure that they keep their responses up to a satisfactory level. If the congregation is quiet and unresponsive, a preacher has various ways to signal his or her dissatisfaction and can thus provoke a more vigorous reaction. Such expressions can range from a gentle prodding ("Can I get an 'amen'?") to somewhat harsher statements; when Eastside Chapel gets too quiet, Reverend Wright will often chide the congregation by saying, "Oh, I wish I had me a church!" and sometimes he will even pointedly switch roles and make the response himself (*"I'll* say it: *'Amen, preacher!'"*).

By using particular resources, performers are able to evoke a response from the congregation. This response increases the intensity and quality of the performer's actions, which in turn evoke a greater congregational response. This "feedback" dynamic is operative particularly during the sermon but also, to a somewhat lesser extent, for all performance segments of the service, especially those that involve a single performer, like the opening prayer or a vocal solo. This structure, in which the actions of one party affect the actions of a second party, which in turn amplify the actions of the first party, and so on, has been called "circular reaction," and it is a hallmark of collective behavior. The overall trajectory of this type of behavior is one of oscillating movement toward higher levels of intensity and participation, culminating in widespread and prolonged shouting. The first two verses of the traditional spiritual "Jacob's Ladder" aptly express this dynamic of upward spiraling: "We are climbing Jacob's ladder" and "Every round goes higher and higher."

"Emotional" Worship and the Transfer of Control

From the above discussion it is apparent that "emotional" worship services are not simply a matter of an energetic preacher or a particular style of music—the congregational response plays a crucial role facilitating the production of "emotion." In fact, we could say that an "emotional" service is a joint creation, produced cooperatively by the designated performer, the organist and choir, the "amen corner" and the rest of the congregation.

One necessary precondition of this collective process is that individual congregants allow their actions to be increasingly influenced by the quality of the performance as well as by the actions of other members of the congregation as the levels of participation become more and more intense. The key dynamic here, one that operates in all forms of collective behavior, is the individual's willingness to transfer control over his or her actions to the group. James Coleman writes:

> [T]he difference between a group that has a potential for extreme collective behavior such as a panic or a riot and one that does not is simply the difference between a group in which the members have transferred large amounts of control over their actions to one another and one in which the members have not done so. (1990: 201–2)

Gerald L. Davis discusses how African American preachers "line-up" the congregation so that their "energies [will be] voluntarily yielded to the preacher for the duration of the sermon" (1985: 17), and members of Eastside also recognize this dynamic, although they put a spiritual slant on their description of it. Darryl Lawson indicated that the more the worshippers had a common desire to worship God, unclouded by factional rivalries or resistance toward the preacher, the more ecstatic the behavior in the service: "If everybody in the church was in one accord—and there have been Sundays that people have been in one accord—God just moves through. But if everybody was on one accord, I mean people—you'd be stepping over people [in the aisle]."

"Two Grand Movements"

Thus far I have shown that this type of ritual can be seen as a stable structure of norms and expectations that act upon individual congregants to collectively produce an "emotional" service. From this perspective, each "emotional" service is a joint creation of both performers and congregation, patterned after cultural standards of what constitutes a "good" or successful service. This leads us to the question of why these standards exist at all. What is the benefit of an "emotional" type of worship service, for the group as a whole or for individual congregants?

In order to answer this question it is important to understand what the members of Eastside Chapel perceive the goal of the worship service to be. As we have seen, the worship service not only provides an occasion where Christians can meet collectively to praise God; it also provides an arena where God can work out his purposes within the congregation. A successful "emotional" worship service is never a one-sided affair with God simply playing a passive role. God is expected to move in the midst of the participants, touching individuals and the congregation as a whole. This understanding of God's role can best be seen through the liturgy of the service itself. For most of my time at Eastside Chapel, the Sunday morning service began with the traditional AME Call to Worship (some of which is quoted at the beginning of chapter 5). One day in early spring of 1992, Reverend Wright mentioned to me that he had written a new Call to Worship that he was having printed in the next Sunday's bulletin. There was nothing wrong with the old one, he was careful to point out, but when anything is repeated too often it can lose its meaning and significance. "When you eat steak 365 days a year, it's not steak anymore," he commented. This Call to Worship is significant because it speaks of the worship service in terms of movement—first on the part of the people, then on the part of God:

Minister: Effective worship consists of two grand movements.
People: The people of God must move toward God and God will move toward the people.

Minister: Therefore, let us worship the Lord with our whole heart.
People: Not only with our hearts, but with our minds and souls.
Minister: Worship is a banquet. God is the host. You are the guests.
People: Let's give God a concert in worship and praise.
Minister: Worship is a drama. You are the actors.
People: God himself is the audience. Let the performance begin, for God waits eagerly.

This liturgy envisions worship in terms of a call and response—the congregation's call through its whole-hearted participation in the drama of the service, and God's response through his presence in the service. The response behavior of verbal cries ("amen"), standing, clapping, running, etc. represents the first movement on the part of the people toward God. Genuine shouting gives evidence that God has responded and is moving upon his people. Thus, the collective effervescence of a worship service at Eastside Chapel invokes the presence of God through the intense participation of worshippers and then provides evidence of his presence through shouting or, more rarely, speaking in tongues. This is why it is almost invariably those congregants who engage in the most vigorous forms of response behaviors who shout, despite the vast difference in consciousness between the two acts that I discussed earlier. Shouting represents the end point of a process that is begun in such simple acts as saying amen or clapping along with a hymn. It is important to underscore the fact that it is this experience of God's immediate and powerful presence, which Eastside members call a "breakthrough," that is the goal of the worship service. Shouting and other forms of ecstatic display are simply manifestations of this experience and not the goal itself. It is necessary to highlight this because many observers have written as if the whole point of the service were to provoke an emotional release among congregants.

I mentioned earlier that while the "emotional" service can be explained by understanding the cultural norms of worship participants, this does not preclude the existence of certain latent functions for the congregation. One of the most important of these was the maintenance of collective identity. Although to the white, middle-class observer, the norms of participation appear similar in all lower-class African American churches, Eastsiders themselves perceived a good deal of variation from one congregation to the next. Even the relatively restrained practice of verbal response during prayers or sermons was not universal among black congregations I observed, and I had several members of Eastside Chapel tell me about other churches where "if you say amen people crane their necks to see who said it." When Reverend Wright spoke in other churches, he would often state at the beginning of his message what he expected in the way of congregational response. For example, at one of the more affluent churches in which he spoke, he politely but pointedly asked, "Are you with me tonight? All right now. I don't want us to have no funeral. I like a live, sassy church. You all get real sassy and I'll be right at home. When you get quiet, I'll preach a long time."

To help ensure the response level he was used to at his home congregation, Reverend Wright generally brought a core group of Eastside members with him when he spoke in other churches. These Eastside members modeled for the host congregation how much response Reverend Wright required. They also helped to prod a more reserved crowd to greater levels of response behavior; much the same way that professional laughers planted in the studio audience of a situation comedy can facilitate greater levels of response among the general audience.

Eastside Chapel prided itself on being a "lively" congregation that maintained a high level of participation and shouting in the worship service. In fact, it was this attribute rather than denominational affiliation or distinctive doctrinal teaching that members used to distinguish themselves collectively from other congregations in the neighborhood. Because a lively service provided evidence of their sincerity in calling to God and God's responsive presence, Eastsiders thought that churches that did not exhibit such fervor were "dead" or lacking in religious commitment. Some members even questioned whether anyone could be saved and still attend an "unemotional" church. Once, when I remarked about several neighboring AME churches characterized by their more somber and restrained worship services, Mother Pinckney exclaimed, "Shoot! All of them churches is dead, man—all of 'em. I mean it's just—I don't think they really know God."

Mother Gadsden had grown up in one of these congregations and told me how she came to be involved at Eastside Chapel. After her daughter started going to Eastside, she began to visit more and more frequently, drawn by the lively nature of the worship service: "So then I just visit and visit and visit. So [my daughter was] going there for about two years. I had been praying, and suddenly I got a taste—oh! Taste and see the goodness of the Lord! [pounds on table] And once you taste, you cannot go sit in no dead, dry, cold church!"

* 7 *

Race, Class, and Religion

It was during an otherwise unexceptional Sunday evening service that Mother Gadsden stood up and told how she found a cancerous lump on her body and treated it herself, without aid from any doctors or hospitals. The story, which Mother Gadsden related in a very matter-of-fact way to the two dozen people assembled, went like this: on a recent morning while dressing she found a lump on her breast and immediately suspected that it was a malignancy. Understandably distressed, she immediately began to pray and "cry out to God" when she was suddenly reminded of a testimony that another Eastside Chapel member had shared during a midweek prayer service some time ago. As Mother Gadsden remembered it, this story concerned a friend who had discovered a tumor on his face. Rather than accept the reality of that tumor, however, he had looked in the mirror every day and repeated to himself, "I don't have a cancer on my face." According to the testimony, the friend's tumor eventually went away. Remembering this story, Mother Gadsden felt that God was telling her to go buy "some stuff" (boric acid I found out later) and tape it up over the affected area. The very next day, she recounted, she took off the bandage to examine the results and found a hole in the place where the lump had been. When she squeezed the hole, blood and pus came out. At that point, "something told her" to squeeze just a bit more. She pressed harder and discovered something in the hole that looked "just like tissue paper." Using her fingers as tweezers, she grabbed hold of it and pulled it out. That, she told the church, was the tumor. She had successfully treated herself for breast cancer with the Holy Spirit's guidance.

As Mother Gadsden finished relating her testimony it was greeted with loud cries of "amen" from the congregation, but I admit that I did not join in with these hearty affirmations. In fact, while Mother Gadsden had been telling it I was experiencing a growing sense of alarm and confusion, a feeling of bewilderment that came into full bloom upon registering the church's positive reaction to the story. Sure, I thought, the kind of faith that she displayed was undoubtedly admirable from a certain point of view, but surely such acts of religious heroism were not really necessary. After all, we weren't in some remote corner of the world without access to modern medicine—in fact, Charleston is the proud home to several major research hospitals. Why, I wondered, didn't she just go see a doctor, at least to determine whether or not it was cancerous?

The disorientation I experienced over this incident signaled my arrival onto the terra incognita of real cultural difference, which is not so much *disagreement* over correct values and behaviors but the more profound inability to comprehend the deeper ideals upon which these values and behaviors rest. But what was the nature and source of this cognitive and cultural divide? Why did my assumptions about the right and "natural" course of action upon discovering a warning sign of cancer seem to diverge so radically from those of Mother Gadsden? It was not attributable solely to differences in religious belief. I did not consider faith healing to be simply the chicanery of white-suited charlatans with bad toupees, or as merely a psychic trick of self-delusion—in fact I had come to Eastside Chapel from a church in Chicago that believed in and practiced healing prayer (but that still encouraged primary reliance on medical care). So what was the problem? Reflecting on the incident over the next few days, what perplexed me most was not that Mother Gadsden had turned to God for healing, but that she hadn't seemed to even consider consulting a doctor at all.

It was only later that I traced the source of our differences to the profound division of race and class that had formed each of our responses to this situation. Most members of Eastside Chapel could not afford adequate medical insurance (if any at all) and had to rely on the local county hospital and free medical clinic for treatment. They were openly critical of the care they received from these institutions and harbored a strong suspicion that the largely white medical staff performed clandestine experiments on their African American patients. Reverend Wright referred to this phenomenon in an off-hand way in one of his sermons, and several times I heard church members tell stories about friends and relatives who went to the hospital for minor ailments and came out in worse shape than when they went in (even, in one case, in "a pine box.") The clear implication of these stories was that the doctors had made them worse and that this had been the result of either casual indifference or outright malevolence on the part of the medical staff. As a white, middle-class person who had always enjoyed reasonably good health insurance, whose own mother had been a nurse for many years, and who grew up with medical doctors as friends of the family, this suspicion of the health care system struck me as bizarrely paranoid—as far out as any right-wing militia fantasy about federal government storm troopers. What I came to realize is that this mistrust of the health care system makes perfect cultural sense, given the history of Africans in America and such documented horrors as the Tuskegee experiments. However, this was a rationality rooted in a people's history and experience that I simply had had no connection to or affinity with as a white middle-class American.

Looking back on it, I really should not have been as surprised as I was by Mother Gadsden's testimony, for it was not my first glimpse into this racial parallel universe. A few months prior to that Sunday night service, I had been talking with Reverend Wright in his office when he causally mentioned that he had just heard an interesting theory about the infamous murders of black children in Atlanta during the 1980s. This hypothesis, which he put forward as a reasonable and plausible alternative to the official view, held that these homicides had not been committed by Wayne Williams, the man eventually convicted, but rather were the work of a pharmaceutical company that had moved to Atlanta from New Jersey just about the time the killings started. The bodies of black male children, the story went, contain a unique chemical compound needed by this company for the manufacture of one of its high-profit drugs and so they had simply "harvested" this natural resource periodically after setting up shop in the South. As I listened, I expressed interest and tried to give an air of serious deliberation over this interpretation, but inside I was experiencing a profound sense of cultural vertigo—how could this highly intelligent, articulate, educated man give credence to such an outlandish tale? This was just before a large segment of the white community became aware of the divide in racial experiences and perspectives as blacks' reactions to the O. J. Simpson verdict made it more apparent to white America.

What these incidents taught me was how much the social location of a congregation—its precise coordinates on the two-dimensional race-class graph of American society—can shape the kinds of experiences that its members undergo and what they consider to be reasonable explanations for these experiences. The location of the congregation in a poor neighborhood had an impact on some of the relational aspects of the church, and this in turn colored some of the experiential and expressive dynamics of religious life.

"Jesus Is My Doctor"

One of sociology's earliest insights and most enduring truths is that an individual's probability of experiencing success, happiness, and good health (his or her "life chances," in Weber's memorable phrase) is tied to his or her position in the social order. Financial, occupational, educational, and even romantic successes are not evenly distributed across the general population, and life for the working poor (and the just plain poor) is comparatively nasty, brutish, and short. Experiences such as being laid off, chronically running short of enough money to pay the bills, being victimized by street crime, having a family member or friend addicted to drugs, facing discrimination in housing and employment, becoming incarcerated, and suffering from an untreated illness are far more common at the lower end of the social class spectrum, and particularly so among African Americans. To the extent that these kinds of situations are treated as having ultimate or proximate supernatural causes (as they often are at Eastside Chapel), and to the extent that human remedies to these situations are in limited supply (as they most certainly are to those with few financial resources), then these problems and their solutions form the basis for a different realm of religious experience among the poor.

Consider the issue of health and medical care raised by Mother Gadsden's story. Compared to whites, African Americans are at greater risk for heart disease and other ailments, and they are less likely to have access to good health care. Therefore, they are more likely to develop serious health problems as they get older. This fact, combined with a suspicion of the health care system based on their racial history, means that God is often a healer of first rather than last resort, the family practitioner for everyday ailments rather than the final desperate hope after the specialist has pulled the last medical trick out of his bag. Thus, the religious experience of physical healing is more common and has more salience among this group of poor and near-poor African Americans than it does in most other segments of American Christianity with its mainstream reliance upon and trust in the modern medical establishment.

For the middle-aged and elderly in particular, health problems were an everyday issue and many, if not most, of the testimonies they offered at midweek prayer services and the occasional Sunday evening service had to do with God's curing some serious illness or permanent disability. When these testimonies did incorporate doctors in the story, they never appeared as actual healers but simply as authoritative diagnosticians, certifying the presence and severity of the ailment in question and thus magnifying the wonder of the miraculous spiritual cure. "The doctors said that I would never see out of this eye again! [Or use this arm, or hear out of this ear, or walk on this leg, etc.]. But glory to God! He has given me full use of [name of body part]!" This substitution of spiritual for medical forms of routine (and not so routine) healing is manifestly clear in the chorus of a popular song I heard at several revivals and midweek prayer meetings:

> Jesus is my doctor
> He write all of my prescriptions, and he
> Give me all of my medicine
> In the prayer room

Under these circumstances, reliance upon God as healer has become a religious marker to the extent that when routine medical help is sometimes available, the use of it can damage one's credibility as a person of faith. Once I was in Sherline Singleton's house when her four-year-old son, Markis, began to complain of an earache. Sherline went to the kitchen and got out some cooking oil, then rested his head in her lap. Tilting his head to the side, she had Markis repeat after her: "In the name of the Father," and then dipped her finger in the oil and dabbed some in his ear, "In the name of the Son," more oil, "In the name of the Holy Ghost," still more oil. Then she had him stand up and sent him in his room to play. When he still complained of the pain several minutes later, Sherline scolded him mildly, saying, "Now Jesus is going to make it all better, but you got to stop thinking about the pain. If you all sad, how is Jesus going to make it better?" After more complaints, she relented and gave him some aspirin, but made it clear to both me and Brother Green (another Eastside Chapel member who was there for a haircut from Sherline) that the medicine was only to help Markis' state of mind. "I don't rely on the aspirin to stop it," she assured us, "but he will think that it is doing something."

God is not only a source of healing but of financial provision as well. This divine work was particularly important in a congregation where the great majority had low-wage jobs, often of a seasonal and unstable nature, so that families' budgets were chronically strained. This, combined with a paucity of public programs, private charities, and any members of an extended family who might be better off, meant that Eastsiders often had to rely on supernatural sources of aid. Reverend Wright often preached about supernatural sources of help in times of extreme hardship and need, combining both medical and financial examples in the following sermon excerpt:

> You don't have to wonder where your God is. Hallelujah! I'm glad to
> serve a God like that! [When you are] in a car and it about to wreck and
> you call on the name of Jesus. And you escape death because you called
> on his name. Some of you had a pain come up in your body that could
> have been a heart attack but you prayed and called on your God, and he
> was there to answer. When you were broke and didn't have no money and
> was wondering where the next dollar was gonna come from. And you got
> down on your knees when you couldn't go to the bank. You got down on
> your knees when you couldn't go to the Food Stamp center. You got
> down on your knees when you couldn't go to your friend. You talked to
> your God, and he opened up a door and made a way. When you're broke
> and you walk down the street, and there's money blowin' on the ground
> that seem to come out of nowhere. When you been prayin', "Lord, Lord,
> Lord," and a check come in the mail that you don't even expect from
> somebody.

Time and again in public and private testimony, Eastside members recounted how God had stepped in and rescued them when they were faced with seemingly insurmountable challenges to their physical and financial well-being. These testimonies were so common that members often relied upon several standard phrases or "sayings" to express gratitude for God's deliverance:

The Lord made a way out of no-way. He didn't have to do it, but He
    did.
He's been better to me than I've been to myself.
He may not come right when you want him, but when he comes,
    he's always on time.

In another commonly heard phrase, members often thanked God for giving them "life, health, and strength" and for providing such tangible benefits as jobs and apartments.

It may seem paradoxical that those on society's lower rungs, who are most prone to financial and physical disaster, would experience God as a powerful healer and provider. From the middle-class vantage point, we might expect that they would have a hard time reconciling their relative poverty and ill health with a belief in a healing and providing God. However, this expectation assumes that these working poor African Americans compare themselves to middle-class living standards. For some this is certainly the case. Yet for others the primary reference group seems to be not those families living in the suburbs and holding down professional jobs, but rather other urban African Americans who are homeless, in jail, unemployed, on drugs, or receiving public welfare. Deborah Watson, who at the time of our interview had a low-wage job stocking vending machines, told me:

> I'm so glad that I didn't get addicted to something [when I was out in the world]. . . . And I really look back on that because as I drive up Meeting St. and around Columbus St., I see so many of the drunks that's sittin' on the corner, so drunk that they don't know what their name is. And I say, "Lord, thank you that you let me live long enough to see that my health and strength lies in the realm of God. That I don't have to sit on no corner selling my body. That I don't have to sit on no corner drinking up a bottle to get my misery and worries off of me." I mean to tell you, I give God the glory!

It is in terms of that comparison—which often includes members of their own extended families, or even siblings, children, parents and spouses—that Eastside believers experience what they see as the provision of God. Darryl Lawson worked as a teacher's aid for the minimum wage, cleaned office buildings five nights a week, and still couldn't afford to move out of his mother's small house. Rather than feeling resentful toward those better off than him, he was grateful to God for not ending up like all of his high school friends who were "either dead or in jail."

"The Devil's Candy"

The social and geographic location of Eastside also shaped members' understanding of the ongoing battle between God and Satan, for it was played out most visibly in the ghetto neighborhoods where they lived— where they could walk down the street and see the small and struggling churches surrounded by neighborhood bars, "juke joints," crack houses, drug corners, and dilapidated buildings full of the victims of unemployment, substance abuse, violence, and other social ills.

Not surprisingly, drugs often played a prominent role in this supernatural struggle and were a constant theme in Reverend Wright's sermons. He often railed against the seductive lure of drugs and alcohol and considered them to be among the most lethal weapons in Satan's arsenal. He had good reason for believing this, as several men (and one woman) had come into the church from off of the street during my time at Eastside Chapel, only to be lured back to their drug habits within several weeks. Even one of the long-standing members of the church, a house painter with his own business and a position on the Trustee Board, had an intermittent problem with drug addiction. He was eventually arrested for possession of crack cocaine and spent several years in the state penitentiary. The sense of being overwhelmed and frustrated by the devastation of drugs and its effects in the African American community can be felt in the following excerpt from one of Reverend Wright's sermons:

> I am so broken up inside when I see the conditions of our people. One of the musicians, well-known in the church community, was talkin' with my brother last night. And he said, "A little girl ten years old came to sell me her body for ten dollars." And beloveds, what is the world come to when a little ten-year-old child who hasn't even lived yet is already destroying her life? And the sad part about it is, the mothers sometime send their children out to sell themselves, because the mothers are hooked on that nasty dope. That filthy, nasty, low-down drug! Beloveds, it's awful, and Jesus told me to go and preach the gospel. Lord, what can I do in a world where people would rather kill themselves with drugs than to turn to you? When the drug dealers are takin' all of their money? And Lord you tell me to preach the gospel. He said, "Preach the gospel anyhow. Preach it if they hear it, preach it if they don't hear it. But, you preach to them that there's a better way. Tell them that the doors of the church is open, tell them that the Lord's table is spread. Tell the drug users that if they come I'll heal them. I'll pick up the broken pieces and put it back together. Go and tell them, because, you see even though they are addicts, they still have their hearing. But somebody has got to cry loud." "What do you do, Lord, when you go to church, and people come and steal the saints' cars?" "Tell them to carry on anyhow. Tell them to let nothing shake their faith. Tell them to let nobody turn them around. Tell them to hold on and to hold out, because all these troubles shall soon be over."

Many of Eastside's members had witnessed the destructive power of drugs in their own families and agreed with Reverend Wright that drugs were one of the devil's primary tools. Mother Pinckney, whose son was in jail on a drug-related charge at the time of our interview, became very emotional when she exclaimed: "[Satan] is loose, and he's walking on the land! And he trying to devour anybody he can. Satan is loose, and he brought that stuff [cocaine] from hell with him when he come. We call that the devil's candy. Yeah! That's what that crack stuff is—the devil's candy!"

White middle-class Evangelicals may subscribe to a theology of evil that looks very similar to that of Eastsiders, but they also live in very different environments, which are not so visibly plagued by the problems of poverty, drugs, alcohol, and crime. They don't have to deal with crack addicts' breaking into churchgoers' cars while they attend an evening service, or groups of young men setting up their drug business on the vacant lot down the street. Winos are not staggering down the cul-de-sacs of middle-class subdivisions clutching forty-ounce bottles of malt liquor, nor are suburban parks littered with needles, vials, and tiny plastic bags. They don't feel anxiety over stray bullets or purse snatchers every time they leave the house to go to work or the store. While middle-class Evangelicals do have a relatively robust sense of evil and its presence in the modern world, it is a force that tends to be conceptualized in terms that are more relevant to middle-class lives and visible within their own social locations. Satan is alive and well, yes, but not so much in terms of street crime or drug addiction, but in the political and cultural realms, pushing such issues as abortion and homosexual rights and pumping up the sex and violence in the media and popular music.

Although Eastsiders consider Satan to be the ultimate cause of all human problems, the lines of attribution for the evils that they see around them are more complex and include many social as well as spiritual forces. For example, experiences of racism and prejudice are not simply swallowed up in mystical talk of demonic activity but seen as an active—and very human—force of oppression in society. As I said earlier, Reverend Wright is very much a "race man" and racial issues were ever-present in his consciousness and conversation. Nearly every interview and informal exchange I had with Reverend Wright turned at some point to the topic of relations between the races and the struggles of African Americans as a people. Since his tenure at Eastside, he had incorporated Afro-centric symbols into life of the church, including painting over the white Jesus on the church's front sanctuary wall, wearing a ministerial stole made from kinte cloth, and choosing a drawing of an African Jesus in a tribal village setting for the cover of the weekly church bulletin.

Sometimes Reverend Wright highlighted the social forces that kept African Americans down and spoke of purely social solutions to the problems of the inner city. The very first time I met Reverend Wright in his study, I asked him about the neighborhood surrounding the church. He replied that there were "lots of drug addicts and alcoholics" in the community and characterized it as "a very negative zone." The neighborhood youth, he lamented, are growing up with "no jobs and no future" and the church simply didn't have the money to offer any alternatives. "See, you got to take them out of these negative zones. You need to get these boys when they're eleven or twelve, before they get into doing drugs and into that type of thing." He led me out the front door of the church, pointed to an abandoned structure across the street, and said that he was trying to purchase it for use as a halfway house for young men from the streets. Turning north and pointing across the intersecting street, Reverend Wright indicated an old and decrepit-looking church with an overgrown cemetery. He said that it used to have a neighborhood youth program run by the Episcopal church in the 1960s and 1970s, and though the program was no longer there, he wished something like that could be started again. Back inside his office, Reverend Wright showed me a picture of the Harlem Boys Choir from a magazine and commented, with some frustration, that

> there are counterpoints to those boys there right in this neighborhood. And because Pepsi sponsored this program, they created an outlet for these young kids. I just need the funds to do something like that right here. . . . A friend showed me a video of some [local] youth gospel choirs and I was so impressed by how much talent there is out there just waiting to be brought out.

During the year I was at Eastside Chapel, Reverend Wright was able to purchase that abandoned house across the street and begin to rehab it. I even contributed to the effort in a small way by applying (mostly without success) for foundation monies to help with the project. He also started a mentorship program for young boys, partnering them with volunteers from the Charleston Naval base. And he was not alone in these kinds of efforts that dealt with the social rather than the spiritual realm. James Ravenel, Eastside's organist, organized a Saturday forum to discuss social and political issues. The speakers represented the local chapter of the NAACP, the Charleston County School District, the former principal of the peninsula's only public (and all-black) high school, as well as one guest pastor, whose talk was called "The Church in the Real World."

At times, however, even explanations of racism and racial history had a tendency to assume a mystical and supernatural quality that went beyond attributions to solely social or historical causes. Reverend Wright had a tendency to invoke spiritual forces as at least partial explanations for patterns of racial domination, and sometimes he portrayed spiritual and social forces as working in tandem with one another. The complexity of interlocking social and spiritual explanations for racial oppression and the continuing problems he pointed to—drug addiction, sexual infidelity, alcoholism, family abandonment, and other social ills—has led most Eastsiders to advocate both spiritual *and* social solutions to these problems. In keeping with the Evangelical emphasis on individual salvation, Eastsiders tried to bring drug addicts, alcoholics, and dealers to a saving knowledge of Jesus Christ because they felt they needed the "heavy fire," in Reverend Wright's words, of God's conviction and the Holy Ghost's work in their life before they could straighten up. Purely human interventions were bound to be inadequate, they believed. At the same time, Reverend Wright had quite elaborate ideas about the kinds of social programs that were needed to address the many social problems that plagued the local community.

The Church and the Street

Observers of extremely poor neighborhoods often report that residents' relationships are characterized by suspicion, distrust, and isolation. This is true for several reasons. First, residents often adopt the images that outsiders have of them, and while community members generally reject these negative stereotypes for themselves, they often apply them to their neighbors (Suttles 1968; Anderson 1990). Second, conditions of oppression and marginality often produce a kind of exploitative individualism as people try to get as much as they can from others without themselves appearing vulnerable to manipulation. In his ethnography of a mostly African American housing project in St. Louis, Lee Rainwater observed: "Techniques of relating to other people are markedly defensive; individuals manipulate and exploit others where possible and at the same time try to ward off manipulation and exploitation by others. This contributes a pervasive tone of guardedness and mistrustfulness to interpersonal relations within the community" (1970: 372). This attitude of competition and exploitation contributes to the formation of street gangs in these neighborhoods (Jankowski 1991), and can be found not only among lower-class African Americans, but also among other ethnic groups and in other industrialized nations (Harrison 1985).

This guardedness and mistrust, which is endemic to the Eastside and neighborhoods like it, is reproduced to some extent within the congregation, although it takes a somewhat different form than it does in the neighborhood. Distrust within the congregation concerned issues of psychic and emotional vulnerability and a fear that being too candid about one's weaknesses might damage one's reputation and perhaps leave one open to exploitation. Ronald Huger, a construction worker in his early thirties and a newer member of Eastside Chapel, told me, "I'm the type of person that I normally hang with myself. I don't hang too much with [other] individuals." I asked him why that was and he replied, "What it is—basically [it] is a lack of trust." He then generalized this to the congregation by saying that many in the church were mistrustful of other members. When I asked him why, he said:

> I think a lot of people are afraid of one another. Now me, I find myself, when I begin to open up, I always find myself weeping. See, I constantly still do that. See you got people look at you and think—a lot of people in the church, when they see you going to the front, they thinking you got a problem. Even when like you go up for prayer, you find a lot of people are afraid—a lot of people got problems in that church, and they are afraid to go up to that altar on Sunday for prayer.

In Ronald's estimation, "Even though they are in the church, a lot of people in the church say they are saved, but [they are really not]." In other words, instead of encouraging and praying for those who have shared their weaknesses, some members will use the information to judge and criticize them. In my conversations and interviews with church members, I was constantly surprised (and dismayed) by the often harsh and critical attitudes that congregants displayed toward one another. For example, Sherman Davis told me that the church was divided up into many small groups, and that these cliques "might do for each other if you're in that group, but not for anyone else." However, just after complaining about these divisions in the church, Sherman went on to criticize several of the lay ministers as well as his own mother-in-law, then condemned one of the older men for "drinking and cursing," and finally denounced the man's son for "putting the flesh before the spirit." Ironically, Sherman himself was notorious for his inconstancy, periodically leaving his job, family, and the church for several months at a time while he returned to his drug and alcohol habits.

As the most visible person in the congregation, Reverend Wright was often a target of harsh criticism, and he would often condemn this type of "backbiting," speaking from the pulpit. In the following sermon excerpt he compares the physical violence of the ghetto streets to the "spiritual violence" of gossip and discord within the church:

> They talking about the violence in the street. But there's another kind of violence—it's a spiritual violence, and it's in the churches. And it's goin' to and fro to tear the churches apart. The devil is out to tear you apart. And it's not a drive-by shooting with a gun, with a Saturday night special. It's a drive-by shooting with this Monday through Sunday special right up here with this tongue on the inside [of the mouth]. It's a trigger and it's always shooting off garbage.

However, Reverend Wright was perhaps the most openly critical person of anyone at Eastside Chapel. He often publicly chastised people for their lack of commitment to the church and other perceived failings, a practice that exacerbated some of the divisions in the congregation and earned him several powerful enemies in the church.

Deborah Watson expressed dismay that the harsh and critical attitudes that characterize street life could also be found to such a large degree within the church:

> There's just as much [criticism and gossip] out in the world as there is in the church. But you know, it shouldn't be in the church. . . . [You] hear that out there, so why hear it when you come inside the church? The church is supposed to be helping and encouraging [people] to get closer with God, not to come in and hear what you done come out from! That throws you back out in the wilderness.

Sherman Davis seemed to think that things were actually somewhat worse in the church than on the street. After talking with him about the divisions at Eastside Chapel I asked if it was the same way with the men he periodically hung out with on the corner. "No, man," he replied, "If they have one bottle or one cigarette, they share it. But in church, if you ask somebody for a quarter, 'No man. I ain't got it.' There is more unity on the street than there is in the church."[1]

One result of the harsh criticism and the distrust it engendered is that, like Ronald Huger, people tried not to appear vulnerable in front of other congregants. On more than one occasion Reverend Wright declared from the pulpit, "Don't ever let anybody know your weaknesses." Deborah Watson acknowledged that all Christians were subject to human frailty and a propensity to sin, yet she upheld the idea that these shortcomings should be a private matter between God and the individual believer: "You know we all fall sometimes, but we don't need to share with our sisters and brothers how we have fallen."

The distrust Eastside members had of fellow congregants and the resulting fear of vulnerability had several consequences for the structure of church events. First, worship services, Bible studies, prayer meetings, and revivals left no room either for "fellowship," or for the informal sharing of personal failures and struggles. In fact, Eastside Chapel members often used very individualistic and antagonistic language to characterize their spiritual struggles. Not only did they not conceptualize themselves as sharing their spiritual journeys with fellow congregants, but they often testified that they were "pressing on" *in spite of* being "talked about" and otherwise "scorned" by other members of the church. The recitation of testimonies, a traditional part of the ritual structure, relied upon heavily formulaic declarations that revealed little personal information. As I alluded to earlier, when the testifier referred to his or her lifestyle before salvation, it was generally referred to in such deliberately opaque phrases as "when I was out in the world, doing whatever it was that I was doing."

One important consequence of distrust within the larger community is that residents tend to keep to themselves. Although the term "social isolation" has come to mean the disconnection of inhabitants of poor neighborhoods from social networks outside of their communities (Wilson 1987), many residents of these neighborhoods remain isolated even from one another (Hannerz 1969; Rainwater 1970), and this isolation could also be found within Eastside Chapel. I asked the members I interviewed if most of their friends were also members of the church. Like Ronald Huger, many people informed me that they didn't have any friends—either inside or outside of the congregation. For example, Mother Pinckney, who had gone to Eastside for over forty years reflected on my question for a few moments before replying, "Well, I don't know. . . . You know I ain't

never been a person to have a lot of friends. . . . I just thought of that."
Deborah Watson, Mother Pinckney's daughter-in-law said, "I don't really
have a friend. . . . I have family through marriage [that attend the church]."
When I pressed further and asked if there were any persons at all in her
life whom she would consider a friend, she replied firmly, "None."

Like Deborah Watson, many Eastside Chapel members did not attend
as individuals but as members of nuclear and extended families, and congregational leadership was dominated by the children and grandchildren
of Eastside Chapel's founding pastor. The presence of these families miti-
gated the level of distrust and isolation in the church to some extent.
However, the social context of the neighborhood also acted to weaken fa-
milial bonds within the congregation. A high percentage of these nuclear
and extended families were composed only of adult women, their grown
daughters, and grandchildren of both sexes. That many of the families
were female-headed reflects the high rate of female headship within the
Eastside community. But even when there was a husband present in the
household, often he either did not attend church or attended the congregation in which he was raised. Several highly visible and active leaders at
Eastside Chapel (including the service leader and daughter of the founding pastor) had spouses who were members of other congregations, a fact
that is consistent with other research on marital role segregation among
the working and lower classes (Gans 1962). The fragile nature of social ties
among church members might have contributed to an even greater emphasis than usual on the traditional Evangelical conception of a personal
relationship with Jesus—for this type of spiritual relationship was often
portrayed as a *substitute* for friendship, kin, and even marital relations.

A *"Church of Prestige"* or a *"Church of Power"?*

As African Americans have gained some economic ground in recent
decades, there is a sense among some that the new black middle class has
lost its spiritual grounding because they have stopped having to rely on
God to meet their needs. Although Reverend Wright reserved his harshest
criticisms for secular musicians and entertainers like Patti LaBelle and
Mike Hammer—whom he saw as pied pipers of the "street" life of drinking, drugs, and promiscuity—he was almost as hard on the churchgoing
black middle class, who he felt had simply kept up the form of religion as
a means of respectability while emptying it of its spiritual power. He often

chastised middle-class blacks for losing their "spiritual desires" and focusing solely on material gain. In one sermon he said, "You know we got a whole lot a folk goin' around—they ain't worryin' about no goin' to no heaven. They're worryin' about gettin' some stocks and bonds." Reflecting on a time when African Americans "didn't have nothin'" but their faith, they were stronger as a people—"you couldn't beat [us]. One of the worse things that could have ever happened to Negroes—and I hate to say it but it's the truth—was for them to start gettin' stuff." The following excerpt from his weekly radio address draws in stark terms what he sees as the fundamental choice facing the contemporary African American church.

> I want to thank our Lord Jesus Christ for sending a great apostle [Paul] who told us not to be a church of prestige—and prestige is a conjurous trick, an illusion, deception. [He told us] not to be a church with elitish people—bourgeois folk who have connections with the governor or the mayor or congressmen; who are in lodges, sororities, or fraternities; who know people in high places, but have no power to change people by the effect of their testimony; [who have no power to change others'] life living from being winos or alcoholics or dope users or whores or prostitutes or pimps or liars—through the demonstration of God in your life—to become righteous people. Don't be a church of prestige, be a church of power and of love and of peace and of sound mind, not of fear. Be a church where the testimony of Jesus Christ is alive and circulating in your midst.

The stark contrast between these two options—a church of prestige or a church of power—reveals much about the social identity of Eastside Chapel, its location among the poorer class of the African American community, and its embracing of shouting and more expressive (and low status) forms of worship. The new middle-class church suffers no embarrassing outbreaks of emotion, no countrified forms of dancing in the spirit, and no impassioned testimonies connoting a simple, uneducated faith. The church of prestige is a refined and sophisticated expression of religion, one well suited to the emergence of an educated and prosperous black bourgeoisie. But, Reverend Wright is asking, is it worth the price? Has the black middle class, like Esau, sold its spiritual birthright for the ephemeral soup of respectability? And has it abandoned the rest of the black community—the "winos, alcoholics, dope users, and whores," in Reverend Wright's graphic language—that remain behind in the nation's blighted urban communities? The trade-off here, as he sees it, is one of social prestige for spiritual power—a power that may look undignified and ignorant to the middle-class world, a power that comes only by a kind of commitment that may disrupt and derail the pursuit of wealth and respectability, but a power that can transform ruined lives and free the poor and oppressed from their bondage and addiction.

Ironically perhaps, this attitude toward religious expression has some affinities to the oppositional culture of the poor neighborhood youth who condemn academic and economic success among their peers as a racially inauthentic attempt to "act white." To Reverend Wright, the black middle classes who are abandoning their religious heritage are simply trying to "pass" and become accepted among the white middle class, a process that has been happening for well over a hundred years. Several times (and always with palpable irritation) in my interviews with him Reverend Wright referred to the legacy of Daniel Alexander Payne. Payne, a Charlestonian by birth, was one of the most important early leaders of the African Methodist Episcopal church and a local hero to many African Americans. To Reverend Wright, however, Payne was nothing more than a race traitor because he had tried to stamp out traditional Negro spirituals (once derisively referring to them as "cornfield ditties"), shouting, and other forms of what he saw as heathenish superstitions and pagan practices from the AME denomination.

The essence of Reverend Wright's message is that the embracing of spiritual power comes at the expense of worldly prestige. This was illustrated in one of Reverend Wright's weekly radio addresses as he announced an upcoming series of revival meetings in the neighboring community of Huger (a Huguenot name pronounced *YOO-gee*):

> You talk about a time—we gonna have it in Huger next week! I want you to tell all the crack addicts that Huger is the place to get some new crack. I want you to tell all the people that's on coke, that's all coked up, to come on to Huger for some new kind of coke. We going to be distributing something next week in Huger. And I want you to tell all the winos, all the people hooked on gin, all the people hooked on Smirnoff vodka, and all that stuff that they been using (and paying good money for) to come on down to Huger next week. We gonna be dealing next week in Huger. I want you to tell them that.
>
> And the police can come and inspect the place if they want and look for drugs, but I declare they won't find any illegal substances there.

There'll be some drugs there all right, but it's going to be the kind of drugs that fell on the day of Pentecost, when the folk came out of the upper room acting mighty strange. And people wondered what they were on. And they kinda figured that they must have been in there drinking some of that Jerusalem Mad Dog wine in the middle of the day. But they tell them, "No it wasn't no Jerusalem Mad Dog, neither was it Wild Irish Rose. But it was the Rose of Sharon kind of wine—the kind that comes out of where the lilies grow in the valley, the kind that when you drink it, it makes you look up and see bright stars—morning stars. That kind of wine we were drinking. The kind that puts a new walk in your feet and a new talk in your tongue and the kind that makes your hands tingle and feel brand new—that's the kind of wine that we been on, and we want you to come and get some of it." And it was so good until 3,000 folk wanted it in the same day. So we want you to prepare to come to Huger next week and be in the midst of this great explosion that will take place there.

In this excerpt Reverend Wright compares the Holy Spirit to a street narcotic and the revival preacher to a drug dealer. These parallels are un-orthodox enough (even if they are metaphoric extensions from the New Testament book of Acts), but even more interesting are the kinds of drugs he mentions and the brands of alcohol that he identifies by name. *Crack?* The very word is synonymous with the underclass and evokes images of emaciated bodies, trash-strewn alleys and abandoned buildings. *Wild Irish Rose* and *Mad Dog?* The brands of winos and street bums everywhere. Metaphors are often used to put a particular slant or spin on a situation, and on several occasions Reverend Wright made very similar references to the Holy Spirit as similar to drugs and alcohol. There are two essential messages conveyed by this association and each of them has to do in some way with the social location of the church.

The first message is that faith should be all-consuming. Wild Irish Rose and Mad Dog are not brands of alcohol consumed by the occasional social drinker, nor are crack users known for having a "take it or leave it" rela-tionship to the drug. These are the substances of the wholly committed, the consumption of which is the defining and ruling aspect of their lives. The second and implicit message is that there is nothing prestigious about this kind of spiritual addiction. In fact, crack addicts and street winos have the lowest conceivable status in every part of our society, including the ghetto. Addicts themselves recognize this, of course, but they have opted to give up any claims on respectability in exchange for the high that they can no longer live without. The power of a feeling, an experience, comes at a high cost of family and friends and status. And there is an affinity here, Reverend Wright is implying, between the addict and the convert. For each it is a total commitment. It is all-consuming. It is a powerful reality changer. And it comes with the cost of position and prestige. The necessity of giving up any desire for social status is simply part of the deal. In another sermon, Reverend Wright drew this parallel between drugs and religion again, this time comparing the relative merits of their "highs":

> I see a lot of people in the world using drugs who call themselves "getting high." But I see some folk in the house of the Lord getting' high, and I tell you what, I like their high a lot better than the high that's in the world. And ah, there's just something about getting high in the house of the Lord! I, I think we ought to let the dope users know that they can get high in the house of the Lord. That's right! [clapping]

He goes on to defend the feeling-oriented aspect of traditional religious ritual from its middle-class detractors:

> People sell their souls simply for a feeling. And I try to figure out, why would people want to use something that's only gonna destroy them? But they're searching for a feeling. Feelings must be awfully important to human beings, and that's why when people tell me that worshipping God is not about feeling, I say you got to be telling a tale. Because feelings are so important that people give their lives for a feeling. Because all drugs give you is a feeling. They don't put money in the bank for you, they don't make you live longer, they don't make you look better, and they don't make you smarter. Everybody I've talked to said it is simply for a feeling. Beloveds, I think the church ought to go and sell the world their feeling. And the thing about the church's feeling, there's more behind it than meets the eye. We get depressed, tossed down, talked about. We have bills like everybody else have bills. We have things that come to hurt us like everybody else have things. We have loved ones who leave us like everybody else have loved ones [who leave them]. But we don't turn to the crack dealer to solve our problems [clapping]. That's right. We had a dealer a long time ago—he dealt for us on Calvary's rugged cross, and his blood has never lost its power.

The primary mission of the church, at least as Reverend Wright and other core leaders of the church saw it, was to bring in the drug addicts, winos, and other "underclass" types living the "street" lifestyle so common in urban ghetto neighborhoods. Indeed, several of the core lay leaders in the church, including Lenard Singleton and Anthony Scott, had been minor drug dealers before becoming saved and joining the church. Reverend Wright deliberately attracted these kinds of people into the church, and this was not popular among some of the more middle-class-oriented families in the congregation. But for Wright, these former alcoholics and drug addicts made better converts precisely because they had long ago abandoned any pretense of social status. They had been at the bottom emotionally, physically, and socially and had nothing to lose from a complete and total commitment to the kind of high-demand, low-status religion championed by Reverend Wright at Eastside Chapel.

I have argued that the social location of Eastside Chapel powerfully shapes members' experiences of spiritual agency, and this has its effects on the ritual style of the church and its sense of mission to those in the neighborhood. Both God's provision and Satan's attacks seem far more immediate and salient when one is living so close to the economic margin and when the symptoms of evil are far more visible. The sense of embattlement that this engenders leads many in the church to embrace spiritual power over worldly prestige because they can see no other way to fight against the strong forces of evil they see operating in their everyday world. One must have a "heavy fire" in Reverend Wright's words, a Holy Ghost fire, to fight fire—the fires of addiction, abuse, and oppression that are so visible along the inner-city streets of communities like the Eastside of Charleston.

Conclusion
Belief, Experience, and Ritual

> It is one thing merely to believe in a reality beyond the senses, and
> another to have experience of it also; it is one thing to have ideas of
> "the holy" and another to become consciously aware of it as an oper-
> ative reality, intervening actively in the phenomenal world.
> —Rudolf Otto, *The Idea of the Holy* (1958)

There is a symbiotic relationship between belief and experience. On one
hand, belief is logically prior to experience, in that the attribution of an
event to a particular cause necessarily rests upon a belief in the existence
of that cause. Yet though experience depends on belief, belief by itself remains dormant. Alone it is abstract, disembodied, lifeless, its power more
potential than actual. It is experience that gives life to the dry bones of belief, and experience through which the abstract word becomes flesh and
dwells among us. By approaching religion merely as a set of ideas, sociologists have tended to take them at face value rather than determining
whether and *how* these beliefs are actually utilized in people's everyday
lives. Sociologically, beliefs are not really beliefs until they are used to
make sense of an actual experience or as a guide to a future action. While a
group's repertoire of beliefs may offer a certain set of *potential* explanations and experiences, this power will remain latent until people grab the
beliefs from the cultural toolbox and actually apply them to real-life situations.

This dynamic is fully recognized by religious believers, perhaps more so
than it is by religious scholars. The following passage from Reverend
Wright's sermon "Do You Believe in Ghosts?" closely parallels the above
quote from Rudolf Otto:

When we say that we believe in [God], that's not enough. We must receive him into our temples to dwell on the inside of us. Sure, there's some people that says, "Well, I believe in ghosts. I've never seen a ghost, but I believe ghosts are real." Well, if you've never had an experience, then you don't know for sure; you just have a belief. And believing is one thing, but having the experience is another.

The church has regarded Biblical stories about the power of the Holy Spirit as inspired Scripture for two thousand years, but only relatively recently, after the Azusa Street revivals in the early 1900s, have they been used to make sense of lived experience. Likewise, belief in the existence of demons has characterized much of Evangelical Christianity throughout its history. Yet, though the supply of belief in demons has hardly increased over the past several decades, the demand for them as explanations of personal troubles seems to have grown (Cuneo 2001). And the concept of karma is ubiquitous throughout India and its sacred writings, yet anthropologists report that it is rarely used by the Hindu faithful to understand actual incidents of misfortune. Instead, fate, "headwriting," ghosts, and witchcraft (or just laziness, stupidity, and other personal attributes) appear to be far more popular explanations (Keyes and Valentine 1983).

Schleiermacher's Legacy

Perhaps the reason that experience has been a neglected topic within sociology is due to its first academic formulation over 300 years ago in German theologian Friedrich Schleiermacher's treatise *On Religion: Speeches to Its Cultured Despisers* (1799). Crafted as a response to Enlightenment critics of religion like Hume and Kant, this book attempted to free "religious doctrine and practice from dependence on metaphysical beliefs and ecclesiastical institutions and [ground] it in human experience" (Proudfoot 1985: xiii). To accomplish this, Schleiermacher argued that doctrines, practices, and institutions were secondary accretions to the primary source of religion: a general and universal religious experience he later identified as "a sense of absolute dependence" (Schleiermacher 1928, first published in 1821–22). He thus established the idea that religious experience was fundamentally private and preconceptual and involved some sense of contact between the experiencing self and the supernatural world. In *The Varieties of Religious Experience,* William James followed in the tracks laid down by Schleiermacher with his assertion that "feeling is the deeper source of religion," and that "philosophic and theological formulas are secondary processes, like translations of a text into another tongue" (James 1902: 431). He went on to argue, as Schleiermacher had done, for the radically individual nature of religious experience and contends that it necessarily involves a sense of immediate contact with the spiritual world.

The legacy of this approach can be easily discerned in more recent psychological and sociological studies of religious experience because they rely as little as possible upon creedal concepts and terminology. Rather than asking about God or Jesus, they inquire about "spiritual forces." Conversions and baptisms of the Holy Spirit are neglected in favor of "moments of awakening" and "insight into the nature of the universe." In taking this course these works assume what the theologians and philosophers before them tried to prove, namely that there *is* such a thing as a universal religious experience, the essence of which can only be revealed by stripping off the encrustation of dogma and belief. These contemporary studies also define religious experience, at least implicitly, as the perception of a *direct encounter* with the spiritual world—an experience often characterized by extraordinary cognitive, emotional, or bodily states.

The analysis of religious experience developed in the preceding chapters goes against both of these legacies from Schleiermacher. First, even if there were some kind of universal religious experience underlying, say, speaking in tongues, people identify their experiences, spiritual and non-spiritual, by the cultural labels placed on them. Thus, sociological attempts to pose such vague questions as "have you ever felt lifted out of yourself by a powerful spiritual force" simply confuse the issue. What known, identifiable experience within any of the major religious traditions could such a question refer to? It is far better to ask these questions in the terms of people's religious traditions, which will give a far more accurate picture of who claims them.

Second, limiting religious experience to perceptions of a direct contact with the spiritual world has limited our understanding of the full range of religious experience and its consequences. Paying attention to indirect encounters with supernatural agency opens up our understanding of the ways in which religion may radically transform everyday life experiences. Though direct experiences of the supernatural can be quite powerful, they are also relatively infrequent, even among Pentecostals and other groups that emphasize them. This does not mean that believers have no experience of God between these fleeting and episodic encounters. Rather, they experience God by seeing his hand in their lives. This happens through the attribution of life events to his intervention, whether personal and relatively trivial (making a parking place available, for example) or collective and consequential (like the destruction wrought by Hurricane Hugo).

Religions are exactly like other belief systems in this respect—they depend upon indirect experience to confirm the "reality" of their constructs. Scientists don't directly experience atomic structures or black holes in space; these entities are known only through the observable effects attributed to them. Similarly, such concepts as "racism" or "adolescence" take on reality because we interpret someone's remark as disparaging of particular racial groups, or we observe a series of patterned behaviors at a particular time in the life course and we attribute them to adolescence. In short, we believe that these things exist not because we can observe them directly, but because we make inferences about them based on their effects in what we can observe. What is unique about religious experience, then, is not that it involves an attribution to forces that are beyond direct observation and whose existence cannot be "proven." This is as unavoidable in science—or in everyday life—as it is in religion. What is unique is that religious forces and beings are in, but not of, this world. The category of "spiritual" that underlies religion is in this sense a residual one, encompassing all beings and forces that are neither purely natural nor purely social, but whose effects can be seen in each of these mediums, like ripples on a pond or wind in the trees.

A Sociology of the Gods

If theories are like searchlights, illuminating one aspect of the social terrain while leaving others in shadow, then Durkheim's functionalist spotlight has played on the solidarity-enhancing aspects of religion for so long that the image has been burned onto our disciplinary retinas. While not denying that solidarity may be one aspect of religious belief and ritual, the attributional approach developed here highlights the explanatory role of religion based upon conceptions of the existence of the supernatural world and the nature of its interaction with human life and history.

This means that doctrinal systems are consequential because they determine the shape and limits of potential human experience; in short, belief matters. Rodney Stark puts it this way: "If the most basic aspect of any religion is its conception of the supernatural, then the most basic aspect of social scientific studies of religion is the sociology of the Gods" (2003: 11–12).

Perhaps the starting point of such a sociology should be to recognize the implications of the fact that in most of the world's religious traditions, the Gods are *persons* with whom one not only *can* but *should* interact. This should particularly intrigue social scientists because human-spiritual interaction can be seen simply as a special kind of "anchored relationship," or tie, between two individuals based on mutual recognition, personal knowledge and face-to-face interaction that constitute society (Goffman 1971). In other words, it is the kind of relationship that is our stock in trade. This point has been made even more forcefully by anthropologist John Caughey who, following A. I. Hallowell, points out that limiting our attention to human relationships "actually represents an ethnocentric projection of certain narrow assumptions" which "may seriously misrepresent the inner worlds of other cultures" (1984: 17). Hallowell had studied the Ojibwa Indians, a tribe whose members interacted regularly not only with each other but also with deceased ancestors, thunder gods, and giant monsters, and Caughey's research on a small Micronesian island uncovered a society in which people reported regular social (and even, in one case, sexual) intercourse with demons and other spiritual beings. These human-spirit relationships, Caughey points out, were such a vital and important part of the culture that one could not understand the society or the behavior of its members without taking these kinds of relationships seriously.

Bringing the Devil Back In

Limiting our concept of religious experience to include only perceptions of a direct encounter with the supernatural misses the fact that not all supernatural beings are to be encountered in this way. As we have seen, Satan has a fairly large supporting role in the spiritual drama at Eastside Chapel, yet most members would not conceive of themselves as having "experienced" the devil, at least not in the same way that they have experienced God. The devil operates both internally—through deception and temptation—and through external events that seem designed to "trip up" believers and cause them to doubt the reality of God's truth or to engage in things he is known to disapprove of.

The works of the devil are powerful because they prey upon our innate and sinful desires. In fact, to the extent that humanity is perceived as fallen and prone to sin, the power of Satan will appear that much greater. This point is an important one because beliefs about the power of Satan bring into sharp relief corresponding beliefs about the power of God. If the strength of a force can be known only through the amount of resistance it overcomes, then a true estimation of God's power requires an appreciation of Satan as a formidable opponent. A religion with a very weak or nonexistent idea of evil (whether conceptualized as a personal foe or impersonal force), need not postulate a very powerful God. And a religion that teaches that humanity is not tainted by evil and prone to sin, however powerful that force may be in the abstract, will not emphasize the necessity of appropriating or experiencing God's power. Eastside Chapel, like evangelical Christianity in general, emphasizes *both* the power of Satan *and* humanity's propensity to sin. Thus, it proclaims not only the power of God in the abstract, but humanity's constant need to appropriate that power, through both individual means like Bible reading and prayer and collective means like attendance at worship services.

It is here that we can see how religious experience contributes to the creation and maintenance of quite intense forms of religious association. Since the seminal works of Max Weber and Ernst Troeltsch, sociologists have distinguished between sectarian forms of religious organization that claim a larger portion of their members' resources, and churchly forms that hold their members more loosely in their grasp. In recent decades Dean Kelley (1972) and Laurence Iannaccone (1994) have tried to explain why Americans seem to flock to sectarian or "strict" churches despite the higher financial costs, time investments, and behavioral prohibitions that these churches impose. Kelley hypothesized that conservative churches provide "more meaning" than their more lax and liberal counterparts, while Iannaccone argued that their behavioral restrictions served to reduce organizational "free riding" and thus are rational mechanisms for strengthening churches.

I want to suggest that Kelley has it more right than Iannaccone, provided that we understand "meaning" in a limited way as the perception of evil and spiritual danger in the world. The sense of evil—experienced as both a powerfully destructive *and* seductive force—is supplied to members of Eastside Chapel by the theology of the church and is continuously underlined by its social location in the violent and drug-infused world of the ghetto. The battle is an invisible, spiritual one, but the casualties are all too real and visible and, in many cases, known to the members of the church. This sense of embattlement is what provides the underlying dynamic of the sectarian impulse, because the feelings of vulnerability engendered by theology and bolstered by experience lead to a greater dependence upon the church and the protective spiritual force that it represents. Dependence is what Hechter (1983) proposes as the foundation of more intense forms of solidarity, which he defines as the extent of a group's obligations over its individual members and which we can extend to include concepts like "strictness" and "sectarianism."

The Complex Role of Experience

Though doctrine is important in shaping experience, it does not determine it. Life events have the capacity to ground beliefs, but they also have the potential to challenge or modify them. The term "theodicy" encompasses all attempts to reconcile experiences of suffering and evil in the world with the concept of an all-powerful, loving, and just God, including personal experiences as well as collective events like wars, earthquakes, famine, and genocide. Theodicy is the nearly constant work not only of academics and professional religious apologists, but of rank-and-file believers as well, as Ammerman's (1987) ground-breaking study of "Bible-believing" fundamentalists vividly demonstrates.

And it is not just the obvious instances of evil and suffering that present these kinds of challenges. The messy and often ambiguous flux of real-world experience can confound easy attributions, even for the most ardent believers. This, combined with the tangled web of spiritual, social, and natural causation, even in the relatively demystified world of Protestant Christianity, means that the process of attribution is more complex and provisional than it might first appear. Table 1 summarizes chapters 3 and 4, showing possible experiences, with examples, and the major spiritual agents to which Eastsiders regularly made attribution.

TABLE 1 *Agency and Experience at Eastside Chapel*

		Agent	
		GOD	SATAN
Root Metaphor		Relationship	War
Experience			
	DIRECT		
	Mind	Visions, dreams, prophecy, shouting, insight/truth	Possession, temptation, illusion/lies
	Body	Tongues, healing, seeing colors, shouting	Possession, illness
	INDIRECT		
	Personal	Provision ($), "testing," "punishment"	Temptation, hardship
	Collective	Provision, punishment (e.g., Hurricane Hugo)	Evil, injustice, sin, and death

Notice that it is the indirect experiences that are the most problematic in this respect. When an employer eliminates my job, is God punishing me for something I did wrong or testing my faith so that I'll become stronger? Is it just Satan out to get me and make me question God's provision for me and my family? Or is it due to impersonal economic and social forces? Support for each of the spiritual interpretations can be found in the Bible, and a believer can hold to the last, nonspiritual explanation *at the same time* as he or she sees a deeper spiritual force at work.

Of course, many religions have a far larger cast of characters that may be drawn upon to account for aspects of life experience, which multiplies the possible layers of explanation. The ways in which people and groups negotiate the complexities and ambiguities of spiritual attribution, the norms that develop regarding their use, and how these norms are applied in individual situations are all issues that deserve far more attention from scholars than they have received.

Encapsulation and Secularization

Eastside Chapel is a congregation for whom we can say that all domains of experience are fairly well encapsulated by spiritual attributions. Even the most mundane and perfunctory, taken-for-granted experiences ("waking up in the morning clothed in my right mind," "being in the house of the Lord one more time," having a body that still functions with the "blood running warm in my veins") are attributed to the active intervention of a

God who "didn't have to do it, but he did." If attribution can be thought of in quantitative terms as the proportion of life experience explained by appeal to supernatural forces, then Eastside surely falls at one end of the continuum. The other end may be represented by Weber's prophecy of the "disenchantment" of the world in which everything is explained by the mechanical operation of natural and social forces. Most religious groups, of course, probably fall somewhere between these two extremes.

But what of the cultural environment in which religious groups must exist? Debates over secularization, or the place of religion in modern society, have focused on individual religious belief and practice, the vitality of religious organizations, and the presence of religious symbols in public life. But the experiential dimension and its place in American culture have yet to be evaluated. It is possible that relatively hyper-spiritualized congregations like Eastside Chapel are quite numerous, especially at the lower end of the social class spectrum, but that these religious cultures are becoming out of sync with a public culture increasingly dominated by the relatively de-spiritualized world of college-educated professionals. If this is so, churches like Eastside Chapel now exist as cultural islands—numerous and populated, even connected to one another in archipelagos of enchantment—but increasingly cut off from the continent of secularity that establishes the societal point of orientation.

Such an argument rests on the idea of cultural power rather than numeric dominance. It may be that, statistically speaking, most Americans do believe in the active provision of God or (less likely) the interference of Satan. But are they free to make such attributions beyond the walls of the church? The issue here is not the relative plausibility or logic of spiritual lines of attribution, but simply their contestability in the public discourse of politics and the media, the school, and the workplace. And here we have the fundamental paradox of contemporary America: charismatic and Pentecostal churches are among the fastest growing of religious bodies and the culture they produce in books, television, and music reach incredibly large audiences. Yet these same institutions and products may be increasingly localized and marginalized—in short, made deviant—within a rapidly secularizing public culture.

Religious Ritual

There is a curious contradiction in the study of religion. On one hand, corporate worship is recognized as the central rite within the Judeo-Christian tradition, and sociologists report consistently high rates of religious participation in contemporary America. Yet while we have an abundance of current and historical data on church attendance, and an appreciation of the importance of weekly worship services, there has been very little attempt to understand just what people actually do once they step inside of a synagogue or church. How has such a central element of religious life come to be so neglected by scholars of religion? One possible reason is methodological. Since World War II sociologists have increasingly relied upon statistical analyses of quantitative data that take individuals and their attitudes, beliefs, and behavior as their units of analysis. While these data are useful for identifying patterns of attendance over time, they are not so helpful in telling us much about the rituals themselves. And yet it is not just quantitative studies that ignore ritual. Most ethnographic studies of congregations limit themselves to descriptions of ritual, while saving their analysis for other aspects of congregational belief and practice. This general theoretical neglect of ritual among sociologists of either preference leads me to believe that the real issue is not methodological but conceptual, a legacy of the powerful influence of Durkheim's treatment of ritual as a solidarity-enhancing mechanism (Stark 2003).

In this book I have taken a very different approach to religious ritual by developing a cultural and experiential understanding of the worship event. I began by simply asking, "What do worshippers believe is going on here?" a question modified from Goffman's more general "What is it that's going on here" (1974). The relatively straightforward answer ("God is present among his people") led fairly quickly to further complexities as I trailed in the wake of such follow-up questions as "Exactly how is God made manifest in the service?" "What are the perceived effects of his presence?" and "How does one know when he shows up?" This approach highlights the continuity between religious experience and ritual because they are both grounded in the same thing: a perception of the interaction between the human and spiritual worlds. Ritual thus can be seen as a particular type of religious experience, one imbedded in a collective occasion rather than solely in individual consciousness and biography or in larger events like hurricanes, wars, and famines.

Transformations

Because they serve as arenas for the intersection of the social and spiritual world, religions develop standard ways of marking rituals as "set apart," similar to yet fundamentally different from other kinds of collective gatherings. How is this done? Goffman wrote that specially framed occasions are usually "marked off" from more mundane activities by conventional markers or "brackets," especially temporal and spatial ones (1971: 250–51). We might call these boundary markers or brackets "transformation devices," as they signal a transformation to a spiritual rather than merely social frame of reference. Sometimes there is such a close association between a particular type of ritual frame and the space or structure in which it is usually housed that the terms can be synonymous, as, for example, in the phrase, "going to church." However, place is merely one common device used to signal a transformation to the ritual frame, and the particular spatial devices used will vary between cultures and over time. Temporal brackets can also be used, and a common device is to schedule rituals regularly at the same time of the year or on the same day of the week. This element of repetition has also been considered one of the hallmarks of ritual, although it too is merely a particular way of creating a transformation, particularly in conjunction with place.

While many rituals are scheduled for a particular day and to begin at a particular time, the clock alone doesn't determine the actual commencement of the ritual, the inner "game" from the outer "spectacle" in which it is imbedded. What cues signal the termination of preliminary activities and announce the official start of the worship service? In many churches, including Eastside Chapel, the organist will end the prelude with a sustained, louder, and more dramatic chord, signaling the processional hymn and the start of the service. Other congregations perform a "call to worship," which the minister and congregation stand and recite together, and still others utilize choral music (Forrest 1982). In more humble rituals like saying grace before the family meal, simple declarations such as "let us pray," combined with bowing of heads and closing of eyes, transform what follows into the spiritual realm.

However, it is not always the place, time, or content of actions and words that signal a frame transformation. The formality of many kinds of ritual can be seen as one way of sending the message that the occasion or action is set apart from ordinary activity (Bell 1992). The use of King James English or Latin in worship is significant precisely because its vocabulary and syntax are archaic, communicating that this is a qualitatively different activity from ordinary conversation. Using outdated instrumentation and musical styles is a similar strategy that transforms singing from diversion and entertainment to worship, and this "time warp" aspect is even more evident among churches that perform such ancient practices as footwashing. Similarly, the practice of dressing in more formal clothing or wearing special uniforms such as the minister's robe is another way of bracketing such gatherings from everyday activities.

Because ritual is a transformed occasion that partakes of spiritual as well as social realities, it is imbued with transformative power. When God is present at Eastside Chapel, the Word is preached, understanding and insight ensue, bodies are healed, and lives are changed. The paradigmatic occurrence here is the sought-after "breakthrough" that brings worshippers, individually or collectively, to a more powerful experience of the spiritual realm, with lasting effects beyond the confines of the event. Scholars of ritual have often commented on the strong restorative powers of ritual (Bellah 1970; Schechner 1977; Turner 1982; Driver 1991; Grimes 1982), and perhaps the most famous passage in this vein is Durkheim's observation that "the believer who has communed with his god is not simply a man who sees new truths that the unbeliever knows not; he is a man who is *stronger*" (1995: 419).

In addition to its powerful psychic and emotional effects, ritual frames can also transform or establish social realities and identities. Christenings, weddings, initiations, puberty ceremonies, and other "rites of passage" (van Gennep 1960) are particular types of rituals that actually call a particular social reality into being. Hearings, trials and other socially binding actions and events, what Bourdieu (1991: 111) calls "rituals of social magic," often utilize what Austin (1975) has termed "performative" utterances— for example, such phrases as "we find the defendant guilty" or "I now pronounce you husband and wife."

While both emotional and social transformations are the result of ritual, they differ greatly in how they achieve their effects. In the former case, control lies largely within each participant because he or she must be fully engrossed in the ritual occasion in order to achieve psychic renewal. Cynical detachment or boredom effectively destroy this type of ritual transformation. However, the opposite is true of the social transformations effected by ritual. Rituals like weddings, trials, and christenings are socially effective regardless of the subjective states of the individual participants. A ritual participant who harbors feelings, thoughts, or intentions considered inappropriate might make the ritual "unhappy" in Austin's words, but not void; the act is still performed (Austin 1975; Rappaport 1979).

Meaning, Motivation, and Ritual

Does this approach to ritual imply a uniformity of meaning and motivation among the participants? To answer this it is necessary to distinguish between two distinct dimensions of belief: intention and motivation. The first is relatively fixed by cultural consensus. Standard beliefs, intentions, and expectations for appropriate behavior are ascribed to participants by the very fact of their participation; they are built into the occasion itself. In attending a funeral one becomes a "mourner," a role enacted by the very definition of the event and implying not only a motivation for attendance but a particular emotional state as well (Hochschild 1979, 1983). Of course, individuals often have quite varied reasons for attending a funeral or a worship service and their subjective emotional states may be far from the situational ideal. In fact, discrepancies between these two levels, what Goffman (1974: 269) calls the "person-role formula," are recognized by ritual participants themselves. Indeed, the sense of anger and even outrage with which Eastsiders regarded the "churchgoers" in their midst who were not "truly saved" gives testimony to this fact, as does the disgust of my fellow church members over the pecuniary motives exhibited a bit too baldly during the Seven Speakers Program.

When there is widespread suspicion of a discrepancy between the dimensions of the ideal and actual, then the term "ritualist" may be used pejoratively to describe "one who performs external gestures which imply commitment to a particular set of values, but . . . is inwardly withdrawn, dried out, uncommitted" (Douglas 1982: 2). However, even rampant ritual hypocrisy need not negate the beliefs and values implied by ritual participation any more than a sudden crime wave diminishes the normative capacities of the law. In fact both situations may serve to *strengthen* public commitments to these norms, either by reshaping the ritual or the law in question to more accurately embody current values (what may be called the liberal approach) or through greater policing of individual belief and behavior (the conservative approach).

Social Location and Ritual Style

Observers of religion have long noted that the kind of "emotional" service described in chapter 6 is more common among the lower class than among the more affluent (see Daniel 1942; Pope 1942; Dollard 1957; and Rubin 1963). To explain this connection between lower class and "emotional" worship style, scholars have argued that this kind of ritual meets the particular psychological needs that are produced by poverty and oppression. This argument takes three main forms.

The most common is the idea of "catharsis," or the need of persons to discharge negative emotional energy built up by the harsh living conditions and oppression endemic to poverty (e.g., Clark 1965). "Catharsis" explanations assume that the worship service helps congregants to subconsciously rid themselves of negative emotional energies produced by their subordinate social position. It allows them to "blow off steam," which, depending upon one's political viewpoint, may either serve a positive therapeutic function or represent a channeling of potential energy away from changing the conditions of oppression.

A somewhat different perspective characterizes the emotional service as a temporary diversion or "escape" from the daily hardships of poverty and subjugation. A variant of this suggests that such escape comes in the form of psychological regression, which explains the "childish" behaviors of worshipers who jump, run, and "babble freely in nonsense syllables" (Eddy 1958).

More recently, a somewhat more sophisticated approach interprets such ritual activity (particularly shouting and speaking in tongues) as a way for the poor to subconsciously express their social subservience and marginality by symbolically articulating their lack of control over their lives. In this way, lower-class worshippers can more adequately adjust themselves to their social realities (Anderson 1979; Wilson and Clow 1981). Whether the perceived need is for catharsis, escape, or symbolic expression, scholars can put forward certain functional equivalents of "emotional" religious services: "hair-raising movies" (Pope 1942); "whiskey, sex, and tavern behavior" (Lewis 1955); or frequenting bars and hanging out on street corners (Clark 1965).

The fundamental premise of all three of these approaches is that the "emotional" character of the service is a simple reflection of the internal emotional states of the participants, whether these emotions have their origin in a need for catharsis, escape, or symbolic articulation. Because middle- and upper-class individuals do not experience the harsh living conditions or blunted life chances of the poor, the argument goes, they do not develop these particular psychological needs. This, in turn, explains the more sedate character of their religious rituals.

There are two crucial issues that all variants of this approach fail to address adequately. First, they assume a simple and direct connection between the observed behavior of congregants and their inner emotional states. Not only does this ignore the fact that such subjective states are not available for empirical analysis (Wuthnow 1987), but it also ignores the existence of the normative order that regulates all aspects of public behavior. Religious activity—even that defined as "emotional"—is not exempt from behavioral norms, as I have shown. Thus, it is extremely hazardous to attempt to "read" internal states from outward behavior and then attribute primary causality to them.

The second difficulty is that these approaches do not recognize the collective nature of "emotional" ritual. That is, the actions of individual congregants are not simple expressions of their own internal states, nor are they simply the reflection of norms that govern participatory behavior; their actions are also affected by the behavior of other congregants. This type of behavioral interaction within the ritual produces an emergent phenomenon that cannot be reduced to the intentions or internal states of individual participants. In this regard, "emotional" worship services bear important similarities to riots, escape panics, fashion crazes, and other forms of what is called collective behavior by sociologists (Coleman 1990; Turner and Killian 1957). In addition, the catharsis theory posits the operation of a peculiar (and unexplained) emotional alchemy that turns the anger and frustration engendered by poverty and racism into positive emotions of love, praise, and gratitude, while the escape thesis fails to recognize how much of congregants' life experience is actually incorporated into the worship service itself, through testimonies, sermons, prayers, and other liturgical vehicles, and not simply left behind in the vestibule.

More fundamentally, academic observers have generally treated the presence of the "emotional" service among the lower class as the phenomenon to be explained, instead of examining the *variation* of ritual style across all socioeconomic status groups. Thus, scholars have used the "nonemotional" worship of the middle and upper classes as an implicit normative benchmark, and treated "emotional" worship as a deviant form of ritual, explicable only by reference to unique psychic needs endemic to life at the bottom of society. We need to make the *absence* of "emotion" among the middle and upper classes as problematic as its presence among the lower classes without resorting to the unsupported (and class-biased) claim that there is simply no "need" for such behavior among those who are better off.

One step in this direction is to recognize that "emotional" behavior is not merely a topic for academic reflection but a source of active contention within many African American congregations. In some churches, emotionalism is absent not simply because parishioners do not have the psychic "needs" to provide it with a hospitable environment; rather, it has been consciously and systematically weeded out by those with the power to suppress it. Both Johnston (1956) and McRoberts (2003) have documented the powerful influence of those who opposed emotionalism in the African American church. This pattern of suppression is not limited to African American churches or even to Christianity. Max Weber (1958: 137) wrote that the Indian Brahmins and the Chinese Mandarins—both classes of "genteel literati"—were alike in removing the "orgiastic and emotional ecstatic elements" from the systems of magical rites that preceded both Hinduism and Confucianism.

Religion, Peter Berger has said, is the audacious proposal that ordinary human life is somehow imbued with cosmic significance. Yet religion goes further, insisting not only that the cosmic takes note of human affairs, but actively intervenes in the everyday lives of ordinary people. Sociologists of religion have generally not considered the kinds of religious experiences that ensue as worthy of serious consideration. Nor have we explored the connection between religious experience and the collective rituals that seem to be so important to religious groups. By attending to religious ritual and religious experience, social science can make a fresh start at understanding religious life and its place within contemporary society. Experience is what transforms belief from a set of provisional hypotheses about human life into a form of knowledge. And it is this knowledge—woven from the combined strands of belief and experience, made alive through ritual—that makes religion one of the strongest and most powerful social forces in human history.

Notes

1. Names of the church and of all persons in the study have been changed.

NOTES TO CHAPTER 1

1. However, this might be somewhat unique to the time and place of research. In the early 1990s Charleston had a relatively low unemployment rate for African Americans, probably because of the expanding tourist industry, the presence of the Navy Yard (which has since closed) and Air Force base and the continuing reconstruction of the city after Hurricane Hugo in 1989. Also, AFDC benefits in South Carolina were among the lowest in the nation, which discouraged participation in the welfare system.

2. Ironically, what academics saw then as the problem of "overchurching" is now taken as evidence of the health and vitality of a "free market religious economy" (Stark and Finke 2000).

NOTES TO CHAPTER 3

1. That the quality of a personal relationship—particularly a submissive one of intimacy and emotion—should be given such prominence in a historically male-dominated tradition is more than a little ironic, though perhaps it does explain the preponderance of women as rank-and-file members.

2. A term referring to physical collapse or fainting, presumably under the power of the Holy Ghost.

NOTES TO CHAPTER 6

1. Spirit possession has long been a focal topic of interest in anthropology as well and continues to absorb much scholarly attention (Boddy 1994).

2. One point of interest I will note, however: observers of African American religion during the nineteenth century all refer to the "ring shout" as the type of "holy dancing" practiced during slavery (Raboteau 1978: 59–75; Taves 1993). After the regular worship service at the Praise House, or meeting place, the participants would clear the benches from the room. Those who wanted to dance would form a circle and begin to sing and shuffle counterclockwise around the room, bending their knees slightly and stamping rhythmically on the floor. Starting slowly, the ring would begin to move faster and the singing become louder until observers reported a frenzy of motion that lasted for hours. The steps of the dance never varied, but were accompanied by an altered state of consciousness that worshippers attributed to the Holy Ghost (Creel 1988: 299). This type of "ring shout" continued for many years after slavery, and forms an interesting contrast to the more individualized shouts I describe here and that others have observed in contemporary African American religious services.

3. According Eastside Chapel interpretation this New Testament term refers to a demon.

4. Actually, responsibility is not evenly distributed across the congregation. Because of their visibility, those in the front pews, in the choir, and the two pews flanking the altar have higher expectations put on them. Those who choose to sit in the "amen corner" feel most keenly the pressure to say amen.

5. Reference to the Piggly Wiggly supermarket chain.

NOTE TO CHAPTER 7

1. However, as Hannerz (1969: 56) notes, these claims of streetcorner solidarity among the men are often exaggerated.

References

Ammerman, Nancy Tatom. 1987. *Bible Believers: Fundamentalists in the Modern World.* New Brunswick, NJ: Rutgers University Press.

Anderson, Elijah. 1990. *Streetwise: Race, Class, and Change in an Urban Community.* Chicago: University of Chicago Press.

Anderson, Robert Mapes. 1979. *Vision of the Disinherited: The Making of American Pentecostalism.* New York: Oxford University Press.

Austin, J. L. 1975. *How to Do Things with Words.* 2nd ed. Cambridge, MA: Harvard University Press.

Back, K., and Linda Bourque. 1970. "Can Feelings Be Enumerated?" *Behavioral Science* 15:487–96.

Becker, Howard S. 1963. *Outsiders: Studies in the Sociology of Deviance.* New York: Free Press.

———. 1982. *Art Worlds.* Berkeley: University of California Press.

Bell, Catherine. 1992. *Ritual Theory, Ritual Practice.* New York: Oxford University Press.

Bellah, Robert. 1970. *Beyond Belief.* New York: Harper & Row.

Bernstein, Basil. 1964. "Aspects of Language and Learning in the Genesis of the Social Process." In *Language in Culture and Society,* edited by Dell Hymes, 251–63. New York: Harper & Row.

Bocock, Robert. 1974. *Ritual in Industrial Society.* London: Allen & Unwin.

Boddy, Janice. 1994. "Spirit Possession Revisited: Beyond Instrumentality." *Annual Review of Anthropology* 23:407–34.

Bourdieu, Pierre. 1991. *Language and Symbolic Power.* Translated by Gino Raymond and Matthew Adamson. Cambridge, MA: Harvard University Press.

Bourque, Linda Brookover. 1969. "Social Correlates of Transcendental Experiences." *Sociological Analysis* 30:151–63.

Bowes, Frederick Patten. 1942. *The Culture of Early Charleston* Chapel Hill: University of North Carolina Press.

Caughey, John L. 1984. *Imaginary Social Worlds.* Lincoln: University of Nebraska Press.

Clark, Kenneth B. 1965. *Dark Ghetto: Dilemmas of Social Power.* New York: Harper & Row.

Clarke, Erskine. 1979. *Wrestlin' Jacob: A Portrait of Religion in the Old South.* Atlanta: John Knox Press.

Coleman, James S. 1990. *Foundations of Social Theory.* Cambridge, MA: Belknap Press.

Creel, Margaret Washington. 1988. *A Peculiar People: Slave Religion and Community-Culture among the Gullahs.* New York: New York University Press.

Crocker, Christopher. 1974. "Ritual and the Development of Social Structure: Liminality and Inversion." in *The Roots of Ritual,* edited by James D. Shaughnessy, 47–86. Grand Rapids, MI: Eerdmans.

Cuneo, Michael W. 2001. *American Exorcism: Expelling Demons in the Land of Plenty.* New York: Doubleday.

Daniel, Vattel Elbert. 1942. "Ritual and Stratification in Chicago's Negro Churches." *American Sociological Review* 7:352–61.

Davis, Gerald L. 1985. *I Got the Word in Me and I Can Sing It, You Know: A Study of the Performed African-American Sermon.* Philadelphia: University of Pennsylvania Press.

Davis, James Allan, and Tom W. Smith. 1991. *General Social Surveys, 1972–1991.* Chicago: National Opinion Research Center.

Dollard, John. 1957. *Caste and Class in a Southern Town.* New York: Doubleday.

Douglas, Mary. 1982. *Natural Symbols.* New York: Pantheon.

Drake, St. Clair, and Horace R. Cayton. 1945. *Black Metropolis: A Study of Negro Life in a Northern City.* New York: Harper & Row.

Driver, Tom F. 1991. *The Magic of Ritual: Our Need for Liberating Rites That Transform Our Lives and Our Communities.* New York: HarperCollins.

Durkheim, Emile. 1995. *The Elementary Forms of the Religious Life.* Translated by Karen E. Fields. New York: Free Press. Originally published in 1912.

Eddy, G. Norman. 1958. "Store-Front Religion." *Religion in Life* 28:68–85.

Edin, Kathryn, and Laura Lein. 1997. *Making Ends Meet: How Single Mothers Survive Welfare and Low-Wage Work.* New York: Russell Sage Foundation Press.

Eliade, Mircea. 1959. *The Sacred and the Profane: The Nature of Religion.* Translated by Willard R. Trask. New York: Harcourt Brace Jovanovich.

Fauset, Arthur Huff. 1971. *Black Gods of the Metropolis: Negro Religious Cults in the Urban North.* Philadelphia: University of Pennsylvania Press.

Fernandez, James W. 1986a. *Persuasions and Performances: The Play of Tropes in Culture.* Bloomington: University of Indiana Press.

———. 1986b. "The Argument of Images and the Experience of Returning to the Whole." In *The Anthropology of Experience,* edited by Victor Turner and Edward M. Bruner, 159–87. Urbana: University of Illinois Press.

Fickling, Susan Markey. 1924. *Slave Conversion in South Carolina, 1830–1860.* Columbia: University of South Carolina Press.

Firth, Raymond. 1951. *Elements of Social Organization.* London: Watts.

Forrest, John A. 1982. "The Role of Aesthetics in the Conversion Experience in a

Missionary Baptist Church." in *Holding on to the Land and the Lord,* edited by Robert L. Hall and Carol B. Stack, 80–88. Athens: University of Georgia Press.

Forsyth, Neil. 1987. *The Old Enemy: Satan and the Combat Myth.* Princeton: Princeton University Press.

Fraser, Walter J., III. 1989. *Charleston! Charleston! The History of a Southern City.* Columbia: University of South Carolina Press.

Frey, Sylvia R., and Betty Wood. 1998. *Come Shouting to Zion: African American Protestantism in the American South and British Caribbean to 1830.* Chapel Hill: University of North Carolina Press.

Gallup, George H. 1978. *The Gallup Poll, Public Opinion, 1972–1977.* Wilmington, DE: Scholarly Resources.

Gallup, George, and F. Newport. 1990. "More Americans Now Believe in a Power Outside Themselves." *Los Angeles Times* Syndicate (27 June).

Gans, Herbert J. 1962. *The Urban Villagers.* Glencoe, IL: Free Press.

Goffman, Erving. 1961. *Encounters: Two Studies in the Sociology of Interaction.* Indianapolis: Bobbs-Merrill.

———. 1971. *Relations in Public.* New York: Basic Books.

———. 1974. *Frame Analysis: An Essay on the Organization of Experience.* New York: Harper & Row.

———. 1981. *Forms of Talk.* Philadelphia: University of Pennsylvania Press.

Goldsmith, Peter D. 1989. *When I Rise Cryin' Holy: African-American Denominationalism on the Georgia Coast.* New York: AMS Press

Goody, Jack. 1961. "Religion and Ritual: The Definitional Problem." *British Journal of Sociology* 12:142–64.

———. 1977. "Against 'Ritual': Loosely Structured Thoughts on a Loosely Defined Topic." In *Secular Ritual,* edited by Sally F. Moore and Barbara G. Meyeroff, 25–35. Amsterdam: Van Gorcum.

Gorsuch, Richard L., and Craig S. Smith. 1983. "Attributions of Responsibility to God: An Interaction of Religious Beliefs and Outcomes." *Journal for the Scientific Study of Religion* 22:340–52.

Greeley, Andrew. 1974. *Ecstasy.* Englewood Cliffs, NJ: Prentice Hall.

Grimes, Kimberly, Dale Rosengarten, Martha Zierden, and Elizabeth Alston. 1987. *Between the Tracks: The Heritage of Charleston's East Side Community.* Leaflet Number 30. Charleston, SC: The Charleston Museum.

Grimes, Ronald L. 1982. *Beginnings in Ritual Studies.* New York: University Press of America.

Hannerz, Ulf. 1969. *Soulside: Inquiries into Ghetto Culture and Community.* New York: Columbia University Press.

Harrison, Paul. 1985. *Inside the Inner City: Life under the Cutting Edge.* New York: Viking Penguin.

Hay, David, and Ann Morisy. 1978. "Reports of Ecstatic, Paranormal, or Religious

Experience in Great Britain and the United States—A Comparison of Trends." *Journal for the Scientific Study of Religion* 17:255–68.

Hechter, Michael. 1983. *Principles of Group Solidarity.* Berkeley: University of California Press.

Heider, Fritz. 1958. *The Psychology of Interpersonal Relations.* New York: Wiley.

Hinson, Glenn. 2000. *Fire in My Bones: Transcendence and the Holy Spirit in African American Gospel.* Philadelphia: University of Pennsylvania Press.

Hochschild, Arlie. 1979. "Emotion Work, Feeling Rules, and Social Structure." *American Journal of Sociology* 85:551–75.

———. 1983. *The Managed Heart.* Berkeley: University of California Press.

Hunter, James Davison. 1983. *American Evangelicalism: Conservative Religion and the Quandary of Modernity.* New Brunswick, NJ: Rutgers University Press.

Hurston, Zora Neale. 1981. *The Sanctified Church.* Berkeley, CA: Turtle Island Press.

Iannaccone, Laurence R. 1994. "Why Strict Churches Are Strong." *American Journal of Sociology* 99:1180–1211.

James, William. 1982. *The Varieties of Religious Experience: A Study in Human Nature.* New York: Penguin. Originally published in 1902.

Jankowski, Martin Sanchez. 1991. *Islands in the Street: Gangs and Urban American Society.* Berkeley: University of California Press.

Jargowsky, Paul A., and Mary Jo Bane. 1990. "Ghetto Poverty: Basic Questions." In *Inner-City Poverty in the United States,* edited by Laurence E. Lynn and Michael G. H. McGeary, 16–63. Washington DC: National Academy Press.

Jenkins, Wilbert L. 1998. *Seizing the New Day: African Americans in Post–Civil War Charleston.* Bloomington: Indiana University Press.

Johnson, Alonzo. 1996. "'Pray's House Spirit': The Institutional Structure and Spiritual Core of an African American Folk Tradition." In *"Ain't Gonna Lay My 'Ligion Down": African American Religion in the South,* edited by Alonzo Johnson and Paul Jersilo, 8–38. Columbia: University of South Carolina Press.

Johnson, Clifton H., ed. 1993. *God Struck Me Dead: Voices of Ex-Slaves.* Cleveland: Pilgrim Press.

Johnston, Ruby F. 1956. *The Religion of Negro Protestants.* New York: Philosophical Library.

Kelley, Dean M. 1972. *Why Conservative Churches Are Growing: A Study in Sociology of Religion.* New York: Harper & Row.

Keyes, Charles F., and E. Valentine Daniel, eds. 1983. *Karma: An Anthropological Inquiry.* Berkeley: University of California Press.

Leach, Edmund. 1968. "Ritual." In *International Encyclopedia of the Social Sciences,* edited by David L. Sills, 520–26. New York: Macmillan.

Lewis, Gilbert. 1980. *Day of Shining Red: An Essay on Understanding Ritual.* New York: Cambridge University Press.

Lewis, Hylan. 1955. *Blackways of Kent.* Chapel Hill: University of North Carolina Press.

Lincoln, C. Eric, and Lawrence H. Mamiya. 1990. *The Black Church in the African American Experience.* Durham, NC: Duke University Press.

Lupfer, Michael B., Karla F. Brock, and Stephen J. DePaola. 1992. "The Use of Secular and Religious Attributions to Explain Everyday Behavior." *Journal for the Scientific Study of Religion* 31:486–503.

Maybank, Johnny. 2001. "Hampstead Village: The Lost Borough of Charleston." *Charleston City Guardian* 4:1, 4.

Mays, Benjamin Elijah, and Joseph William Nicholson. 1933. *The Negro's Church.* New York: Negro Universities Press.

McClenon, James. 1984. *Deviant Science.* Philadelphia: University of Pennsylvania Press.

McRoberts, Omar M. 2003. *Streets of Glory: Church and Community in a Black Urban Neighborhood.* Chicago: University of Chicago Press.

Mitchell, Henry H. 1975. *Black Belief: Folk Beliefs of Blacks in America and West Africa.* New York: Harper & Row.

Morland, John Kenneth. 1964. *Millways of Kent.* New Haven: College & University Press.

Nadel, Siegfried Frederick. 1954. *Nupe Religion.* London: Routledge & Kegan Paul.

Nelson, Timothy J. 1997. "The Church and the Street: Race, Class, and Congregation." In *Contemporary American Religion: An Ethnographic Reader,* edited by Penny Edgell Becker and Nancy L. Eiesland, 169–90. Walnut Creek, CA: Alta Mira Press.

Orsi, Robert A. 1997. *Thank You, St. Jude: Women's Devotion to the Patron Saint of Hopeless Causes.* New Haven: Yale University Press.

Ortony, Andrew, Gerald L. Clore, and Allan Collins. 1988. *The Cognitive Structure of Emotions.* Cambridge: Cambridge University Press.

Otto, Rudolf. 1958. *The Idea of the Holy.* Translated by John W. Harvey. New York: Oxford University Press.

Paden, William E. 1994. *Religious Worlds: The Comparative Study of Religion.* 2nd ed. Boston: Beacon Press.

Poole, Jason. 1994. "On Borrowed Ground: Free African-American Life in Charleston, South Carolina, 1810–1861." *Essays in History* 36, http://etext.virginia.edu/journals/EH/EH36/poole1.html.

Pope, Liston. 1942. *Millhands and Preachers.* New Haven: Yale University Press.

Powers, Bernard Edward. 1994. *Black Charlestonians: A Social History, 1822–1885.* Fayetteville: University of Arkansas Press.

Proudfoot, Wayne. 1985. *Religious Experience.* Berkeley: University of California Press.

Proudfoot, Wayne, and Paula Shaver. 1975. "Attribution Theory and the Psychology of Religion." *Journal for the Scientific Study of Religion* 14:317–30.

Puckett, Newbell N. 1931. "Religious Folk-Beliefs of Whites and Negroes." *Journal of Negro History* 16:9–35.

Raboteau, Albert J. 1978. *Slave Religion: The "Invisible Institution" in the Antebellum South*. New York: Oxford University Press.

———. 1995. *A Fire in the Bones: Reflections on African-American Religious History*. Boston: Beacon Press.

Rainwater, Lee. 1970. *Behind Ghetto Walls: Black Family Life in a Federal Slum*. New York: Aldine.

Rappaport, Roy A. 1979. *Ecology, Meaning, and Religion*. Berkeley, CA: North Atlantic Books.

Rogers, J. A. 1957. *From Superman to Man*. New York: Amereon Ltd.

Roof, Wade Clark, and William McKinney. 1987. *American Mainline Religion: Its Changing Shape and Future*. New Brunswick, NJ: Rutgers University Press.

Roth, Andrew L. 1995. "'Men Wearing Masks': Issues of Description in the Analysis of Ritual." *Sociological Theory* 13:301–27.

Rubin, Morton. 1963. *Plantation County*. New Haven: College & University Press.

Russell, Jeffrey Burton. 1981. *Satan: The Early Christian Tradition*. Ithaca, NY: Cornell University Press.

Schechner, Richard. 1977. *Essays on Performance Theory, 1970–1976*. New York: Drama Book.

Schleiermacher, Friedrich Ernst Daniel. 1928. *The Christian Faith*. Edinburgh: T. & T. Clark.

———. 1958. *On Religion: Speeches to Its Cultured Despisers*. New York: Harper & Row.

Smart, Ninian. 1972. *The Concept of Worship*. New York: Macmillan.

Sobel, Mechal. 1979. *Trabelin' On: The Slave Journey to an Afro-Baptist Faith*. Westport, CT: Greenwood Press.

Spilka, Bernard, and Greg Schmidt. 1983. "General Attribution Theory for the Psychology of Religion: The Influence of Event-Character on Attributions to God." *Journal for the Scientific Study of Religion* 22:326–39.

Spilka, Bernard, Phillip Shaver, and Lee A. Kirkpatrick. 1985. "A General Attribution Theory for the Psychology of Religion." *Journal for the Scientific Study of Religion* 24:1–20.

Stark, Rodney. 1965. "Social Contexts and Religious Experience." *Review of Religious Research* 6:17–28.

———. 2003. *For the Glory of God: How Monotheism Led to Reformations, Science, Witch-Hunts, and the End of Slavery*. Princeton: Princeton University Press.

Stark, Rodney, and Roger Finke. 2000. *Acts of Faith: Explaining the Human Side of Religion*. Berkeley: University of California Press.

Stark, Rodney, and Charles Y. Glock. 1968. *American Piety: The Nature of Religious Commitment*. Berkeley: University of California Press.

Stevens, William Oliver. 1939. *Charleston: Historic City of Gardens.* New York: Dodd, Mead.

Stump, Roger W. 1987. "Regional Contrasts within Black Protestantism: A Research Note." *Social Forces* 66:143–51.

Suttles, Gerald D. 1968. *The Social Order of the Slum.* Chicago: University of Chicago Press.

Taeuber, Karl E., and Alma F. Taeuber. 1969. *Negroes in Cities: Residential Segregation and Neighborhood Change.* New York: Atheneum.

Taves, Ann. 1993. "Knowing through the Body: Dissociative Religious Experience in the African- and British-American Methodist Traditions." *Journal of Religion* 200–222.

Taylor, Robert Joseph. 1988. "Correlates of Religious Non-Involvement among Black Americans." *Review of Religious Research* 29:126–39.

Thomas, L. Eugene, and Pamela A. Cooper. 1978. "Measurement and Incidence of Mystical Experiences: An Exploratory Study." *Journal for the Scientific Study of Religion* 17:433–37.

Turner, Ralph H., and Lewis M. Killian. 1957. *Collective Behavior.* Englewood Cliffs, NJ: Prentice Hall.

Turner, Victor. 1982. *From Ritual to Theatre: The Human Seriousness of Play.* New York: PAJ.

Twining, Mary A., and Keith E. Baird. 1980. "Introduction to Sea Island Folklife." *Journal of Black Studies* 10:387–416.

U.S. Bureau of the Census. 1990. http://www.census.gov/main/www/cen1990.html.

van Gennep, Arnold. 1960. *The Rites of Passage.* Translated by Monika B. Vizedom and Gabrielle L. Caffee. Chicago: University of Chicago Press.

Wade, Richard C. 1964. *Slavery in the Cities: The South, 1820–1860.* New York: Oxford University Press.

Weber, Max. 1958. *From Max Weber: Essays in Sociology.* Translated and edited by H. H. Gerth and C. Wright Mills. New York: Oxford University Press.

Welch, Michael R. 1978. "The Unchurched: Black Religious Non-Affiliates." *Journal for the Scientific Study of Religion* 17:289–93.

White, James F. 1990. *Introduction to Christian Worship.* Rev. ed. Nashville: Abingdon Press.

Wikramanayake, Marina. 1973. *A World in Shadow: The Free Black in Antebellum South Carolina.* Columbia: University of South Carolina Press.

Williamson, Joel. 1965. *After Slavery: The Negro in South Carolina during Reconstruction, 1861–1877.* Hanover, NH: Wesleyan University Press.

Wilson, John, and Harvey K. Clow. 1981. "Themes of Power and Control in a Pentecostal Assembly." *Journal for the Scientific Study of Religion* 20:241–50.

Wilson, William Julius. 1987. *The Truly Disadvantaged.* Chicago: University of Chicago Press.

Wood, Peter H. 1974. *Black Majority: Negroes in Colonial South Carolina from 1670 through the Stono Rebellion.* New York: Knopf.

Wuthnow, Robert. 1987. *Meaning and Moral Order: Explorations in Cultural Analysis.* Berkeley: University of California Press.

Zierden, Martha A. 1990. "The Past and the Present: Urban Archaeology in Charleston, South Carolina." In *Cultural Heritage Conservation in the American South,* edited by Benita J. Howell, 66–78. Athens: University of Georgia Press.

Index

About the Author

Timothy J. Nelson is Lecturer in Sociology at the University of Pennsylvania.